Haunted Ground

Haunted Ground

Journeys through a Paranormal America

Darryl V. Caterine

 PRAEGER

AN IMPRINT OF ABC-CLIO, LLC
Santa Barbara, California • Denver, Colorado • Oxford, England

Library of Congress Cataloging-in-Publication Data

Caterine, Darryl V.
  Haunted ground : journeys through a paranormal America / Darryl V. Caterine.
    p. cm.
  Includes bibliographical references (p.   ) and index.
    ISBN 978–0–313–39277–1 (hard copy : alk. paper) — ISBN 978–0–313–39278–8 (ebook)
1. Parapsychology–United States. I. Title.
BF1031.C444   2011
130.973—dc22   2011015116

ISBN: 978–0–313–39277–1
EISBN: 978–0–313–39278–8

15 14 13 12 11   1 2 3 4 5

This book is also available on the World Wide Web as an eBook.
Visit www.abc-clio.com for details.

Praeger
An Imprint of ABC-CLIO, LLC

ABC-CLIO, LLC
130 Cremona Drive, P.O. Box 1911
Santa Barbara, California 93116-1911

This book is printed on acid-free paper (∞)

Manufactured in the United States of America

Copyright Acknowledgments

All photos courtesy of Darryl V. Caterine.

For Jana, Hilary, and Spencer

Contents

Prologue

The traveler along America's highways will search in vain for the equivalent of a Jerusalem, a Mecca, or a Bodh Gaya—some *axis mundi* where the national community as a whole connects to the power and mysteries of a sacred world.[1] There are, of course, the great monuments to the country's so-called civil religion: places like the Lincoln Memorial, the Gettysburg Battlefield, or Mount Rushmore commemorating the larger-than-life figures and events in United States history. Here Americans may reflect on the providential moments in the making of their nation, but even in their most pious light, memorials to magnificent feats of human achievement fall short of gateways to the invisible realms recounted in religious myths.

This book is a record of my experiences and reflections at Lily Dale, a Spiritualist camp in New York; the Roswell UFO Festival in New Mexico; and the American Society of Dowsers (ASD) conventions in Vermont. It is the result of repeated visits to places and immersion in movements often brushed aside as tangential to the more serious issues in American religion. Compared, for example, to the role of faith in national politics, the topic of the paranormal might seem just a tad bit quirky. As a scholar of American religions and after more than two years of research, however, I have come to see the "paranormal hot spots" along the American roadside as the nearest analog our nation has to the pilgrimage centers of more traditional religions, sites where we stop to wonder if there is not something really akin to the miraculous afoot, right here in our modern midst.

I say the "closest we come" to sacred centers and "akin to" the miraculous because these places are not, in fact, oriented to the supernatural. They are rather designed to draw our attention to Nature, something that is both ordinary and extraordinary at the same time. At Lily Dale,

Roswell, and the ASD conventions, visitors ponder the sublime—though not transcendent—ground beneath their feet and the amazing galactic expanses above their heads. The sites I have visited, taken together, reveal themselves as shrines to Nature, which I write with an uppercase "n" to denote its association in the paranormal context with ineffability, ultimacy, and mystery. Spiritualists, ufologists, and dowsers alike push the edges of a broader American quest to fathom this cosmic enigma, although they each explore it from their own distinctive perspectives. I have organized my own accounts of their gatherings according to some particular aspect of this *je ne sais quoi* that both motivates and is illuminated by their investigations.

Lily Dale, Roswell, and the ASD conventions are but nodes in a much vaster network of preternatural places memorializing the wonder that is American Nature. These extend throughout the United States. Every state has dozens of its haunted groves, one-time UFO landing sites, chupacabra lairs, and the like. Only a few have become, like Roswell, the modern-day equivalents of destinations along the medieval pilgrimage routes of Christendom, mandatory stops along a tour through America's popular culture. But the hundreds of other locales are lesser known, listed in collections of roadside attractions, often bearing the word "weird" in their titles—*Weird New England*, *Weird Carolinas*, *Weird Texas*, and so on—and subtitled "your local guide to [enter your state's, or even America's] local legends and best kept secrets."[2]

The terminology of the "weird," like that of the "paranormal," is misleading. These labels suggest something that is beyond our "normal" experience, marginal to our everyday lives as modern Americans. And yet nothing could be further from the truth. I am hard pressed to think of another subject that can so easily stir up controversy, fascination, or uneasiness in virtually every nook and cranny of American society. Almost everyone, it seems, has a paranormal story to share or at least has taken the time to formulate an opinion about the matter. UFOs are as familiar to Americans as the Gettysburg Address, maybe even more so: the paranormal is a public discourse. The real question is, why?

In my travels throughout paranormal America at every turn, I came upon unexpected numbers of images, stories, and allusions to Native Americans. There are Indian spirit guides at Lily Dale. There are modern-day versions of the Indian captivity narrative at Roswell. There are haunted Native American grounds in Vermont—as there are throughout the rest of the nation—that have transformed dowsing from a search for water to a search for a pre-Columbian past. These lingering traces of the Native Americans provide a clue to understanding the nation's collective obsession with and derision of the paranormal. For a moment, let us block off all the familiar exits and refuse to brush the subject off as someone else's trivial concern. Let us consider the possibility raised by Renee Bergman: that modern America is collectively haunted, unnerved by some aspect of the past that gives shape to the present before and even as we name it.[3]

There is a second, related clue: the uncanny similarity between the typical paranormal narrative and the earliest descriptions of America as recounted by early voyagers to and colonizers of the New World. In both cases, there are claims of a wondrous natural world on the one hand and accounts of a preternatural Native American presence on the other. Consider just one of the typical portrayals of the newfound continent recorded and published by Spain's Peter Martyr d'Anghiera in the early 1500s:

> Every creature in the sublunary world ... that gives birth to something, either immediately afterwards closes the womb or rests a period. The new continent, however, is not governed by this rule, for each day it creates without ceasing and brings forth new products, which continues to furnish men gifted with power and an enthusiasm for novelties, sufficient material to satisfy their curiosity.[4]

As for the Native American inhabitants, they were positively out of this world, alternating between sublime and savage. In Martyr again, we read,

> They go naked, they know neither weights nor measures, nor that source of all misfortunes, money; living in a golden age, without laws, without lying judges, without books, satisfied with their life, and in no wise solicitous for the future. Nevertheless ambition and the desire to rule trouble even them, and they fight amongst themselves, so that even in the golden age there is never a moment without war.[5]

The "discovery of America" was indeed for Europeans a preternatural event, an unprecedented encounter with radical alterity.[6] They did not know where they were and so called the place Eden. They did not know whom they had encountered and so named the Others Indians. In the terminology of religious studies, the narrative of America was a new myth, an authoritative and paradigmatic reckoning of the modern West's origins and orientation to the world.

In time, this New World metaphysics[7] came to vie with and in many instances replace the inherited cosmology of Europe's and America's dominant Christian culture. Starting in the 1700s, during the rise of the Enlightenment, it became increasingly common to speak of ourselves as living in and originating from Nature. The myth became institutionalized in the language of modern nation-states and the emerging discourse of science. The trope of nature is so ubiquitous that it is easy to forget its historic emergence as a metaphor. It is even easier to forget that it is a symbol that perennially erases the violent subjugation of non-Europeans on the "other side" of Western discovery.

Five hundred years after Columbus, the myths and tales of America's wondrous and haunted ground are alive and well in our collective obsession with the paranormal. In this modern-day discourse, Nature remains what it was to the original discoverers: a marvel for all to behold, satisfying those with an "enthusiasm for novelties, sufficient material to satisfy their curiosity." By now the Indians have been displaced to the geographic and historical sidelines of Euro-American mythology, but new kinds of fantastic beings have come to stand alongside and sometimes to replace them. In the paranormal variant of the Columbian myth, the spirits, extraterrestrials, and ghosts metamorphose into Native Americans and back again, trading places and sharing masks. Together, they take turns unnerving the inhabitants of Nature's nation.

These vital clues to understanding the cultural significance of our collective fascination with the paranormal are completely absent from the more rarefied, second-order debates over the "scientific reality"—or lack thereof—of so-called paranormal phenomena. All three of the topics encompassed by this book began—and today continue—as homegrown American cultural movements. It is only by traveling to the gatherings of Spiritualists, ufologists, and dowsers on their own haunted ground that one sees and hears and participates in the rich symbolic milieu in which accounts of preternatural beings, Indian or otherwise, take shape and thrive.

But in all this talk of metaphors, symbols, and tropes, I do not want to leave the reader with the impression that this book is simply an excursus into linguistics. The myth that the New World voyagers unwittingly bequeathed to their modern descendants leaves us all with a problem that cannot be so easily be analyzed away. The gap between ourselves and the Other is real enough and grows only greater as the New World becomes a global one, displacing those who stand in Nature's way. In venturing into the paranormal, we come face-to-face with this disconnection from the Others-as-yet-to-be-understood, which is simultaneously a confrontation with our own homelessness and exile. This is an experience by turns exhilarating, disorienting, and deeply disturbing.

For some, the paranormal becomes a path that winds its way out of Eden altogether. As Stephen Greenblatt has observed, "[Wonder] erects an obstacle [to understanding the Other] that is at the same time an agent of arousal. For the blockage that constitutes a recognition of distance excites a desire to cross the threshold, break through the barrier, enter the space of the alien. . . ."[8] Alongside the many instances of "playing

Indian"[9] I have encountered in my travels, I have also met those with a genuine desire to "enter the space of the alien," those for whom a curiosity about the interconnection between ourselves and the rest of the world was initially awakened by preternatural beings and Indian ghosts. They go to meet the living Others. America's long obsession with the paranormal can and does lead into another chapter in the post-Columbian tale, which is the story of interreligious exchanges in a global society, most commonly between "the East and the West."[10]

For others, the paranormal simply undercuts any sense of safety and security in the mythic world of Nature, leaving us haunted without reprieve. I have written this book somewhere in between these two extremes. While it could not have taken shape without referencing the misunderstood Other, ultimately my account is the record of a rendezvous with the gap between ourselves and the Other, an abyss that Nature can conceal only in part.

Acknowledgments

I would like to express my deepest gratitude to the following people: Anthony Chiffolo, John Kavanagh, Richard Seager, Frederick Stecker, Alba Valeriani, and Judith Weisenfeld for their support from the very beginning; Christina Michaelson for introducing me to the Lily Dale community and for her constant encouragement; Martie Hughes and Frank and Shelley Takei of Lily Dale for their incredible hospitality and assistance as well as the many hours shared pondering the enigmas; Charles F. Emmons for his helpful and clarifying readings of the ufological chapters; Scot Foxx of the ASD Bookstore in Danville, Vermont, for his generous assistance in granting me access to early ASD newsletters; Maura Brady, David Gove, and Tony Lisi for the ongoing conversations about the paranormal in America; Jennifer Glancy for her ongoing advocacy and invaluable assistance in reading drafts of each chapter; Chip Callahan and Melissa Click, Geoff and Joan Rutkowski, and Rob Cohen and Christine Roth, once again and always, for their friendship on and off the road; Hilary, for almost never forgetting to leave me dessert; Spencer, for teaching me about the things that matter; and finally to Jana, without whom none of this would matter very much at all, for her guidance, patience, and faith throughout the project and for her support and companionship all along.

Introduction: Afoot and Lighthearted[1]

I can see them in my mind's eye, shimmering like the reflections in a rear-view mirror.

There are great gatherings in the woods of upstate New York, crowds assembling to hear messages from beyond the veil of death, news of loved ones now passed on, guidance from the spirit world. There are assemblies convening in the deserts of New Mexico, sharing news of visits from beyond our sun, tales of beings from far away and long ago, forebodings of coming contact. There are odd alliances of farmers and urbanites in the Green Mountains of Vermont, searching with sticks and rods for water and wisdom and wealth. Together they dowse.

As I speed now east along modern interstate highways, I feel less certain of my bearings than when I set out two years ago, less confident in my certainties. I travel toward home but cannot say for sure it will still be there in the same way I left it. And I am not quite sure how to remember what I have heard, seen, and felt or what to call it all. It shimmered when I was there, and it slips through the space of language now, as I name it back into another kind of being, equally gossamer-like, evoking words.

I have been to Lily Dale, the Spiritualist camp in New York, several times now since 2007. I have twice attended the Roswell UFO Festival and have also made two trips to the American Society of Dowsers conventions in Vermont. For two years, I have immersed myself in a world where conventional boundaries slip and slide; the clear lines between religion, science, and technology grow thin; and one cannot even say with certainty which came first: the media or the mediums, the tales of such things or their widespread acceptance among the American public. Attempts to unravel this riddle or the many others surrounding the worlds of ephemera are themselves lures into the further Abyss.

Camp Chesterfield, Indiana.

Many have been seduced. Skeptics, demanding hard facts, have brushed these things into the dustbin of science gone awry. Religious thinkers, predisposed toward acceptance or denunciation, have debated where they fit—or if they fit—in the received theological schemes of things. Academics have seen them as continuations of older "metaphysical religions" in the

West, specimens of new religious movements, or residues of now stigmatized folklore in modern times.[2]

These and other observers have left behind an abundance of labels: "pseudoscience," "the paranormal," "the occult," "magic," "metaphysics," and good old-fashioned madness, to domesticate the enigmas, unwittingly destroying in the process of naming the very things they are trying to name. Herein lies my uneasiness with words. If I identify an unidentified object—flying or otherwise—I am no longer faithful to the subject matter I am trying to describe.[3]

And so, despite my training as a scholar of religion, I have decided to jump off the solid platforms of observation altogether. I have become one of the many millions of rank-and-file Americans who are drawn like moths to the flame into the worlds of ephemera precisely *because* they are impossible to pin down. And I have tried to explain why it is I think that the inhabitants of these strange worlds—mediums and spirits, extraterrestrials and outer-world denizens, unusual energies, and "weird vibes"—are an integral part of what it means to be a modern American. Is it even possible to list all the books that have titillated, part bemused, and part enthralled readers for nearly two centuries with titles like *Confessions of a Medium*, *The Flying Saucers Are Real*, or *Stonehenge Decoded*? Or such recent films as *The Sixth Sense*, *Close Encounters of the Third Kind*, or *Indiana Jones and the Temple of Doom*? Or the rash of present-day television shows like *Ghost Hunters* and *Paranormal State*?

Is it sufficient to explain this all-pervasive interest by settling on a single word or explanation, say, for example, "interest in the occult"?

Every study begins with a methodology, a particular angle of approach. My own is based in the arts of night vision. To see in the dark, do not stare directly ahead. Look through the corners of your eyes. Or, if you prefer a less visual metaphor, listen to what Julia Kristeva called the semiotics of speech rather than the words themselves. Pay close attention to the undertones, rhythms, and innuendos in conversation.[4] Let the ephemera be what they are and follow them into their own terrain to learn something unexpected.

I first realized this a few hundred miles west of Oklahoma City where the Trail of Tears comes to an end, and the things that had eluded my understanding suddenly came back in droves of memories. This, I imagined, was a reward from the wild things for promising not to domesticate them in intricately woven nets of words, at least of the analytical variety.

Before Oklahoma, I was still ensnared in thoughts about *heirophanies*. The great historian of religion Mircea Eliade described a hierophany as a sudden eruption of divine power into our ordinary world of space and time.[5] They are perceived revelations of spiritual force in everyday things:

God speaking to Moses through the Burning Bush, a lock of Shiva's hair descending as the River Ganges. But the concept of hierophany turned out to be of little help along the American roads. There is no consensus among Spiritualists about what constitutes a "spirit," no agreement between ufologists over the unidentified nature of the objects they chase, and no coming together among dowsers over the nature of the energy that guides their tools to desired things. Some would say that these are divine powers erupting into our midst. Others would say that they are ordinary features of our world already.

And so I parted ways with Eliade at a prehistoric burial mound near Chesterfield, Indiana. Farther south, as I pondered the clairvoyant readings of Edgar Cayce in his home of Hopkinsville, Kentucky, I finally embraced the idea of *wonder* as a more fitting concept. But even here, I wield the term lightly. According to another influential religious philosopher, Rudolf Otto, wonder is the essence of religious experience and the foundation of religious belief. Like Eliade, he too is looking for a bridge between the world we can see and feel and the posited realm of the gods or God. Otto, in fact, wrote eloquently about ghosts, hoping we might find in their haunting some basis for faith in God.[6]

I do not go as far as Otto went. Ephemeral things are wondrous only insofar as they ask us to suspend certainties, to develop a sustained tolerance for ambiguity. The great American philosopher and psychologist William James concluded his study of Spiritualism with the refreshingly honest confession of finding himself *baffled*. Fraud and wish fulfillment abounded, but he was left with the distinct impression that something else was going on. The problem, for James the academic, was that he could not say what that "something else" was exactly.[7]

The search for phantasms always ends where James left it. Each "conclusive" study for or against the "reality" of spirits, UFOs, or anomalous energies undermines the next. Together they baffle the reader. At Lily Dale, Roswell, and Killington, Vermont, the rendezvous with wonder falls short of finding a reliable highway to heaven as Otto had hoped. Here, there are no hierophanies or bridges to the gods. Instead, we are left suspended, indefinitely, between the phenomenal world of the senses and the transcendent world of the gods, in an extraordinarily ordinary realm.[8] Among Spiritualists, ufologists, and dowsers, the common name for this ambiguous setting is Nature. It is a wondrous thing because no one really knows what, exactly, it is.

And here is where the foray into the seemingly fringe interests of our culture leads into the innermost sanctum of modern America. If we chase the ephemera long enough, they begin to show us the ambiguous nature of Nature and the ghostly dimension of dwelling in its midst. Nature has remained a central obsession of the United States ever since the Enlightenment. The Declaration of Independence, for example, invokes the Laws of Nature and Nature's God in authorizing the colonies' separation from Great Britain. During the nineteenth century, the romantic authors of the American Renaissance—Ralph Waldo Emerson, Nathaniel Hawthorne, and Hermann Melville, to name just a few—articulated a vision of American culture as rooted in and nourished by the wellsprings of Nature. Modern scientists today seek to uncover the secret wonders of lowercase "nature," even as environmentalists seek to imbue it with more value before we destroy ourselves. Nature connotes the sense of bedrock reality. It is the ontological constant of our modern world.[9]

And yet its meanings slip and slide. Here it is universal political truths, as in the Declaration; there it is awesome cosmic power, as in the romantic writers. Science studies physical constants, while environmentalism probes cultural ideas. What is the nature of Nature? If we could answer that question definitively, perhaps we could say what ghosts and UFOs and dowsing are. And yet the answer fades in and out of our understanding, like a spirit, an unidentified object, a weird vibe.

We don't know where it is, exactly, that we are.

I lost myself at Lily Dale, Roswell, and the ASD convention. Chasing down enigmas, I encountered, quite unexpectedly, a conversation about America as Nature's Nation. Ghosts and the like were phenomena—or were they states of mind?—that stood in for a much wider and pervasive mystery, which turns out to be the very ground of the ordinary world. Reflections on spirits at Lily Dale were never far from questions of who we are as modern Americans, enmeshed in those ambiguous Laws of Nature and Nature's God. At Roswell, UFOs led us into the madness of modern scientific mapmaking, the never-ending quest to chart the cosmos, the perennial rewriting of our physical certitudes. And in the Green Mountains of Vermont, dowsing for energies led us down the rabbit hole into the magical world of machines, the sublime nature of modern technology. Things that I had previously taken for granted as modern "realities" were suddenly revealed as wonders. Modern America, Nature's Nation, was itself the *mysterium tremendum et fascinans*, the Mother of All Mysteries.[10]

And everywhere the ground was haunted. The ghosts of Native Americans lurked in the midst of our assemblies, at the end of our telescopes, and in the power of our machines. Glimpsed through the corners of our eyes, the other worlds of native civilizations unsettled the foundations of Nature's Nation. Cast in fantastic guises, Indians peeked up through the cracks in the ground. The dark side of our wondrous creations, their histories are a record of collective sacrifices made to inaugurate this New

World, their persistent presence in our midst a reminder that we are perennially lost without the Other. We speak of wonders in troubled tones, lamenting our estrangement from the very places on which we stand.

These thoughts come to me on the road as I try to find a route back home. Utterly dependent on what dowsers call "the grid" of technology for my movement and bearings, I am nevertheless set loose to wander free. It is finally in this grounded and yet unbounded space of the road that I understand Nature in all its phantasmagoric splendor, a translocal and boundless space. When the ancient Greeks spoke of nature, they did so in contrast to customs. Nature was the locus of universals—customs of particular places, languages, and mores. Despite their many divergent meanings, the American conceptions of Nature also carry the same sense of universality. But unlike the Greeks, who cultivated customs, Americans increasingly live and move and have our being in Nature. Our translocal nation (now seen as a part of a global village), our constantly evolving sciences, and our limit-defying technologies all give rise to a milieu in which we can—or must—think of ourselves as being from nowhere in particular. Our customs are changeable, arbitrary, and unreal.[11]

My maternal ancestors lived for a time in what could properly be called a world of custom. Hanging on the wall back home is an old postal route map of Wilmot, New Hampshire, where they lived for seven generations. The houses from the map, dated 1892, are unnumbered. Instead, they bear the names of the families who lived there down through the years. This is a map reflecting a community where neighbors knew certain intimate details of each other's lives as well as where their forebears were buried. There was not so much a sense of "history" as a living past, perpetuated anew with each generation. There were common centers—churches, town halls, and greens—where collective memories were evoked and passed on.

Unlike my Wilmot ancestors, I am a resident of Nature's Nation, as are the people I have met in my travels. We are fixated by beings—or the idea of beings—that fade into and out of space-time, defy boundaries, and dwell in mysterious lands. One cannot say with certainty what amazes us more: America-as-Nature's-Nation or the spirits, aliens, and elusive energies that have come to take their place alongside baseball and apple pie as its icons.

Modern America and the craze for phantasmagoria in fact emerged in tandem. The tradition of Spiritualism still celebrated at Lily Dale started in 1848, at the tail end of the tumultuous Second Great Awakening. This latter religious movement saw an upwelling of cosmological innovations in large part as a response to the incipient industrialization of America. Especially among the middle-class clientele who were the mainstay of

Spiritualist gatherings, these were the times when Nature was first becoming a lived reality, as the translocal and rootless nation began to usurp connections to local places. Spirits emerged as doppelgangers, ghostly doubles, of "ordinary" Americans living under unprecedented conditions. And as the processes of modernization have continued since that time, crazes for the paranormal have erupted periodically, as in the UFO panic of the mid-twentieth century or the New Age movement of the 1980s. Presently, as the country goes global at the eleventh hour of modernity, interest in the paranormal is enjoying a veritable renaissance.

The progressive transformation of America into Nature's Nation fulfills what Europeans first hoped the New World would be: a utopian space, a dreamscape, a world with no limits. While the full story of this dream lies beyond the event horizons of my road trip, somewhere north of Roswell I realize nevertheless that the Great Admiral has been haunting me all along. As I roll along highways—wandering, wondering, and writing ephemera into being—I remember Columbus. I remember his journals, filled with the first descriptions of New World wonders: the marvelous trees, the Indians. I recall the shock of future voyagers, as they came to understand there was no going back to their medieval Christian *oikoumene*—literally "world home"—a cosmological map of the earth, its peoples, and their relationship to the supernatural world.[12] I ponder how Nature came to replace this cosmology, at first as a fantasy of the New World and later as a social reality made possible by modern nation-states, institutionalized science, and machines. Nature's Nation is the legacy of the Age of Discovery: a wonder for those who came to America in its wake and a graveyard for those who were here before.

As for myself, I have grown quite comfortable with the idea of ghosts and aliens and energy lines. They are somehow more familiar than I had first thought they would be. I am wary of both the skeptics who deny their existence and the "true believers" who domesticate them too hastily into fictive solidities. I prefer to let them remain as I found them, in the borderlands between politics, science, and technology, perfect reflections of our modern American selves. And if there is ultimately no such thing as going home, then at least I can revel in the fascinating and disturbing wonder of Nature, shimmering now behind me in the rearview mirror.

I

Lily Dale: To Wonder Is to Wander

I.

I am approaching Lily Dale from the west, skirting along the southern shores of Lake Erie, on the final leg of my second "paranormal road trip" across America. I let the GPS do the navigating for me, trusting in the robot's voice commands as I turn onto back roads I have never seen before. She—or it—has been a faithful companion these past few weeks, guiding me in that crisp British accent of hers across thousands of miles of highway. I have come to imagine my invisible GPS scout as a member of the Royal Air Force, wearing a starched woolen suit complete with a pillbox-style hat, her light brown hair tied up in a knot behind her head.

Lily Dale is one of a handful of surviving Spiritualist summer camps in the country. In the decades between the Civil War and World War II, there were dozens of them. Like the one I am going to now, they were typically located in bucolic settings: by pristine lakes, in remote forest groves, or overlooking an ocean. Lily Dale, more affectionately known as "the Dale" by residents and repeat visitors, was built in 1879 on the eastern shore of Lake Cassadaga, in the far western regions of upstate New York.

The camp began as a woodsy tent community, but with the early endorsements of Elizabeth Cady Stanton and Susan B. Anthony and the financial backing of wealthy business tycoons, it quickly expanded. By 1900, Lily Dale was a 37-seven-acre, self-sufficient settlement (then called the Cassadaga Free Lake Association) with a full-service hotel, two grocery stores and bakeries, a meat market, a hardware store, a bowling alley and a billiards hall, a library, a printing press, and a post office. Except for the hotel and post office, these amenities are now gone, but Lily Dale remains as a handsome gated community of some 220 Victorian homes within the town of Pomfret. Today, by some estimates, approximately 25,000 visitors still frequent the camp each summer.

The Gate.

A large sign on the front gate touts Lily Dale as "The World's Largest Center for the Religion of Spiritualism," but this is only part of the truth. Lily Dale is more accurately described as a community of mediums. Mediumship, the formal practice of communing with the dead, first emerged as a cultural craze in 1848, not far from here, in the small hamlet of Hydesville, New York. From the United States, the movement jumped across the Atlantic and then, with a few alterations, back again to the Caribbean and into Latin America. With the influx of Latino immigrants to the United States, Espiritismo, or Spiritism, has once again become part of the lively religious landscape of America, mingling with African and Spanish Catholic beliefs and practices.[1]

In the European American context, Spiritualism did not become a legally incorporated, national religion until 1893. In the intervening decades, the American penchant for séances underwent many transformations. One of these was the emergence of summer camps like Lily Dale. Here it is still possible to encounter mediumship not simply as part of an American religious denomination, "the religion of Spiritualism," but also as an open-ended wonder—an underdetermined performance evoking fascination, doubt, skepticism, and in some cases fear.

Among modern self-identified Spiritualists, the meaning of mediumship is already understood, couched within various "principles" or creedal formulas about the nature of the universe. For most everybody else, mediumship evokes lively discussion and debate and often merges (as it once did in the nineteenth and early twentieth centuries) with preestablished religious beliefs about the afterlife. For most of the people I have met in my travels to Lily Dale, mediumship is appealing precisely because it is shrouded in an air of mystery.

When I stopped by the Dale for the opening weekend of the 2009 season, a camera crew from New York City–based Stick Figure Productions was there, collecting footage for the HBO documentary, finally aired in August 2010 as *Nobody Dies in Lily Dale*. Their final product turned out to be less about organized Spiritualism and more about communion with the dead as an enigmatic cultural practice. It is a lingering Puritan bias to assume that serious religion and good entertainment have nothing to do with each other. Mediumship has always been part of both, a subtlety that has not been lost on the producers of popular media.

Back in an earlier era, when Lily Dale could boast of itself as the premier Spiritualist camp in the country, "physical mediumship," such visual demonstrations of human-spirit interaction as levitating objects or spontaneously manifesting ectoplasm, was all the rage. The emergence of Spiritualist summer camps and the cultural obsession for material "evidence" of spirits were in fact coterminous.[2] At Lily Dale, visitors from New York to Chicago once came to Lake Cassadaga to ogle at an array of spectacular and typically fraudulent materializations of spirit beings. The dearly beloved dead came to the Dale, or so it was believed, to write messages on slates, to paint self-portraits on blank canvasses, or to prance about in darkened séance rooms.

But those days are now long gone. By the 1940s, rampant fraud and deception among physical mediums had tarnished the reputation of Spiritualism, and the accoutrements of their arts—the slates, the cabinets, and the trumpets—were perfunctorily packed away and hidden from public view. Fortunately at Lily Dale, this rich material culture has been preserved in a museum, housed in a former one-room schoolhouse. But it is no longer in the forefront of camp life today. I watched the crew of Stick Figure Productions scramble to capture something as sensationalistic as a hogtied medium locked in a cabinet or a trumpet floating through the air. But their efforts were in vain. Mediumship at Lily Dale and throughout the country has returned to its antebellum roots as a gossamer performance, made up of words and the imaginations of its participants.

I had been duly warned against taking too materialistic an approach during one of my first visits to Lily Dale—not by any of its resident mediums but by a visitor from Miami, a Cuban-born practitioner of Santeria and a medium herself. She and her friend from Buffalo were paying a visit to the camp in the summer of 2007 to see how Anglos negotiated their own dealings with the dead. The three of us met on a park bench outside the Lily Dale auditorium as I exited a Spiritualist message service, lost in thought over the information I had allegedly just received from my dead father. Isabella called out to me in Spanish, beckoning me over with a request to light her cigarette.

Twenty-four hours, two meals, and one Espiritismo-style séance later, I finally managed to ask her what she thought about the cultural differences between mediumship at Lily Dale and communion with the dead in the Cuban/Cuban American context. Taking a long drag from her cigarette, she looked at me with mild disgust. "If you want to know about culture, read your books," she said in Spanish. "If you want to know about spirits, learn about energy."

In attempting to record my impressions of Spiritualism and Lily Dale, I have gradually come to appreciate the wisdom of Isabella's curt remark. Like a member of the camera crew, I first came to the camp obsessed with its more solid, visual aspects: its museum artifacts, its architecture, its printed historical pamphlets and brochures. Similarly, in describing its visitors and residents, I was unduly focused on their external appearances, the dry, staid markers of sociological analysis: they were mostly white, disproportionately female, 30 years of age or older, and hailing from local American states and the Canadian province of Ontario.

None of these facts is completely irrelevant, but they become secondary to more subtle considerations. The first of these has to do with motion.

I begin to understand Lily Dale now only as I move toward it, a modern traveler speeding in my Tacoma truck with Roswell far behind me. I am pleased by the route my British GPS has chosen for me, through dairy country, the land of small farms. The month is July, and the warm air is blowing in through the windows smells of sweet, freshly cut grass. Silos and barns dot the well-watered green fields, and occasionally I drive through small towns built at the crossroads of rural routes, passing modest nineteenth-century homes, graveyards with white stones, and steepled churches.

Today, the only way to get to Lily Dale is by car, but once upon a time, visitors traveled here by train. The New York Central Railroad ran along the western edge of Lake Cassadaga, with a depot just a short walk away from the main gates. The railroad company had built a three-story hotel, the Iroquois, alongside the tracks to accommodate the thousands of annual visitors to Lily Dale during the Spiritualist heyday. Guests could also stay in the hotels built on the grounds of Lily Dale: the Maplewood, built onto the camp's original horse stable, or the Leolyn Inn, once a farmhouse and stagecoach stop and the house where the idea for a Spiritualist camp on Lake Cassadaga was first hatched. Both of these buildings still function as hotels today.

As I drive, I am afforded a glimpse of how upstate New York must have appeared to earlier visitors. I am not simply referring to the physical layout of the farms and towns, which are monuments in their own right to American pastoralism. I am referring rather to their foreign quality. I am not a member of any of the communities I drive through. If I ran out of gas or needed directions, I could not ask for the name of a local neighbor (which is why I, like an increasing number of modern Americans, carry a GPS gadget). The family names on local gravestones or local gossip would be completely lost on me.

From the perspective of a truck or a train, speeding passengers must be content to call most of what they see through their windows "Nature," an abstract, amorphous category born from a lack of any local social context. And like the millions of visitors before me, I will finally arrive at Lily Dale to behold a shrine to American Nature, which the anonymous road has already partially revealed to me. In a secluded grove together with other modern travelers, I will spend a few days by Lake Cassadaga and try to figure out (with the help of spirits) where the hell we are, anyway. (A memory from my recent visit to The Very Large Array, an impressive collection of radio telescopes clustered in the San Agustin Valley of New Mexico, built to help us figure out how the Universe—or Nature—came to be: a particular T-shirt in the gift shop caught my eye. In a sprawling field of stars, a large arrow points to a dot indicating our sun. The caption reads, "I have no idea where I am.")

It is 7:30 in the evening when I finally pull up to the gates of Lily Dale. I put the truck in neutral and jam on the emergency brake. I pause once again to consider the weird power of this gate. In classic religious studies analysis, the sacred is set apart (Hebrew: "qadosh") by a threshold like this, distinguished from the profane world all around it. But in the case of Spiritualist camps like Lily Dale, what is inside the gate is an exact replica of what lies outside it: a carefully laid out community of Victorian houses, parks, and churches nestled in the woods of upstate New York— just like the small towns I have driven through.

At the same time, the gates do signify a passage into something extraordinary. In the words of journalist Christine Wicker, Lily Dale is, after all, "a town that talks to the dead."[3] Am I crossing over into a profane place, a nineteenth-century version of a contemporary "gated community," or a sacred one—some sort of mystical grove?

The answer, I have come to understand, is both. Spiritualist camps are uncanny in the sense that Freud dissected the term: familiar and unfamiliar at the same time.[4]

Today, Lily Dale has become something of a cultural oddity. But back in the golden age of Spiritualism, camps like these reflected back to their visitors a widespread belief that all of modern America was an uncanny zone, a place where spirits could infiltrate their porches and parlors. Any and all towns could—and often did—talk to the dead and were proud of that fact.

I drive through the gates and take a sharp right. I want to see the Leolyn Woods before the sun goes down. On the one hand, Lily Dale lacks anything approaching what might be called a sacred "center." Its acreage is covered, instead, with a number of spots where spirits like to come and go: its haunted Maplewood Hotel, a Fairy Trail winding through the woods with dioramas of sprites and elves, a labyrinth made of evergreen bushes. On the other hand, Leolyn Woods commands attention in a way these other spaces do not. Once used as the picnic grounds by the original founders of the camp, this grove has been allowed to mature into a towering stand of old-growth trees.

In the depths of these woods, at the end of a long gravel path, stands a stump covered with concrete and surrounded by a small wrought-iron fence. Permanent wooden benches are arranged to face "Inspiration Stump" as it is called, the most impressive site here where mediums stand to deliver outdoor messages. Until a few decades ago, visitors also ventured into Leolyn Woods to touch a "healing tree," eventually removing so much of its protective bark coating that it died.

I have come to realize that Leolyn Woods truly encapsulates the main wonder that Lily Dale seeks to celebrate and understand—and this is Nature. Wondrous because we can never pin it down; we remain inside it, immersed within it. Nature is the fixation of all modern travelers, Spiritualist or otherwise, who lack a stable community and cosmology that might tell them something more specific about where they came from, who they are, and where they are going. Like the T-shirt at The Very Large Array, the Leolyn Woods reminds us, "We have no idea where we are."

There is no cosmology or mythology vaster than Nature, one that might fix its meaning once and for all. It is beyond signification. It is sublime. It is, at Lily Dale, a cause for celebration. In and through this uncanny ground of being, spirits come and go to help us find our way, busy travelers themselves.

II.

Lily Dale is a place for people in constant motion. Visitors come and go from all over the country. Spirits come in from destinations left unspecified, at least in readings. Visible and invisible beings unite to share stories, insights, and reflections on our journeys. The living exchange addresses and phone numbers, building a network of community.

The legend of Lily Dale's founding is a story of these crossing paths, and it begins with an itinerant mesmerist named Dr. Moran. In 1844, traveling on the lyceum circuit, Dr. Moran came to Laona, a town about six miles north of present-day Lily Dale. The son of a local minister invited Moran to his home for a private demonstration of the mysterious powers of mesmerism, the original precursor to modern hypnotism.

One of the neighbors, Jeremiah Carter, afflicted with health problems, came to watch the show. Moran mesmerized Carter. Carter went into trance and was transformed into the learned "Dr. Hedges." He went on to give advice to his bewildered townsfolk and waxed eloquent on the benefits of hands-on healing, which turned out to be the cure for Carter's illnesses.

In the heady climate of the day, this single occurrence was enough to ignite a sustained and unsupervised theological conversation among the locals. After Moran left Laona, Carter and his friends organized the "Religious Society of Freethinkers." Unfortunately, there are no records of their regular meetings together, but their interests can be deduced from what we know about the religious culture of mid-nineteenth-century upstate New York.

Laona was located in an area that has since come to be known as the Burned-Over District of western New York.[5] This was the place where the Bible met the Erie Canal, where American Protestant Christianity first grappled with the various upheavals of early industrialization—particularly the erosion of traditional social groupings and an information overload wrought by new scientific and technological discovery. During the first three decades of the nineteenth century, millions of Americans took solace

Monks at Lily Dale.

in a new interpretation of Christianity that came to be known as evangelical Protestantism.[6] For other Americans like Carter, the wonder of mesmerism held out a similar hope of spiritual renewal as well as the promise of restored social cohesion.

Wherever they were mesmerized, entranced Americans like "Dr. Hedges" suddenly seemed to know things about their neighbors—their secret pains and problems—that they did not or could not know in their ordinary waking consciousness. For its enthusiasts, mesmerism redressed the anomie of social isolation by making evident the invisible "chords of sympathy" binding modern communities together.[7] And for many entranced subjects, mesmerism also proved to be a Philosopher's Stone, unlocking insight and understanding into the dizzying array of scientific inquiry that was just beginning in the mid-1800s, in fields as various as astronomy, geology, engineering, and biblical studies.

When Carter and his friends first assembled in 1844, the birth of Spiritualism was still four years away. But sometime in the mid-nineteenth century, they embraced the movement with gusto. In 1870, they purchased the local Universalist church in Laona and converted it into a Spiritualist meeting-house. In 1877, Jeremiah Carter received a directive to "prepare for a camp meeting" at a forest grove in Pomfret, New York (today's Leolyn Woods), from a spirit speaking over his shoulder. The morning after this revelation, Carter walked six miles to see the owner of the land, his fellow freethinker Willard Alden, and the plans for a Spiritualist summer camp by Lake Cassadaga were launched.[8]

To what extent the Laona Freethinkers were "Spiritualists" in today's sense of the term is now an open-ended and sometimes contentious topic of conversation at the camp. The argument boils down to how we define "Spiritualism" in the first place: as a cultural movement or as a religious denomination.

Historically, Spiritualism did not become a permanent, nationally recognized denomination until 1893, with the formation of the National Association of Spiritualists (although a number of state organizations were then already in existence).[9] As a legal watchdog, the association played an invaluable role in defending Spiritualism as a legitimate "religion, philosophy, and science" in the era of physical mediumship, when frauds were threatening to undo the movement. Thanks to its efforts, mediums received protection under the law to practice what was now recognized as a "religion." After its formation, even debunkers began making polite distinctions between con-artists-posing-as-mediums and the earnest believers in organized Spiritualism.

In the process of transforming a cultural movement into a religious denomination, however, the National Association of Spiritualists was obliged to formulate clear creeds that froze an amorphous cultural movement into a stable system of belief, one that did not do justice to the rich and eclectic innovations of the earlier nineteenth-century Spiritualists.

I emerge from the woods and amble over to the Lily Dale Museum to learn more about the early days of the camp. There, I leaf through faded brochures from the late 1800s and early twentieth century. Lily Dale once hosted America's most famous suffragettes, including Elizabeth Cady Stanton and Susan B. Anthony, whose politics had earlier been endorsed by spirits speaking through trance speakers in the 1850s. The suffragettes are billed alongside some of the best-known physical mediums of the day—like the Bangs Sisters or the Campbell Brothers—who presided over the mystifying materializations of spirit paintings. Early residents of Lily Dale included former members of John Murray Spear's Harmonia community from Kiantone, New York, where members had heeded spirits' urging to dig for the remains of an ancient civilization of Celtic, web-footed Indians.[10]

As the twentieth century approached, Spiritualists began venturing into Asian religious thought as well. Theosophists—the metaphysical cousins of Spiritualism—came to lecture on reincarnation. In 1894, there was even the guest appearance of a Jain philosopher from India, touring the

United States in the wake of the World Parliament of Religions, held the previous year in Chicago. Starting in 1916, a Mohawk man named Oskenonton—a well-known opera singer of the day who was billed as the "Indian Enrico Caruso"—became a regular summertime resident of the Dale, setting up a tipi on the camp grounds where he healed Anglos using traditional Iroquois methods.

As I read over the brochures, I am reminded of the famous barroom scene in the original *Star Wars* movie, where creatures from all over the universe sip drinks together while waiting for their spaceships to leave port. Spiritualism emerges from the records as a momentary freeze-framing of the accelerated social exchanges of late nineteenth-century America, a snapshot of early globalization from one rather bucolic corner of New York.

As the twentieth century unfolded, however, American Spiritualism took pains to fashion itself as an imitation of Protestant denominational-ism. It emphasized stasis, issuing formal creedal statements of belief and eclipsing its own eccentric and theologically innovative past. As I continue to peruse the brochures at Lily Dale, I see a clear transformation in the 1930s: the camp becomes more "serious." Gone are the advertisements for the old bowling alley and Ferris wheel and promises to visitors of the health-restoring properties of its well waters. In the 1940s, physical mediumship was banned altogether. Instead, there are dry "declarations of principles"—those adopted by the National Association of Spiritualists (now renamed the National Spiritualist Association of Churches)—which read as follows:

1. We believe in Infinite Intelligence.
2. We believe that the phenomena of Nature, both physical and spiritual, are the expression of Infinite Intelligence.
3. We affirm that a correct understanding of such expression and living in accordance therewith, constitute true religion.
4. We affirm that the existence and personal identity of the individual continue after the change called death.
5. We affirm that communication with the so-called dead is a fact, scientifically proven by the phenomena of Spiritualism.
6. We believe that the highest morality is contained in the Golden Rule: "Do unto others as you would have them do unto you."

And added in 1909,

7. We affirm the moral responsibility of individuals, and that we make our own happiness or unhappiness as we obey or disobey Nature's physical and spiri-tual laws.

8. We affirm that the doorway to reformation is never closed against any soul here or hereafter.

And in 1944,

9. We affirm that the precepts of Prophecy and Healing are Divine attributes proven through Mediumship.[11]

Throughout the middle of the twentieth century, these principles became the public face of the camp. A quick perusal of books donated by Dale visitors to the library paints quite a different picture, however, revealing a continuing taste for the eclectic or spectacular: James Churchward's *The Lost Continent of Mu*, bequeathed in 1953 (on the antediluvian civilization, an offshoot of Atlantis); Gray Barker's *They Knew Too Much about Flying Saucers*, donated in 1977 (the first sustained discussion of the Men in Black); and John A. Keel's *The Mothman Prophecies*, donated in 1981 (on creatures from other dimensions, UFOs, and psi-induced paranoia).

Nevertheless, throughout the twentieth century, scholars followed the lead of the brochures in writing about Spiritualism. Sociologist George Lawson came to Lily Dale in the late 1920s and published a full-length book on the camp in 1930, *The Drama of Life after Death*. His main focus was on Spiritualist creeds and their appeal to modern Americans. As for the more sensational displays of physical mediumship still being practiced at the time, he simply ignored them. "The occurrence of messages, rappings, movements of objects at a distance, materializations, [and] photographs of 'spirits' does not prove the Spiritualist hypothesis of disincarnate spirits enjoying an eternal life in a spirit world which is a perfected reproduction of this one," he briefly summarized in the introduction, before proceeding to his main focus on Spiritualist ideas.[12]

In 1980, sociologists came to Lily Dale again, producing another tract on Spiritualist creeds. Michel P. Richard and Albert Adato were interested in resolving the academic debate over how to classify Spiritualism: as a denomination, sect, or cult. They took an interest in mediumship only to discount a former characterization of Spiritualism as "thaumaturgical" or miracle based and wrote a monograph on the Lily Dale community as a religious sect with historical ties to liberal Protestantism.[13]

But in the past 30 years, something at Lily Dale has changed. The camp seems to be returning to the more libertine culture of its Freethinking foundations, and a narrow focus on Spiritualist creeds hardly does justice to what I encounter. Since the 1980s, two independent Spiritualist churches have emerged on the grounds, competing with the older national church for members. While these new congregations have their own declarations of principles, they are less invested in preserving denominational identity. Elected to the Lily Dale Assembly, the camp's autonomous governing board, they have imparted an unmistakable "New Age" style to the camp's culture.[14]

For the past several years, the Gyuto Monks from Nepal have been invited to inaugurate the Lily Dale summer season, sculpting sand mandalas in buildings bedecked with the daguerreotypes of nineteenth-century mediums and suffragettes. In 2007, the first year I visited, summertime workshops were being held with titles like "Past Life Regression," "Indigo and Crystal Children," and "Understanding Challenging Tarot Cards." The Good Vibrations café offers vegetarian wraps and fresh fruit smoothies in a Pagoda building, built in the 1890s in homage to Eastern culture.

In 2009, I have tea with one of the Gyuto monks in the Lily Dale auditorium, a large barnlike structure whose walls unfold like accordions to let in the outside air. Hundreds of guests are gathered here to celebrate the 130th anniversary of the camp. Dressed in formal clothes or retro Victorian-era outfits, we snack on hors d'oeuvres to the background music of big-band swing. Tenzin, the Tibetan translator, and I chitchat about mediumship and channeling in Nepal and India and compare it casually to the goings-on in Lily Dale. Tenzin seems unfazed. I mention my college trip to Gujarat and Rajasthan, back a million years ago in the 1980s, before Madras leveled its architectural past and became high-rise Chennai.

What does this have to do with Spiritualism? Nothing at all, if Spiritualism is defined in terms of this or that number of principles. But it has everything to do with the ongoing and ever-accelerating social dislocations and information overload that first sent upstate New Yorkers like Jeremiah Carter into cosmological overdrive in the 1840s.

The turn toward religious pluralism taken by Lily Dale in recent years has boded well for camp business. According to several longtime residents of the camp, by the late 1970s Lily Dale was barely hanging on. Many of its Victorian homes and cottages were in various states of dilapidation, and a few were even boarded up, left abandoned by self-identified Christian Spiritualists who had lost a court case that attempted to steer the camp toward a more biblically centered future. But with the turn toward a broader range of religious themes, visitors began to trickle in to the premier American Spiritualist camp once again, after several decades of relative neglect.

Over the years, I have talked to dozens of visitors to the camp. Most of them have been raised in Christian faiths, both Protestant and Catholic. A few of Lily Dale's registered mediums and healers are even former Catholic clerics: one ex-priest and two former sisters. Without fail, those who find themselves at home in Lily Dale are men and women who revel in the radically democratic ethos of the Spiritualist culture, where critical reflection on theology and religion is a virtue. Many of the visitors are academics like myself, trying to locate Spiritualism within the broader landscape of American religious culture.

One metaphor that might accurately describe the Lily Dale crowd is the term "spiritual seekers," explored at length by sociologist Wade Clark Roof in his study of the baby-boomer generation.[15] Leigh Eric Schmidt has in fact used the concept of "seeking" to frame nineteenth-century metaphysical religiosity.[16] He casts the turn toward unmediated encounters with the divine in religions like Spiritualism as the epitome of America's culturally Protestant ethos of individualism.

For myself, I prefer the slightly less goal-directed metaphor of spiritual homelessness. The people I meet at Lily Dale seem dislodged from any cosmological home. And they are not particularly seeking a new one. Rather, they are learning to enjoy the free fall of not knowing, wandering without an end in sight, and helping others like themselves along the way.

We come to the camp as sojourners fresh off the road, both literally and existentially, cast adrift from the clear certainties of preestablished religious cosmologies. Together with its encouragement of do-it-yourself theologizing, what makes the camp so appealing is its attention to hospitality. As a traveler myself, I notice the attention to detail, the soft sheets and strong coffee in the hotels and bed-and-breakfasts. The word "hospice" comes to mind: not in its most common association today as end-of-life care but in its older sense as a place of respite for wandering pilgrims.

In faithfully describing the Lily Dale of my own experience, better than the sociological studies of Spiritualist beliefs is E. Lyell Earle's 1899 article written for *The Catholic World*. Earle's overview of late nineteenth-century mediumship in upstate New York stands out from the hundreds of other garden-variety exposés of physical mediumship so common during that period. As an American Catholic, he saw the gatherings at Lily Dale as a search for something the Church had long sanctioned as official doctrine: the notion of a "communion of saints" in the afterlife, responsive to the needs and prayers of the living.

Although I do not share Earle's interests in mounting a Catholic polemic against Spiritualism, I find the following summary of his stay at Lily Dale deeply resonant with my own: "All around us are spirit forms with whom we may hold immediate converse, solace ourselves with their company, find guidance in their counsels, and courage in the thought of their victory. In everything else concerning the nature of these spirits, their origin, their destiny, their manner of manifesting themselves, all is chaos."[17]

Solace, guidance, and courage. All of these are, in fact, resources that present-day visitors to Lily Dale seem to find. And except for the word "chaos," Earle's summary of religious belief at Lily Dale is accurate. There is no consensus at Lily Dale, even among its mediums, as to the nature, origin, and destiny of the spirits.

But all is not chaos.

Think instead of well-worn paths and routes, steps traced and retraced. At Lily Dale, all is in motion.

III.

The Great Mystery of Spiritualism is that we are, all of us, extensions of the primordial ground of Nature cordoned off in Leolyn Woods. And this Nature of late seems to resemble a Great Information Highway, through which messengers from other realms speed to deliver information.

In 2008 and 2009, I attend two seminars offered through Fellowships of the Spirit, one of the two independent Spiritualist churches that has led Lily Dale into its present-day "New Age" instantiation. Located in a former Italian restaurant just outside the main gates, Fellowships has been training mediums and healers and ordaining Spiritualist ministers since its founding in 1988.

Our teachers include Elaine and Mark Thomas, the cofounders of Fellowships. Both are members of the baby-boomer generation who have sought to breathe new life into the traditional methods of cultivating mediumistic abilities, still taught at the Morris Pratt Institute on Lily Dale's main grounds. In both schools, the practice of mediumship is deceptively simple. It rests on allowing ourselves to be moved by the impressions we receive from our inner nature and communicating them to other people with the intention of consoling or guiding them. The bearer of this message is the medium; the recipient is known in Spiritualism as a "sitter."

As it is taught to us at Fellowships, these impressions are nothing more or less than the daydreamlike perceptions that float through our minds as a matter of course, most of the time. Inner vision is labeled "clairvoyance"; inner hearing, "clairaudience"; and inner feeling, taste, and smell, "clairsentience."

It is the first of my two weekend seminars at Fellowships. I sit on a metal folding chair across from a perfect stranger, in the midst of delivering my first message. It had something to do with swing sets and pineapples. I look despairingly at the woman sitting in front of me: "Does this make any sense to you?" She is kind. It will be her turn next. "Well, we do have a swing for our son in the backyard, and I do like pineapples. ..." I return the favor.

Inspiration Stump.

"Well, I don't have a father named Earl, but I did know someone in college by that name. . . ."

Reverend Elaine has already shared with us her own story of studying mediumship with a British-born resident and medium of Lily Dale who came to Spiritualism through an acquaintanceship with Sir Arthur Conan

Doyle, of Sherlock Holmes fame.[18] A spiritual seeker of the 1960s, Elaine was struck by the idea that the traditional development of mediumistic abilities could be sped up by incorporating techniques gleaned from various meditation traditions and modern hypnotism. We can do something to hone our receptivity—loosen up. The Morris Pratt method depends more heavily on sheer patience, requiring would-be mediums to wait, sometimes for years, for the spirits to finally show up.

During my first weekend at Fellowships, we are taught about changes in posture, breathing, and eye movement that correlate with subtle changes in human perception and cognition. We break up into groups of threes to practice what we have just learned. Claire, a co-owner of two pizzerias in Rochester, New York, retrieves and concentrates on a powerful memory from her past and assumes a bodily position to accompany the memory. Susan, a Buffalo schoolteacher, sits opposite Claire, mimicking her posture. I take on the role of the sculptor, moving Susan's body to create as exact a replica of Claire's position as I can. Then I ask Susan to tell me what Claire is remembering. The results are impressive. Susan guesses that Claire was somewhere near water on a sunny day, trying to relax but disturbed by something nearby. Claire then shares that she was remembering the first time she had seen a jellyfish at the ocean, frightened as a child by what she had seen. We repeat this and other exercises several times, making forays into the interpretation of nonverbal communication.

In the second weekend, we learn meditation practices based on Pantanjali's *Yoga Sutras*, which are said to clear the pathways of inner seeing (clairvoyance), inner hearing (clairaudience), and inner sensation, including touch, smell, and taste (clairsentience). Together, we meditate before breaking up into smaller groups to refine and practice the skills we learned in our first introduction to mediumship and healing. The meditation exercises, like the experiments of the first weekend, reduce our inhibitions and ease us into a more playful mode of mediumship.

Reverend Elaine is on to something. By the end of each weekend, we are all experiencing something of the *jouissance* that fuels improvisational theater or stand-up comedy. Whether or not the readings are true or really come from spirits is for the moment beside the point. We are all now relaxed and adept at making sense of the spontaneous impressions flying out of our own and each other's mouths. We are making connections and finding associations with impressive speed. We have learned to "read" each other and ourselves, more finely attuned to the nuanced cues of communication that undergird everyday interactions. And in the process, we have been transformed from perfect strangers into more intimate ones.

The bare bones of a Spiritualist narrative consist of the following parts: the invocation of a memory of an ancestor, brushstroked in words (e.g., "there is a woman here who used to love to play cards"); a vital connection made between the ancestor and some present-day concern of the sitter ("she says you are having difficulties with the people at your school or office"); and some consolation or guidance from the deceased ("the card-playing woman [now identified by the sitter as an ancestor] tells you to enjoy the game of life, despite its difficulties.") These components make up a beginning, middle, and end of a Spiritualist vignette, respectively.

Within this basic narrative structure, mediumship entails spinning meaning out of metaphors and metonymy. It is a language made up of highly fluid symbols, akin to free association or poetry. So cards, for example, are symbolic of hands; hands represent work; and as cards are a game, so too is life a game as well.

There is one important difference between the readings given by the more traditional Spiritualists and those given by the graduates of Fellowships, and this has to do with the raison d'être of a reading itself. Emerging out of the religious confusion of the Second Great Awakening, Spiritualism originally addressed itself to the public's concerns about the afterlife. Well into the mid-twentieth century, mediums reassured sitters that their dearly beloved had survived the transition of death and were progressing along into higher stages of spiritual development.

Those Spiritualists still faithful to this tradition today will therefore deliver readings that identify the deceased with physical or psychological descriptions of their personalities. Consoling the bereaved is the purpose of the reading. In contrast, mediumship at Fellowships is taught as a method for guiding and encouraging the living through their everyday trials and tribulations. Guidance rather than consolation is the primary purpose, and less emphasis is put on elaborate descriptions of the spirit itself.

In neither case, however, do the Spiritualists concern themselves primarily with information. Whether they pertain to the dead or the living, mediumistic messages are first and foremost a peculiar kind of interpersonal communication. Much of the religious and scholarly confusion surrounding the veracity of messages stems from ignoring this basic social fact. What is the truth of a conversation? Who, aside from the conversationalists themselves, is in a position to arbitrate this issue?

I remember the advice of the Cuban-born Santera in keeping my own focus riveted on energy. We have come to Lily Dale as bodies in motion, hurtling in our moving machines and unmoored from any stable cosmology. *I have no idea where I am.* And at the end of the day, what saves us all from vertigo is spinning yarns, talking ceaselessly, about who we are and how we are related to that Nature outside the window—at once so familiar (we can see Lake Cassadaga through the Fellowships windows) and yet so strange (what is the nature of Nature?). Those gossamer things called words turn out in the end to save the day from total disorientation. All of us moderns weave tales about each other and the world around us, always just a few steps ahead of the *horror vacui* behind us—the lurking possibility that none of this makes any sense at all.

Spiritualism is a chapter in a much longer story mapping the boundaries of the modern self, also known as "human nature." In a tale with many tellers, each one clamors for ultimate authority. Before there were tales about spirits, mesmerists stumbling on trance states claimed to have unlocked the innermost mysteries of the human soul. The story of mesmerism eventually became the story of modern psychology, with its fictive inner chambers of the subconscious and unconscious.[19] Parapsychology—rooted in the efforts of nineteenth-century scientists to find an empirical basis for mediumship—tells yet another tale about a mind allegedly located beyond space and time altogether.[20] Skeptics write the whole thing off as irrelevant psychic white noise, even as neurobiologists collect new physical evidence for mental processes in general, telling a particular story, through science's own complex language of symbols and signifiers, about the human brain.

Although neither Elaine nor Mark mention his name, the author of the most important story about spirit beings in Spiritualism was Andrew Jackson Davis, yet another upstate New Yorker of the nineteenth century who was swept into the mesmerist craze of his times. Beginning in the mid-1840s, Davis was periodically mesmerized over a two-year-long period during which he dictated *The Principles of Nature, Her Divine Revelations, and a Voice to Mankind.* It was in this tome, which covered subjects as vast as the origins of the universe, the history of humankind, and the topography of the afterworld, that the entranced Davis described the ongoing telepathic communication between spirits of the deceased and the living.

Davis's visions were especially reassuring to an audience of American Protestants, raised on the hellfire-and-brimstone theology of their Puritan ancestors. In Davis's vision, there was no hell. There was only the halcyon Summerland, Davis's name for the spirit realm, an ethereal replica of life here on Earth and an afterworld of souls progressing indefinitely in their spiritual development. For the most liberal or rationalized sects of American Protestantism, Unitarians and Universalists, Davis's words only echoed what they had already been espousing. Spiritualism came to be, in part, a liberal Protestant church for the masses, enticing crowds with its alluring demonstrations of communion with the dead before educating them in its theological tenets.[21]

Lily Dale has a building named after Davis, the Andrew Jackson Davis Lyceum, which is used today for educational events. It stands just down the road from the remains of the Fox Cottage, the building memorialized in Spiritualist histories as the site of the first modern séance. (In 1915, the old Fox Cottage was shipped on barges and trains from its original location in Hydesville, New York, to Lily Dale. There it stood as a shrine until 1955, when it burned to the ground.) Davis unknowingly provided the Spiritualist cosmology when *Principles of Nature* was published in 1847. One year later, the Fox Sisters—Maggie and Kate, both young girls—modeled the first modern séance by talking to a poltergeist that was then terrorizing their home. Invoking Davis's theory about "spirits," bewildered witnesses reframed the Fox Cottage fracas from a ghost story to a tale about tutelary spirits conversing with the living.

The cultural movement of modern Spiritualism was therefore set in motion by spontaneous acts of storytelling. First there were stories about the spirits in the afterlife, recounted by Davis in mesmeric trance like so many lullabies to console the Protestant living. Then there were the widespread demonstrations of mediumship, the majority of them unfolding in private home parlors and back porches, that contemporary participants folded into Davis's master narrative about the afterlife. The mass media of the day picked up these stories as well, starting with favorable coverage of the Fox Sisters by Horace Greeley's *New York Tribune* in 1848, and circulated them throughout the nation. Finally, a vast array of independent Spiritualist newspapers emerged in the wake of the Fox Sisters' séances, keeping Americans abreast of the movement as it took root in particular towns and cities.

I have pored over various studies (primarily American) of parapsychological or "psi" phenomena—extrasensory perception, psychokinesis (mind's power to influence matter), and remote viewing—conducted at various laboratories over the past 80 or so years. These highly contested experiments typically use statistics to separate "lucky guesses" and coincidences from allegedly genuine incidences of psi, sometimes known as "hits" or "odd matches."[22] But at Fellowships of the Spirit, spirits chat with Americans in decidedly vernacular English. And an alleged message from Abraham Lincoln, conveyed through automatic writing and etched on a slate in the late 1800s, came with a grammatical error that would have raised the hackles of nineteenth-century schoolmarms like my own great-grandmother. Today on display in the Lily Dale Museum, the president's message uses "should of" instead of "should have."

Spiritualism continues at Lily Dale as an intimate ritual, an act of storytelling between and by perfect strangers. Following the example of the mediums themselves, we mediums-in-training are taught to trust our own insights and inspirations as inviolable and to weigh the words of others heeding the same calls. Together, we weave our own meaning in and around the stories others are telling about Nature, human and otherwise. Here there are no statisticians or grammarians to interrupt our tales.

IV.

"May I come to you?" The woman in front of the stump is talking to me.

I am back at Leolyn Woods, and the benches are now full of spectators. It is noon in August, and one of the Dale's daily displays of mediumship is now in session. Here I come to watch and listen to the virtuosi of improvisational storytelling in action, weaving together simple vignettes to the members of large audiences with amazing grace, speed, and ease. Visitors to Lily Dale who want a full-fledged "reading," a longer and even more intimate message, are welcome to make appointments with the some 40-or-so registered mediums who reside at the Dale. But these outdoor services give visitors a telltale glimpse of the individual mediums' skills in short messages lasting just a few minutes.

"May I come to you?" or some similar request for permission is supposed to inaugurate all public performances of mediumship. I have been to dozens of public readings at Lily Dale, and so far I have never heard a sitter turn down the request.

The people sitting all around me in this green cathedral of old-growth forest are here for a variety of reasons. Some who come to Lily Dale are grieving. Others are the religiously homeless, mostly Protestants and

Nature Temple.

Catholics (in equal numbers) disaffected from their own traditions and piecing together private theologies. Others still are simply looking to be entertained. All of us, however, seem eager to be approached.

"May I come to you?" I remember the gate separating Lily Dale from the outside world, the threshold marking off a space that is uncannily a replica of the pastoral American landscape and a portal to the Summerland. In a Spiritualist reading, the electric charge surges most strongly precisely at the moment the stranger crosses the threshold into the most intimate, psychological space of the sitter.

Listen to the content of a reading given another: it is, just as some critics of Spiritualism have alleged, invariably banal. So-and-so's grandfather is here, having transcended space and time wearing the same tweed coat he used to sport in church. He has defied the known laws of science and dogmas of modern religion to comment on the frayed caulking in an upstairs bathroom. He comments on the lack of mechanical prowess in the family, makes reference to a local plumber, and departs with a message of love.

But the content of the message, its odd match with the details of one's everyday life, is only part of the allure of Spiritualism. More primordially, "May I come to you?" is an invitation to transgress the boundaries separating that most sacred of all American spaces, the autonomous region of the private self, from the profane world around it. It is this transgression of privacy that magnetizes visitors to Lily Dale like moths to the flame and unnerves the detractors of Spiritualism.

And so we invite the mediums to talk *to* us and about us, again and again, despite the not-so-infrequent experience of receiving "bad readings," ones that seem to have no clear connection to the details of our lives. The hope, of course, is for a good reading, in which case the details of *your* ancestors and *your* leaking bathtub drain are no longer banal but now charged with a weird thrill of having granted a total stranger permission to help script your own life narrative, if even for a short time.

"May I come to you?" the medium asks me, and I give her permission to enter. Suddenly, her voice is inside the deepest recesses of my memory and imagination. As she describes a male figure with dark hair who once worked with his hands, I imagine she is talking about my father, now deceased for more than 20 years, who was once an artisan and woodworker. The suggestive details about his physical appearance and eccentric personality she gives me are enough for me to create a vivid real-time recollection of Dad. She then goes on to create a story about his opinions on what I am doing now (writing a book) and leaves me with reassurance of his approval and love.

The medium has become a midwife for my memory, now freshly brought to life and suffused in a wash of bittersweet emotion: longing, affection, and sadness alike. I do not even hear the next several messages. It is not until after the service has ended, as I walk along the gravel path back out through the entrance to Leolyn Woods, that I will talk to others who were similarly touched. Our inner lives having already been aired in the grove beside Inspiration Stump, we continue on disclosing more of ourselves than we might otherwise do outside the gates of the camp.

Leolyn Woods is one of two outdoor venues for the display of mediumship at Lily Dale. The other is at Forest Temple, a veranda-like structure facing out toward rows of wooden benches on the west side of the camp, just a few hundred feet from the remains of the Fox Cottage and the entrance to the sylvan fairy trail. At these two sites especially, the performance of mediumship returns to its unbounded status before Spiritualism became an established denomination.

There are, of course, the Spiritualist churches at Lily Dale: one affiliated with the National Spiritualist Association of Churches, and two nonaffiliated, independent ones. During the summer season, the association conducts afternoon services inside the Lily Dale auditorium for visitors. Its Unitarian-Universalist style of service, complete with old American hymns (including "Amazing Grace" and "God Bless America"), is distinguished only by the mediumistic messages delivered at the end. In the context of Spiritualist services, the links between mediumship and theological principles is made most explicit: communion with the souls of the departed is but one of many gifts (both natural and spiritual since there is ultimately no distinction between these two terms) possessed by the offspring of Infinite Intelligence.

But here at Leolyn Woods, the bones of American Spiritualism are laid bare for all to see. There are only the trees and strangers interacting with each other in a most unconventional way, relative to white middle-class American social etiquette. It is unclear exactly what kind of performance we are participating in, a fact that is underscored every time the sitters applaud for a reading. The chairperson of the outdoor service, who opens and closes with a prayer (usually dedicated to "Spirit" or "Mother-Father God"), intervenes to remind us that this is a religious service; applause is inappropriate. But in the three summers I have visited Lily Dale, the applause continues nonetheless.

Shorn of any theological context, mediumship seems to be the ritual par excellence for engineering an experience of what Victor Turner called *communitas*—a viscerally felt and affectively charged feeling of being connected to others.[23] It is a great leveler, unmasking, with the sitters' permission, the social personae of all who participate. Visitors to Lily Dale leave comments in bed-and-breakfast notebooks recounting "life-changing" experiences at Lily Dale, describing the camp as "magical," "amazing," "wonderful," "restorative," and "fantastic." It is difficult to understand the power of this place—what the Santera would call the camp's "energy"—until one has welcomed a stranger, the medium, into one's midst. Transgression of privacy is the key to grasping the camp's power.

The threshold separating public and private space is lowered in the ritual of mediumship, and now we who have come to Lily Dale will follow the mediums' lead in our interactions with each other. Lily Dale acts as a kind of echo chamber where the central rituals of mediumistic readings reverberate for several days after they are first performed. What was common in the nineteenth century has now become remarkable; there are so many places here simply to sit, talk, and listen. There are seven parks, two restaurants, and a coffee shop. Televisions and radios have yet to be installed inside the Maplewood Hotel and the camp's sundry bed-and-breakfasts. Instead, there are porches and parlors with chairs. In these quiet nooks and crannies of the camp, first-time visitors share their experiences and perceptions with more seasoned guests, the members of the Spiritualist churches, and self-taught metaphysicians.

During our stays at Lily Dale, we do not so much express our belief in spirits as pool our collective resources to analyze what has just happened to us during public message services or in private readings. Visitors to the camp are a well-read lot. Theological, parapsychological, skeptical, and even anthropological interpretations whip around the parlors and porches, reaching no definitive conclusions. But even the most skeptical visitors cannot help but wonder out loud if seemingly chance coincidences, or dreams, or pictures found aslant, or coins discovered on sidewalks, or books falling off shelves, have not all along been neglected signs of an extraordinary world nudging up against the contours of everyday life. Our conversations awaken what sociologists call "memorates," personal tales of unusual or as-yet-to-be-explained events that build on each other with increasing intensity. Together, we wonder.

The experience of *communitas* at Lily Dale reaches its crescendo in the camp's twice-daily energetic healing services, held at the Healing Temple, a white-clapboard building resembling a Protestant church or meeting-house and built in the 1950s for the Spiritualist version of the laying-on-of-hands. I have been there many times. As soothing music plays softly over the Temple's indoor speakers, visitors approach available seats set up in the altar space. Here again, licensed healers ask permission to lay their hands gently on or near parts of the body with a simple request: "May I touch you?"

As I sit in a folding metal chair under the Temple's cobalt-blue lamps, awash in a sea of good feelings, I begin to understand how and why Spiritualism veered off its moral bearings as the history of the movement unfolded. Alongside the ever-present difficulty of discriminating between "genuine" and "fraudulent" readings lies a host of anxieties relating to our vulnerability, as the protective shield separating self from others is progressively let down.

Back in the Spiritualist heyday of earlier decades, Lily Dale earned an unsavory reputation as a place where mediums conned wealthy patrons into handing over large sums of money. In 1908, the *New York Times* published a lengthy exposé of trickery at the camp, disclosed during a visit by the American Society of Psychical Research. The article included the story of a Dale medium who had convinced a client to donate farm equipment, including large harvesters and even his own horse and buggy, which the medium promised to dematerialize and send to the inhabitants of Jupiter for the cultivation of the planet.[24] Especially during the Victorian era, darkened séance rooms figured perennially in the pubic imagination as places of illicit sexual activity, although Lily Dale stayed clear of such charges.

The energetic laying-on-of-hands is now over, and the healer whispers a prayer for good health and blessings in my ear. I walk past the other visitors waiting for their turn and step outdoors again. I am beginning to feel more and more like a spirit myself, exposed, slightly light-headed, unsure of my bearings.

About a year or so before this most recent visit to Lily Dale, I was visiting my father's grave in New Hampshire when my cell phone rang. It was one of the Dale's mediums. She asked me what I was doing, so I told her, "I'm standing at my father's grave." Without being asked, she proceeded to deliver me a message from him. "Louis wants to know when you're going to finish that book."

The timing of the call was an odd coincidence, some might even call it an "odd match." But it made me nostalgic for the days before Spiritualism, when the living still had a clear place for the dead. I like knowing where both my parents are buried. I like driving to New Hampshire and having heart-to-heart conversations with them, imagining them hovering around the headstones and thanking me for watering their geraniums. I also like leaving them there, imagining them resting in peace, finally released from the suffering of the last days of their painful illnesses.

There are no gravestones in Lily Dale, save for a few reserved for animals in its pet cemetery at the outermost edges of Leolyn Woods. Because the dead are nowhere in particular, they are everywhere in general, with mediums rather than the headstones serving as the only anchors of memory. And if Andrew Jackson Davis was right, the dead cannot exactly be said to be "resting in peace." In fact, as message bearers, they may even be busier than I am now, in my travels across America.

After yet another sustained look at Nature here at Lily Dale, both within myself and in the woods all around me, I am no closer to knowing where I am than when I arrived or, for that matter, where the dead are located. In a word, I still feel ungrounded. The only constants are motion and the endless spinning out of words. Energy.

It is a good state of mind to begin to think of the road again.

And so I pack up my bags at the Angel House bed-and-breakfast and return to the surety of my Toyota Tacoma. I drive through the uncanny gates of Lily Dale, back into a modern world that is as unstable as the one I am leaving. At the very least, I am refreshed from my time spent here by the shores of Lake Cassadaga and assured that there are other travelers out there not so unlike me: rootless children of Nature.

2

Lily Dale (Cont'd): Inner Wandering

I.

Oma is here.

It is shortly past dusk, and about 20 of us are gathered inside Assembly Hall. A few moments ago, a soft-spoken woman from Kentucky named Frankie Z. Avery, dressed in a single-piece, dark blue tunic, was expressing her gratitude for being invited to Lily Dale, extolling its mediums as her role models and heroes. Now she is gone. A middle-aged man sitting beside her had counted backward from 10, and the persona known as Frankie Z. Avery disappeared. For a moment, she seems to be fast asleep, but suddenly her eyes open wide. She sits up straight, looking around the room and smiling.

"Greetings! I am Oma! You have come here for a reading, yes?" She speaks in a slightly altered accent, possibly British, though not as crisp as the voice in my GPS. She is positively beaming.

I heard rumor of Oma's upcoming visit back at the Angel House bed-and-breakfast a few days ago, during a discussion about "trance speaking" in Frank and Shelley Takei's living room. Frank, now retired, once taught philosophy at a small college in Pennsylvania. Shelley is a licensed psychotherapist and writer who offers workshops at Lily Dale based on transpersonal psychology. Together, they run the Angel House during the Lily Dale summer season, and their living room has become something of a modern-day salon, Spiritualist style. Here, in a cozy carpeted nook of plush couches and chairs, resident Dale mediums and visitors from a wide range of professional pursuits—academe, journalism, politics, and medicine—stay up late into the night, smoking cigarettes and drinking wine or coffee, trying to get down to the bottom of spirit communication.

When I first heard about "trance speaking" at Lily Dale, my mind conjured up images of the bygone Spiritualists discussed by Ann Braude, those somnambulistic women of the nineteenth-century lyceum who spoke in the

Spirit Painting of Abraham Lincoln.

name of spirits to condemn a variety of social injustices, including slavery and the political disenfranchisement of women. It is not until now, as I am talking directly with Oma, that I realize that the terms "trance speaking" and "channeling" have been used interchangeably at the Angel House. "Channeling" is a general term that can refer to the relaying of messages from any kind of invisible being through a human messenger.

Frankie Z. Avery speaks now not on behalf of the departed ancestors but rather on behalf of other kinds of entities altogether. The exact nature and origins of Oma are unclear. The being has described itself as a cluster of interdimensional intelligences. Some observers have described her—or them—vaguely as a "collective universal energy." Throughout the twentieth century, other channelers have delivered messages to earthlings from angels or extraterrestrials on matters of great import.[1] Presently, Oma is exhorting me to take up drumming and to play the flute as I once did, although I never have.

Against the backdrop of the Assembly Hall daguerreotypes—brown-and-white images of former Dale mediums, many of whom may have worked, in fact, as trance speakers—the connection between nineteenth-century somnambulists and channelers becomes clear. We are waiting for Oma to speak eloquently on the collective fate of the human race, just as Spiritualist trance speakers once addressed the state of the union. Though she is not addressing them now, Oma has before spoken prophetically on a number of present-day planetary crises, including global warming and the influenza pandemics. We are no longer in the realm of Leolyn Woods, where spirits can be trusted to guide us through the ordinary struggles of everyday life.

Channeling of Oma's variety was popular at Lily Dale during the 1980s and met with a mixed response. Precisely because the range of issues covered by channeling is broader than those of a modern-day Spiritualist medium, reaching beyond mere personal issues into social ones, its messages tend toward generalities. In a culture already saturated with apocalyptic prophecies, the exact whereabouts of a deceased grandmother's wedding ring packs a greater cognitive wallop than yet another pronouncement of a coming cataclysm. The interest in channeling thus died down at the Dale after a brief spike in interest. Oma is my first encounter with a medium of this particular kind after three years of visiting the camp.

Its brief rendezvous with channeling aside, it has been a very long time since Spiritualism has taken a public, political stance against social issues. After the 1850s, nothing ever came to replace the wave of trance speakers. In Braude's analysis the emergence of Spiritualist camps like Lily Dale— and the sensationalist displays of physical mediumship they showcased— sounded the death knell for the movement's political significance.[2] On the one hand, there can be little doubt that mediumship took a turn toward the apolitical—and burlesque—in its new instantiation as a stage spectacle after the Civil War. Radical spirits disappeared from public discourse, and Andrew Jackson Davis, scandalized by the stage gags and sexual indecencies of fraudulent mediums, broke with the movement in 1878, taking his socialist endorsements of Spiritualism with him. In the meantime, a number of new metaphysical movements that arose to compete with Spiritualism either emphasized personal enlightenment or kept many of their secrets hidden from public view, open only to initiates.[3]

On the other hand, there are signs aplenty at Lily Dale and at other surviving camps that Spiritualists, even during this new phase, identified themselves as quintessential American patriots. In the back of Assembly Hall, a framed picture of the Revolutionary War hero Thomas Paine includes a short paean clipped from an old edition of the *Psychic Truth* (the date of the Lily Dale newspaper article is missing) praising him as the first advocate for American independence, justice for women, and retirement pensions. A precipitated spirit painting of Abraham Lincoln, brought through by the Campbell Brothers, still hangs in the Maplewood Hotel, and a nonprecipitated painting of George Washington hung until recently in the Lily Dale Museum. American flags fly proudly throughout the camp, and a plot of land just outside the Healing Temple has been set aside as a memorial garden for American veterans.

In its more recent transformation into an extension of New Age spirituality, the political agenda of Spiritualism has simply changed tactics, opting for a more guerilla style of social reform than the mass movement–oriented vision of Spiritualist founders like Davis. As Elaine Thomas previewed the two-year Spiritualist licensing program offered by Fellowships, she gave many examples of how "spiritual insight" (a new name for mediumship) has borne fruit in a variety of modern-day professions, usually behind the scenes and therefore unnoticed. Policemen use their heightened intuitive skills to identify criminals, physicians read auras as they diagnose their patients, and teachers visualize protective light shields around classrooms of unruly students. Once the notion of "politics" is broadened to include what French theorist Michel de Certeau called "the practices of everyday life," we can see that Spiritualism's political aspirations have not disappeared completely.[4]

And yet for all its focus on personal politics, even contemporary Spiritualism still speaks on behalf of something vast, even cosmic. In order to understand the continuous political thread running through all of Spiritualism's incarnations—from lyceum to summer camp to organized church to New Age—it is necessary to know something more about this central wonder of Nature that permeates the camp. The portraits of Thomas Paine, George Washington, and Abraham Lincoln already suggest the starting place. Lily Dale celebrates an American society founded, in the words of the Declaration of Independence, on the Laws of Nature and Nature's God. But from the vantage point of Lake Cassadaga, this is an ephemeral reality indeed.

Soon, it will be time for a visit to the Lily Dale Museum. There, I will find all around me tantalizing clues about the nature of this nation, its ghostlike quality, its wondrous ability to elude classification. Do not let the ubiquitous American flags fool you. Despite the outward displays of patriotism, there is nothing at the Dale approaching the triumphalism of what some scholars have called "American civil religion," a strident vision of the United States guided and blessed by God. On the contrary, throughout the history of Lily Dale, Nature's Nation has been celebrated as a mystery and a riddle, in the playful spirit of the carnival. It is seemingly so solid, there at the basis of modern political discourse, scientific inquiry, and even *spirituality*, and yet nobody can find it.

This looming and pervasive cultural vertigo makes some of us giddy. We stay up late into the night, pondering questions about the modern world that as yet have no answers. Will democracy prevail in the world, or will religious institutions rear their heads again as self-appointed leaders of modern nations? And is there a scientific basis for the claims of parapsychological phenomena being spoken all around us? Are we witnessing, as official Spiritualist principles claim, some still ill-defined aspect of the natural world?

We sip our beverages, smoke cigarettes, and wonder.

But inside Assembly Hall, the soft-spoken woman from Kentucky named Frankie Z. Avery has just passed out.

II.

I come to my senses somewhere west of Big Savage Mountain. I glance down at the odometer: 50 miles have passed by, unnoticed. Interstate 68 rolls forward west through Maryland like a ribbon, undulating down through valleys and over summits toward West Virginia.

I have been lost in road trance for the good part of an hour, one eye on the highway, the other surveying the swirling memories of my last trip to Lily Dale as they condense into new patterns. My satellite radio is set, as it almost always is, to receive the high-definition waves of electronic music. The pulsating tempos of trance, 130 to 150 beats per minute, synchronize perfectly with the speed of the truck's motion, intermixed with major and minor chords of layered melodies and repetitive chants. The harmonies build up and splash away, dissipate out into the surrounding blurs of green hillsides, dark against the dome of a blue sky.

I have been speaking into my small Sony digital recorder, trying to capture fleeting insights before they pass away altogether. As soon as they dissipate, new ones coalesce into being. At night in a generic motel room of a Comfort Inn, I will scribble them down into a journal, where they come to assume the appearance of solidity. But for the past 50 miles, awareness has been a dreamlike stream. There have been times when the optical illusion has taken hold that I am perfectly still, that the road has been moving toward and past the truck.

On the road, I am narcotized by the rhythmic flow of traffic. Occasionally, west of the Rocky Mountains, the movement of trains will become visible in the distance, adding to the cascade effect of people, freight, and even information circulating unceasingly through the veins and arteries of the land. At some point—I can't remember where—I become aware that 18-wheelers and motor homes have been reciting, mile after mile, a particular version of European American history to those of us enmeshed in this web. The highways are distant heirs, via rivers, of the old Atlantic trade routes, and on them ride Mayflower moving vans, named after the Pilgrim ship, hauling the insides of family homes from one locale to another. There are the meandering recreational vehicles

Tree on Fairy Trail.

named Magellan, Discovery, Expedition, or Conquest. Others recall the more recent land journeys of pioneers, bearing names like Prairie-Schooner, Wilderness, or Trailblazer. As driven by cultural romanticism and marketing as it may be, this plastering of historical markers on the sides of motor vehicles gets one thing right. It is our collective freedom, or doom, as modern Americans to wander, and this has been so for more than 500 years.

The anthropologist Victor Turner once suggested that pilgrimage is "extroverted mysticism" and that mysticism is "introverted pilgrimage."[5] Pilgrimage, like the names on the sides of trucks, is easy to identify. Routes can be charted and demographics tabulated as bodies move toward sacred centers in the landscape: Mecca, Benares, Jerusalem. Mysticism is more elusive. For travelers to these places, at the very least we can say it is a way of talking about inner experience that is modeled on the outer journeys. Muslims, Hindus, Jews, and Christians journey to a "center" within themselves where Heaven and Earth connect.

In the mid-nineteenth century, a new language of mysticism, which is to say a new way of talking about inner experience, emerged in America. True to Turner's observations, this new story about the inner landscape was an introversion of an exterior journey. But unlike many other forms of mysticism, this was an inner journey without a fixed center. It echoed the European American experience of traveling, without end, through the vast and boundless expanses of an uncharted world. This particular kind of mysticism was introverted wandering, memorialized in a quote by Henry David Thoreau: "Be a Columbus to whole new continents and worlds within you, opening new channels, not of trade, but of thought."[6]

For some moderns wishing to take such a voyage, an altered state of consciousness first called "artificial somnambulism" afforded a way aboard in the early 1800s. This mode of trance was first induced in a French peasant by the Marquis de Puysegur, a protégé of Franz Anton Mesmer. In 1774, Mesmer had accomplished his first cures of what today would be called mental illnesses by intensifying and releasing the nervous crises of his subjects. He sat directly in front of individual patients, locking his knees against theirs, staring deeply into their eyes, moving his hands across their arms, and pressing his fingers against their upper abdomens, sometimes for hours. He would wait for the illness to manifest visibly in various contortions and pains and then—knees still locked and hands held firm—allow it to pass away.

The Marquis de Puysegur, using the same techniques, effected a remarkably different state. Popularly known as "mesmerism" in the United States, it was first demonstrated to a New England audience in 1836 by one of Puysegur's students, Charles Poyen Saint Sauveur. Poyen's subjects seemed to fall asleep, their waking personalities dissipating before the passes of the "operator," but the subjects in fact remained conscious. In this new space of trance, highly attuned to Poyen's suggestions, weary and diseased Americans experienced a release from the confines of time and space. They remembered their own pasts with remarkable clarity and ease. They looked into the minds and bodies of those gathered around them, reading thoughts and diagnosing illnesses. Sometimes, they saw events transpiring in distant locales.[7]

In a few rare cases, they left the earth altogether. They set sail for the uncharted lands of distant planets and beyond, amazing the earthbound with wondrous tales of newfound discoveries. One of these mesmeric virtuosi was Andrew Jackson Davis, whose tales of mystical wanderings became the prototype for the future journeys of mediums first and, still later, of modern channelers. Davis's 1847 *Principles of Nature* was a cosmic travelogue, recounting the origins of a sentient cosmos, the univercoelum, from a primordial burst of mind-matter into a series of six concentric worlds with the "Sensorium" at its core. *Principles* told of the transformations of terrestrial minerals, plants, and animal life into their current configurations. It reconstructed the emergence and metamorphoses of human civilizations—Asia, Africa, Europe, and pre-Columbian America. Lulled into trance by the operator S. S. Lyon, Davis overcame the barriers of space and time, passing, in his own words, into the fourth and deepest state of mesmeric trance, "the mind becom[ing] free from all inclinations which the body would subject it to."[8]

Davis took care to explain at the outset of *Principles* that his experience of flight was an optical illusion. As was true for the Swedish mystic Emmanuel Swedenborg, whose visionary flights Davis discussed at length, knowledge came to him. He was but the passive receptor, perfectly still, who absorbed information communicated through what Mesmer called animal magnetism, an ethereal and all-pervading cosmic substance. But while Swedenborg was content to catalog his visions, which came in the form of visitations from supernatural beings, Davis addressed the public and spoke of himself in the language of exploration and adventure. Before elaborating on the technicalities of mesmerism, for example, he explained, "A man intending a journey to some foreign country, would, if a judicious traveler, familiarize himself with the geography of it, and acquaint himself with the maps and charts of the various ways by following which he might reach the place of his destination." And as the mesmerized mind entered its deepest, most receptive regions, it was "launched from its nidulated [i.e., nested] state . . . pass[ing] into a new sphere of existence."[9]

In *Principles of Nature*, there is no privileged center, no Heavenly Jerusalem to which Davis travels and from which he returns. Like his contemporary Ralph Waldo Emerson, he is drawn to the image of circles and spheres as an image of totality.[10] He frequently explains that any and every point of the universe is a center of a new world. At times the idea seems almost to overwhelm him: "No possible combination of figures would be adequate to present to the human mind the number of spheres contained in the broad ocean of the stellar system. If each particle of matter composing this sphere could be numbered, the whole world would not even convey an idea of the number of worlds contained in infinite space!"[11] And yet, undaunted, Davis ventures on, clearly exhilarated by the thrill, or the illusion, of movement through the vastness. The result of his two-year initiatory tour of the univercoelum is a Byzantine, highly ordered cosmology. At the same time, these pioneering forays leave the door wide open for future cosmonauts to connect the dots—the infinite set of all spherical centers—in new and unending ways.

The evolution of what American religious historian Catherine Albanese has called American metaphysical religions tells the story of modern mystics taking up the invitation that Davis implicitly extends in *Principles of Nature*: come fly with me. In 1848, Spiritualist mediums found in Davis's description of the afterlife a cosmological motif in which to conceptualize their dealings with the dead. One of Davis's visionary discoveries was that spirits take up residence on other planets and further make their way back through the concentric spheres of the univercoelum toward its center. Along the way, they are at liberty to "*by permission*, descend to any earth in the Universe, and breathe sentiments into the minds of others which are pure and elevating."[12] Mediums typically referenced Davis's writings to explain their remarkable abilities and elaborated on his own descriptions of afterlife realms in various depictions of the Summerland.

In 1888, Helena Blavatsky, a Russian-born émigré to the United States and cofounder of Theosophy, took her own visionary flight into the cosmos to produce *The Secret Doctrine: The Synthesis of Science, Religion, and Philosophy*. This time, the dots were connected in fundamentally different ways. One of Blavatsky's new additions was the introduction of reincarnation into the drama of life and death. Further, she claimed that a race of ascended masters—enlightened souls that had transcended the rounds of rebirth—guided over the spiritual evolution of humankind. An especially advanced race of these masters had in eons past imbued our protohuman predecessors with reason, steering the course of human evolution as we now know it.

Blavatsky's repartee with advanced intelligences opened the door for a slippery slide from mediumship to channeling. Future Theosophists would learn in trance that Blavatsky's advanced masters were actually the indigenous inhabitants of Venus. In the early 1930s, these Venusians appeared directly to a Californian named Guy Ballard, one-time Theosophist and founder of the I AM Activity. Again in 1950, they made contact with George Adamski, first telepathically and then in physical form. His best-selling books popularized the idea of channeling to an American audience, and since that time the list of extraterrestrials communicating with "contactees" has been lengthening.[13]

Frankie Z. Avery's warm reception at Lily Dale is historically fitting. Mesmerism, reconceptualized in modern psychology as hypnotism, is no longer the popular method for inducing altered states of consciousness that it once was. The trance mediums are gone, but new generations of cosmonauts have emerged to take their place, still managing to elude the confinements of ordinary waking consciousness. Channelers describe their ecstatic release from the body—literally an *ek + stasis* (no longer still)—as blissful. Their subsequent flight through the cosmos continues as an introverted story of outward movements that began to accelerate in America at the beginning of the 1800s, into the frontier, toward the factories, and away from religious certainties. Unbounded mystical flights through Nature embody the thrill of speed and dislocation in the modern era.

As 6:00 P.M. arrives, the satellite radio begins broadcasting the daily program, the Subterranean, heard around the world through the Sirius XM channels 38 and 80, Dance Radio GR and Radio Safari in Greece, Radio DJ.RO and Radio Flash FM in Romania, and Trance Base FM in Germany.

The show begins as it always does, with the sonic layering of a countdown to transmission, an arrangement of sound bites from science fiction movies, and an escalating rhythmic melody in the background:

We have been confirmed for take-off. Please take your seats. This will be your only advisory. Countdown to transmission: five . . .

If it doesn't send you to a psychiatrist, it will send you at least to a mirror. . . .

Four . . .
It seems to be related to the substructure of space. . . .

Three . . .

This is not a human being. He's from another planet, another solar system. . . .

Two . . .

I don't think this body's really a body. I think it's some kind of transport unit for something else altogether. The question is, what . . . ?

Prepare for ignition . . .

I saw him with my own eyes. He disintegrated himself into a beam of light and passed through the hall window without breaking it . . .

And then the San Diego–based DJ identifies himself. He is Zoltar, the Brother from Another Planet.

One. Zero. Welcome to Subterranean.

Zoltar begins to spin the world into trance. What a wonderful way to travel. I hurtle over the border into West Virginia, but my mind is hundreds of miles behind me, back in upstate New York in that fabulous wunderkammer, the Lily Dale Museum.

III.

The sheer abundance of material objects stuffed into this room is stunning.

To my right, on the high ledge beneath the frosted windows, are a number of collapsible spirit trumpets arranged in a row. Beneath them hang black-and-white photographs documenting the history of Lily Dale in the first decades of its existence: the original "bough house," made of saplings, where Spiritualist speakers once lectured; a man peddling atop a "water bike" or hydrocycle on Lake Cassadaga, dressed in a full suit and bow tie; and the "healing tree" that once stood in Leolyn Woods.

To my left, the wall is covered with colorful paintings and drawings of spirit guides, composed by various psychics and mediums while in trance. Straight ahead of me on the wall are the white metal placards that mediums once hung outside their cottages, bearing their names in raised black lettering. In one corner stands an old pump organ, in another a Victrola record player, both encased in dark-stained hardwoods.

And all along the walls are display cases, filled with bits and pieces of Lily Dale gone by. An old wooden Ouija board sits next to a set of goggles once donned by mediums to read auras and a pair of Billy Turner's grandmother's reading glasses that he wore when he wanted to slip into trance. There is a bowling ball from the old Bunch Club bowling alley and billiards hall, which once stood on the camp grounds; swan- and camel-shaped china gravy boats once used in one of the Dale's hotel dining rooms; a book of World War II ration coupons; glass medicine bottles; a copy of *Woman's Home Companion* from 1911; a Lily Dale Post Office receipt book from 1903; the mallet used at the first meeting of the Dale's Medium League; a 1928 edition of *The Book of the Hand: A Complete Grammar of Palmistry for the Study of the Hands on a Scientific Basis*; a horseshoe; and the complete works of Andrew Jackson Davis.

Ron Nagy, the museum curator and an eminently knowledgeable historian of Spiritualism, stands beside me, calmly eating fruit cocktail in a can. He chats casually about the marvelous feats of the camp's bygone mediums. It is a slow day at the Dale, and the other visitors must be eating lunch. Nagy and I are the only two people in this former one-room schoolhouse. The bitter smell of mildew is sealed in the walls and faded

Lily Dale Museum.

paisley-designed linoleum floor. It permeates the room, mixing with the sweet scent of Nagy's fruit cup.

Nagy probably has the most difficult job at Lily Dale. As a practicing member of the National Spiritualist Association of Churches, he has to account for the overwhelming evidence of fraudulent mediumship assembled in this room in a way that does not undermine the credibility of his own religion. Two glass cabinets are filled with "spirit slates," still bearing the original messages from the dearly beloved dead etched in white and colored chalks. Like the messages I have heard in outdoor public readings, they are tender and humorous. "God Bless You on this Holy Sabbath Day Ethel—Did you expect me?" one of them begins. "I have never forgotten you. Say isn't this ikey [*sic*] a case. He certainly doesn't use any common stuff for his writing. He seems to be a gold miner. I wish you would develop slate writing—you can. I am with love, Mabel Evans."

Many of the spirit drawings hanging on the walls are examples of Lily Dale's famous "precipitated spirit paintings." These images originally manifested like Polaroid pictures on blank canvases, before the eyes of amazed spectators. Several of the more spectacular precipitated paintings hang in the lobby of the Maplewood Hotel (Abraham Lincoln and Napoleon Bonaparte) and a spirit guide of the Campbell Brothers medium duo named Azur, an elderly bearded man raising his right arm to the sky, index finger pointing upward, dressed in white tunic and headdress, towering on a massive canvas more than feet high.

Other residents of Lily Dale have the luxury of sidestepping the issue of fraud that goes hand in hand with physical mediumship. "We don't do those kinds of things any more," they can say. But Nagy is alone with a stash of smoking guns—and he is the perfect man for the role. Quite simply, I never know when to take him seriously. During my first visit here three years ago, I carefully explained that I was an academic scholar of American religious history, working now at a Jesuit college, writing a book on things parapsychological. In that introduction, Ron developed a shtick that has continued to define our interactions ever since: he addresses me as a Jesuit priest.

Earlier today he emerged from his backroom office, spooning the fruit cocktail out of the can to inaugurate our act for maybe the tenth time. "H-e-y-y—I remember you! Aren't you *that Catholic priest?*"

"Hey, Ron. Nice to see you again. Good memory! Yeah, I'm the professor from the Jesuit college. Except I'm not a priest, remember?"

"Yeah, right. Yeah, I remember you—you're that *priest* from the Jesuit college down the road."

And here we are again.

Ron has taken the rather risky position of defending the reality of physical mediumship in two self-published books: one on spirit slates, the other on precipitated spirit paintings. After reading them, I have no doubt that he wants his readers to take seriously the *possibility* of spirits intervening in the physical world. He takes pains to emphasize unusual or anomalous features of the slates and paintings, posing riddles for his readers to solve on their own. But after meeting and talking with Ron, I remain more convinced that he is one of the world's leading experts on Spiritualist history than the "true believer" that his books might imply. His wry sensibilities run through many of the displays of the museum and in the presentations he gives to visitors.

Take, for example, the display case housing the relics of the former Fox Cottage, where, according to legend, mediumship was born in the taming of a poltergeist. Only a few objects were salvaged from the cottage fire in 1955, now showcased here: the Fox family Bible, a few foundation bricks, and a tin trunk. The last artifact is of particular significance since it is believed by some to be the trunk carried by the itinerant peddler whose angry ghost was the first spirit to commune with the Fox Sisters. The spirit told the Sisters that its body had been buried underneath the cellar floor. Despite a long and painstaking effort to find the peddler's remains, none was found, until 1904, when a wall of the cottage collapsed to reveal a heap of bones.

As for the trunk, it was alleged some 20 years later that this, too, had been found alongside the bones, although no mention of it is included in the original journal reports of 1904. In an interview with Joe Nickell for the *Skeptical Inquirer* in 2008, Nagy admitted quite frankly that there was no proof for its discovery in 1904 and that its exact origins are unknown.[14] And yet he allows it to sit alongside the family Bible and cottage bricks as a historical artifact of Spiritualism. If visitors ask of its significance, as they invariably do, he simply replies that *people say* this is the trunk that belongs to the peddler. So Ron has put *somebody's* trunk in the case, next to the Bible.

Or consider the framed photograph of the Mitchell-Hedges crystal skull, which is prominently displayed in the Museum's alcove, kitty-corner from daguerrotypes of the suffragettes who used to congregate at Lily Dale in its early decades. The full-sized likeness of a human skull, carved from a single block of clear quartz, was put on display at Lily Dale in 1996, when the Assembly invited Anna Le Guillon Mitchell-Hedges to conduct a workshop at the camp. Mitchell-Hedges claimed to have discovered the skull in the 1920s, buried underneath the altar of an ancient temple in Belize. She made a career for herself touring with it. Mitchell-Hedges also told her audiences that Mayan informants had explained to her that their pre-Columbian ancestors had used the skull as part of a magical ritual that inflicted death on the enemies of the ancient Mayans.

But in 2007, skeptical researcher Joe Nickell again uncovered documentation that Mitchell-Hedges had purchased the skull from a London art dealer in the 1940s.[15] Tests by the Smithsonian Museum subsequently determined that the object had been manufactured using late nineteenth-century machinery. The evidence clearly pointed to an elaborate hoax, one that had bamboozled visitors to the 1996 Lily Dale season out of their hard-earned dollars. Case closed.

Or almost. I am not quite sure how to interpret the positioning of the picture of the Mitchell-Hedges skull as it hangs in the museum alongside the images of the suffragettes, as at least two readings are possible. Am I to understand this photograph as "evidence" of the spirit world on the one hand or as documentation of the recent history of Lily Dale on the other? In other words, am I to understand Anna Le Guillon Mitchell-Hedges as a pioneer of the paranormal or as one of the entrepreneurial women who, like the suffragettes beside her, rose through the ranks of the Spiritualist subculture as a popular lecturer? Surely, Nagy is aware of Nickell's research, having been interviewed by him a year before? If he were, would he tell me?

I have watched Nagy here in the museum giving lectures on the spirit trumpets that once floated through the air in darkened spirit cabinets, voices of the deceased blaring out messages to the living. Once he balanced a trumpet on its end when suddenly, without any prior warning, he slammed his hand down on it with a loud *bam!* The thing collapsed into a small disc of metal—a convenient design, Nagy explained, for concealing trumpets in a knitting kit.

Ron seemed bemused, or so I thought, by the visitors' startled reaction to the small sonic shock. Speaking as a Catholic priest, I can only say that his overall delivery struck me as rather deadpan.

But perhaps it is the Lily Dale Museum that is misnamed. The former one-room schoolhouse strikes me as reminiscent of the seventeenth-century European wunderkammern, or "cabinets of curiosities," that flourished in the wake of the New World voyages. These were eclectic collections, housed in a number of royal courts throughout northern Europe and Russia, of the odd and exotic, natural and man-made, real and fake. Wunderkammern crammed together in a single showcase such diverse objects as minerals, fossils, flora and fauna, skeletons, clockwork automata, artistic miniatures, paintings of deformed human beings, Catholic relics, Native American ritual objects, and even specimens of plants purported to sprout sheep. Here, the natural world was showcased in a space collapsing distinctions between the empirical and the imaginary.[16]

In fact, as several historians of science have recently demonstrated, it was the prevalence of wunderkammern that provoked Enlightenment distinctions between the real and the fake to begin with.[17] Throughout the seventeenth century, rational empiricists devised the earliest taxonomies of modern science to make sense of the nonsense in the cabinets of curiosities. In the wake of their efforts, the *real* artifacts of science and history went on to be housed in modern museums. For modern-day debunkers, the Lily Dale Museum is an abhorrent leftover from this earlier era of confusion, blurring the categories between museum and funhouse. Professional skeptics like Joe Nickell are there to warn us all: *the objects inside this room are not what they purport to be.*

But what have they purported to be?

I ask Ron Nagy, "Is that crystal skull *real?*"

He sticks his thumbs in his pants pockets and looks at me askance: "What do *you* think?"

I do not answer. A photograph of the medium Jack Kelly has just caught my eye. I ask Nagy, "Is this *the* Jack Kelly, of Mae West fame?" This time he gives me a straight answer. It is.

I recognize Kelly's face from my research at Harvard-Radcliffe's Schlesinger Library archives, where I once rifled through Mae West's papers in between my visits to Lily Dale. West's involvement with Spiritualism typifies the stories I have heard repeated in my visits here to the camp.

Midway through her life, disenchanted with the material trappings of modern American society and disillusioned with mainstream Christianity, the bawdy diva of film and vaudeville found answers to her spiritual questions in the marvelous feats of Lily Dale medium Jack Kelly.

Born in Wales, Kelly had exhibited a penchant for trance and clairvoyance from an early age. He first stupefied his own family members with a spontaneous demonstration of remote viewing, describing the details of a horse team mired in a pond some distance from his Welsh home. As an adult, Kelly became a professional psychic and medium, electrifying Americans like West with fantastic displays of clairvoyance, mediumship, and telepathy. He was both a close friend and a spiritual guide to West, nurturing her beliefs in the reality of an afterlife and the worldly applications of psychic powers in this one.

The Mae West papers at Radcliffe include bits and scraps of their correspondence, affidavits from Kelly's family swearing to the authenticity of his psychic and mediumistic abilities, and notes for West's 1975 book, *Mae West on Sex, Health, and ESP*. After reading through her book, I find nothing suggesting that she approached Kelly and Spiritualism with the same sense of camp and double entendre that defined her acting career. *If I asked for a cup of coffee, someone would search for the double meaning.* Nevertheless, it is precisely this sense of double meaning, one explicit and the other implied, that defines the culture of Lily Dale.

Ron Nagy is not the only one with a deadpan sense of humor. The mediums of Lily Dale embody the spirit of the double entendre. In anthropological terms, they are involved in "ludic" activity, a term denoting the paradox of "serious play."[18] In the first Spiritual Insight Training workshop for cultivating mediumistic abilities, Reverend Elaine Thomas spent much of the weekend reflecting on the strange powers of improvisation, when arresting insights and premonitions seem to emerge from apparently random associations. "Sometimes when you seem to be making things up, it turns out that you're making up reality," she mused. The mediums at Lily Dale revel in play and understand its potency in breaking down calcified notions of "what is real." Particularly in the context of bereavement, ludic activity acts as a powerful solvent in dissolving the emotional and cognitive complexes that surround grief.

Debunkers expose the "tricks" of a former era at Lily Dale in a somber tone, lamenting the rise of scientific illiteracy in America and warning the public of the "con artists" in our midst. But there is little in Lily Dale to suggest that we should approach Spiritualism with utmost seriousness to begin with. I remember the first inspirational talk I heard at Lily Dale, when the middle-aged man at the lectern, dressed in his Sunday best, broke out into a five-minute, spot-on Katharine Hepburn impersonation from *Suddenly, Last Summer*. Or when the Lily Dale medium corrected me for taking seriously a public reading, delivered by her friend and colleague, that my truck tire was flat—*That's his throw-away line!* Or when I learned that the "Campbell Brothers" duo who brought through some of Lily Dale's most famous precipitated spirit paintings were not brothers at all but lovers all along.

This is, after all, a place where middle-class Americans are invited to participate in an elaborate masquerade, doffing and donning masks. The performance of mediumship models social protocol for the entire camp. Ordinary citizens are stripped of their public personae, while mediums metamorphose from the neighbor next door into liaisons with the dead or channelers from other planets. The process is repeated ad infinitum; the unmasked become the masked, as visitors take their own turns reading each other. Just when you think you have someone figured out, you learn that they are on speaking terms with Napoleon Bonaparte.

For a culture raised on the value of knowing the truth, the whole truth, and nothing but the truth, Lily Dale's infinite regress of masking and unmasking is maddening, for some even immoral. Professional debunkers attempt to short-circuit this infinite regress by pronouncing mediumship as *absolutely fake*, to invoke the allegedly solid ground of scientific method, to interrupt the masquerade. But, as it turns out, even institutionalized skepticism—today represented by the Committee for Skeptical Inquiry, of which Joe Nickell is a member—is involved in a shtick of its own. The committee poses as a scientific institution but is not a scientific institution at all. It avoids scientific experimentation on claims of the paranormal as a matter of institutional policy. Instead, it enlists the support of celebrity scientists. Over the years, its more prominent members have included astrophysicist Carl Sagan, psychologist B. F. Skinner, and geneticist Francis Crick, all of whom vouch for the authenticity of the organization but are themselves not particularly interested in conducting scientific studies of the paranormal.[19]

In other words, we are led to believe that skeptics are scientists in the same way that we are led to believe the tin trunk belonged to the peddler or that ancient Mayans crafted the Mitchell-Hedges skull.

It is as if Lily Dale has brought out the gamer in all who venture near to its gates, leaving the question of the spirits' "reality" an ever-unfolding riddle. As soon as you think you've found solid ground, you find that there is another layer of meaning. Here the trickster reigns, and everyone speaks in the tones of Mae West. *It isn't what I do, but how I do it. It isn't what I say, but how I say it, and how I look when I do it and say it.*

IV.

The ground ceases to spin.

Zoltar, the Brother from Another Planet, has finished DJ-ing for the day. I snap back into my body, rising and falling over the dramatic hills of West Virginia.

The GPS announces that I am nearing my destination of Point Pleasant. Here, I will spend two days in the capital of Mason County, on the eastern bank of the Ohio River. Nearly half a century ago, residents on both sides of the Ohio were terrorized by a wave of bizarre events that lasted more than a year—sightings of strange lights in the sky, widespread poltergeist phenomena, and encounters with an awful bird-man hybrid with glowing red eyes. Journalist John Keel, who came to Point Pleasant in 1966 to investigate the phenomena, memorialized the events in his paranormal classic *The Mothman Prophecies*.[20]

Tonight, I will be one of just two guests staying at the four-story Lowe Inn in downtown Point Pleasant. The hotel was built in 1901 and still preserves a turn-of-the-century decor. It has a reputation for being haunted. The cashier at the Mothman Museum, located in the same building as the Lowe Inn, shows me a strange photograph that a friend of his took

Native Guide.

of the hotel lobby. In the foreground, light seems to coalesce into the shape of a woman wearing a bonnet or hat. "She used to be the maid of Lowe Inn," the cashier explains, watching my reaction. I am quite sure there is a rational explanation for this photo but later will sleep with the lights on.

In the evening as the sun goes down, I take a stroll along the Ohio River. I am struck by a sweeping series of murals painted on the half-mile-long flood wall separating downtown Point Pleasant from the river bank. From left to right, Louisiana artist Robert Dafford has depicted scenes of the Shawnee Indians in various stages of contact with Virginian pioneers and, from right to left, murals of the English colonists in various phases of their settlement in Shawnee and Mingo Indian lands. Almost directly behind the Lowe Inn, these two panoramas meet in the center, with Natives and European Americans massacring each other at close range, wielding guns and tomahawks.

The scene depicts the 1774 Battle of Point Pleasant, the culminating battle in a long series of pre–Revolutionary War struggles between Native American and European nations for control of the Ohio River valley. On October 10, 1774, the Shawnee chief Cornstalk instigated the last of these fights with raid against a Virginia militia at the confluence of the Ohio and Kanawha rivers. Under the leadership of General Andrew Lewis, the militia held its ground throughout the day but suffered at least 75 casualties. The next day, they began their pursuit of the Shawnee, who had retreated to Chilocothe, some 20 miles north up the Ohio. The Americans subsequently forced Cornstalk to sign a peace treaty that ceded vast tracts of land in what is now West Virginia and Kentucky to the settlers.

Several people in Point Pleasant tell me Chief Cornstalk has cursed this corner of the country. After all these years, they still remember the story of his murder by the settlers, after he had sworn peace and laid down his arms. Residents recall the strange events of *The Mothman Prophecies*, which culminated in the 1967 collapse of the Silver Bridge between Point Pleasant and Gallipolis, Ohio, across the river. A man who works in the Mothman Gift Shop and Espresso Bar shows me photographs he captured of orb lights in the abandoned army storage bunkers back behind the nuclear power plant on the outskirts of town. Enlarged on his computer, they vaguely resemble the heads of gargoyles and ghoulies. He gives me a hand-drawn map to the storage bunkers so that I can check them out myself.

In one sense, I could not be any farther away from Lily Dale than I am now. Point Pleasant has yet to produce its own version of the Fox Sisters, who might tame the local poltergeists into benevolent spirit guides. Except for photos of last year's Mothman Festival over at the museum, there is very little that feels "playful" in this town. And yet the specter of the Indian dead, memorialized in the statue of Chief Cornstalk and the paintings of the Shawnee warriors, is quite familiar. The Indian ghost is a stock item in Spiritualist summer camps as well. Back at the Lily Dale Museum, Native American guides appear in several of the precipitated paintings, figure in wooden busts of fierce-visaged warriors, and still leave messages for anyone who cares to read the spirit slates. Chief Oskenonton, a Kahnawake Mohawk man who practiced healing at Lily Dale from 1916 to 1955, has an entire display case of his own. Among other memorabilia, it houses the scrapbook he collected while on tour throughout Canada, the United States, and Europe as a professional opera singer.

Point Pleasant and Spiritualist summer camps memorialize different Indians from different wars. Here in West Virginia, it is the prerevolutionary Lord Dunmore's War that is remembered. In the latter case, Native Americans made their debut as spirit guides in séances immediately after the Civil War, as battles between the U.S. government and the Great Plains peoples were raging west of the Mississippi. This was also the era that introduced vanquished Great Plains warriors in "Wild West" equestrian shows and, in major metropolitan areas, red-face vaudeville actors posing as Natives. But in neither Point Pleasant nor Lily Dale is the Indian intended to be a historical figure. In the eyes of the white civilization that conjures up their spirits, the Indians signify what has been left behind or surpassed by modern civilization. The "vanishing Indian" and Indian ghost has thus become enmeshed with American national identity since the days of James Fenimore Cooper and *The Last of the Mohicans*. Their displacement from the landscape was—and remains— the necessary condition for the existence of modern nation-states throughout the Americas.

Literary critic Renee Bergland has studied the prevalence of Native American ghosts in American art and literature as a sign of the originary crime lying at the heart of the nation's origins. She suggests that American citizens are caught in an insolvable paradox. In order to commemorate America, they are obliged to remember the initial encounters between European and Indian peoples, and yet the remembrance of these events undermines the moral authority of their nation. And so the paradox is repressed from political discourse, resurfacing in fiction as the Indian ghost, charged with its uncanny power to horrify (haunted Native burial grounds) and fascinate (sage Indian elders). "The land is haunted," Bergland writes, "because it is stolen."[21]

I have just begun my travels through Nature's Nation, but already the Indian dead are beginning to emerge as a key to understanding the common cultural issue that Spiritualists, ufologists, and dowsers are attempting to work out. I find Bergland's analysis compelling on many levels: first, that the Indian ghosts are projections of the white American psyche; second, that the Indian ghost is a legacy of America's repressed foundations in violence; and, third, that the Indian ghost raises an insoluble question about American identity. And yet I have not yet seen any particular signs that white Americans are wracked by guilt over this issue. The more striking problem here begins—and ends—with the question of origins. Where does the American nation come from? More particularly, where *in the world* does the American nation come from?

The answer is, we will never know.

We will never know because the New World was founded on an erasure of all that preceded it.

Both power and ideology figured in this originary event. In my travels, it is the ideological dimension that confronts me—the way that European Americans think about their origins as a society and their place in the world. Spiritualism is closer in time to the "closing of the frontier" heralded by Frederick Jackson Turner at the 1893 Chicago World's Fair, just three years after whites and Natives had been brought into contact for the last time through the contingencies of warfare. When the last Native Americans "vanished" (which is to say, when they were politically and geographically displaced), it was really the white man who disappeared, at least as he had defined himself as an inhabitant of the New World up until that point. The presence of the Other was waning. The absence of the Other was overwhelming. Even as they communed with Indian specters, white Americans were completing their dissolution into ghostlike beings. They had at last realized Europe's old utopian dream of living alone in a virginal New World.

A precipitated spirit painting in the Lily Dale Museum bears the signature of a Native American guide named Grey Wolf. He walks alongside the shores of a lake that appears to be in the lush woodlands of the Northeast, yet he wears a headdress common to the tribes of the Great Plains. Grey Wolf is a self-portrait of a Spiritualist in trance. He comes from nowhere in particular—maybe the Seneca's land, maybe the Nakota's. Origins are irrelevant. He hails from Nature. He is alone. He is a ghost.

Surely, somewhere in America, Frankie Z. Avery has passed out again.

It is now night. I look up to the darkened sky, and a strange light floats across the field of stars. I feel compelled to move again. I stand facing west, toward Roswell, New Mexico.

3

Roswell: Cast Adrift

I.

It is early July 2007, and I am making my way through a malevolent night-time storm along the high deserts of Arizona. The windshield wipers are set on manic speed, whipping back and forth through solid sheets of rain and hail that blow down from the inky blackness enveloping Interstate 40. The lighting of the GPS console has switched over to its evening setting; tendrils of interstate highways and secondary roads are lit up in yellow against a darkened gray background.

I am bound for Roswell. In two days, the 2007 UFO Festival will begin there, commemorating the sixtieth anniversary of an alleged crash and retrieval of a downed flying saucer and its extraterrestrial crew on the outskirts of town. As legend now has it, the American military retrieved the debris and bodies and whisked them away to a secret base—perhaps in Ohio, perhaps in Nevada—and has since been reverse engineering space-ships, conducting autopsies on alien bodies, and perhaps even entering into secret pacts with extraterrestrial races bent on dominating the human race.

I steady my eyes on the red taillights of the 18-wheeler ahead, the only object visible on the road between sporadic flashes of lightning, bracing myself for the jolting blasts of wind that periodically batter our highway caravan. I turn on the satellite radio for company, spinning the dial to XM 165. The digital airwaves play *Coast-to-Coast AM*, America's most famous paranormal talk show. I listen to the host, George Noory, interview his guests on tonight's topic, which is "Web Bot Predictions of the Future." George Ure and Cliff High have developed sophisticated software pro-grams that track recurring key words on the Internet, allegedly scanning the collective unconscious of the nation. I learn that the Web Bots have already predicted the Northeast blackout of 2003 and the September 11 attacks and are presently picking up on something especially ominous for the year 2012, possibly a reversal of the earth's magnetic poles.

Boynton Canyon Vortex Spot.

Outside, another flash of lightning lights up the sky to my left. Twisted silhouettes in the distance, perhaps of clouds, appear in the sky. Then again, all is darkness.

As I listen to *Coast to Coast AM* in the midst of this storm, I am in a sense at Roswell already. More than just a collection of weird tales, ufology is a terror-stricken narrative about Nature. Early in the twentieth century, the Protestant theologian Rudolf Otto wrote a highly influential essay that redefined the way scholars in my field look at religion. In *The Idea of the Holy*, Otto argued that religions originate not in ideas about God or the gods but in primal experiences of awe. The idea of the holy is born in an apprehension of the *mysterium fascinans et tremendum*, an encounter with a mystery that simultaneously provokes feelings of rapture and dread, ecstasy and horror. The referents of this experience change from one time and culture to the next, but the anatomy of this encounter stays constant. It is revealed in universal statements about the dual nature of divinity, the paradoxical descriptions of the sacred as both compassionate and wrath-ful, loving and unapproachable.[1]

In modern America, Nature itself has perennially stood in for God as the referent of religious experience.[2] And, true to Otto's analysis, it has been cast in turns as sublime and forbidding. As I traverse the miles between Lily Dale and Roswell, I am leaving one representation of Nature and entering another. The spirit world of the mediums has been from the start a place filled with kindly grandmothers and Indians who lay down their hatchets to make peace with the white man. But where I am going, America is haunted by dreadful things. Aliens arrive unbeckoned, confusing and tormenting its citizens. And in their wake, the aliens have left a popular conversation about the awe-inspiring depths of the physical cosmos. Nature is a dark wonder, the terror-inspiring Other.

In my encounter with Oma back at Lily Dale, I realized what a fine line separates a spirit guide from an alien. Frankie Z. Avery and other channelers have simply ventured further out into the imagined vistas of Nature than the Spiritualist mediums. They bring through messages from interplanetary and intergalactic intelligences dwelling on its outermost borders. Historically, however, their rendition of extraterrestrials has been much tamer than what we find in twentieth-century ufology. The channelers' extraterrestrials are wise and caring, not unlike spirit guides, and the channeled messages are filled with hope and helpful advice.

Channeling is a modern-day legacy of a bygone era when human beings were confident that, working together, human reason and the perceptions of the five senses could uncover the underlying structure and order of the physical universe. As vast and sublime as nature was, faith in empirical science helped ground us in it. By the end of the nineteenth century, there was no reason to doubt that, given enough time, further observations and experiments would eventually render a complete map of our cosmic coordinates. Reason, nature, and progress went hand in hand; another day, another piece of the bedrock charted, onward toward omniscience. Extraterrestrials like Oma are as straightforward and predictable as Newton's physics. The fact that they inhabit some distant galaxy does not stop them from seeing the universe in more or less the same way that we do.

A few days ago, I stopped in Sedona, Arizona, overshooting the UFO Festival by a few hundred miles to the west. While I was there, I received an unexpected initiation into this older world of metaphysical ufology through a series of conversations and private rituals with a psychic named Bev. Sedona is the perfect way station between Lily Dale and Roswell. It has one foot in nineteenth-century metaphysics and another in expectations of the Apocalypse. Since the 1980s, it has become a popular destination for New Age spiritual seekers who believe that the city, nestled in the gorgeous red rock country of Verde Valley, lies atop a system of "vortexes." I paid Bev several hundred dollars to escort me down a trail in Boynton Canyon to one of these fields of anomalous Earth energies in search of release from my smoking addiction. As it turned out, we spent more time talking about extraterrestrials than the nature around us.

Bev was a channeler, a confidant of aliens, and a master cartographer of the universe she has spent many years traversing.

Most of what I now know about the living tradition of metaphysical ufology I learned that day, on my back, head spinning. I lay on an Indian-weave blanket that my guide had spread out on the ground, breathing in fumes from her sage smudge stick. On her cue, I began to purposefully hyperventilate for several minutes, until the tips of my toes and fingers were tingly and my head was light. Bev prayed to the earth spirits of Boynton Canyon, sprites and fairies and ultradimensional dolphins that once swam through the red rock valleys millions ago, when Sedona was just a corner of a vast and deep primordial seabed. She called out to her extraterrestrial guides as well, asking them to come down and guide me through an inner journey to loosen those energetic knots whose outward and visible signs were a particular fondness for nicotine.

In my mind's eye, I saw what Bev, the masterful storyteller, gently suggested I see: the angelic faces of aliens radiating beams of light down to the trailheads of Sedona, right through my skin, and into my central nervous system. I floated high above the earth in the delicious trance stratosphere. I saw connections where I had never seen them before: between the extraterrestrials, distant geological eras, mermaids perched atop of buttes, interstate highways, Oma, the loving face of my own maternal grandmother, Lily Dale, and more.

For just a few hours underneath the live oaks of Arizona, I imagined a world whose sundry parts connected in a seamless and unified tapestry.

And with the impending UFO Festival on my mind, Bev's mention of extraterrestrials caught my attention especially. When my carbon dioxide and calcium levels slowly returned to their normal levels, I asked her about this. She explained,

> The aliens are our own ancestors. They were here on Earth before, millions of years ago. They mated with human beings; human DNA is infused with the stuff of extraterrestrial races. But they have never left us. Now they hover around the earth in their ships. People see them. They are here to raise the vibration of the earth, and all the beings who dwell upon it, until consciousness is transformed. At that moment—which is coming soon, most recently calculated at 2012—human beings will know ourselves to be one with the cosmos and each other.

But this is nothing more or less than an elaboration on Madame Blavatsky's Theosophical cosmology. Blavatsky was that successor to Andrew Jackson Davis, a visionary extraordinaire. Beginning in the 1870s, Blavatsky started to fly to the farthest reaches of Nature and back again, bringing us back a map of all she had seen and heard both on Earth and on other worlds, from the beginning of time. According to her, humanity has and will continue to evolve through a total of seven eras and by the nineteenth century had already reached the end of the fifth age.[3] Lunar intelligences jump-started evolution at the beginning of the first age, creating the progenitors of the human race, who were similar to us in form but lacking intelligence.[4] A class of advanced beings called the Lords of the Flame imbued these beings with sparks of intelligence during the third era, when our ancestors lived on a now-sunken continent named Lemuria.[5] According to Theosophists, Blavatsky's disclosure of this information in the 1888 publication of *The Secret Doctrine* signaled the inauguration of the next two eras of higher consciousness.

The explicitly extraterrestrial flourish to Blavatsky's cosmology came several decades later. In 1925, Charles Webster Leadbeater, one of Blavatsky's leading students and intellectual heirs, explained that the Lords of the Flame originally inhabited the planet Venus. Since imbuing humankind with the light of their own intelligence, the Lords, whom Leadbeater also referred to as the Masters, returned to Venus, but one of them remained connected to the earth. Sanat Kumara, the world's "Spiritual King," guides the spiritual evolution of select individuals—the students of Blavatsky's metaphysical tradition, who continue an esoteric lineage dating back to the days of Lemuria.[6]

Sure enough, as Bev and I talked further, she told me that she had begun her formal study of metaphysics decades ago in Mount Shasta, California. Mount Shasta is a renowned site in Theosophical circles. It is the place where, in the 1930s, Guy Ballard, an American student of Theosophy, claimed to have met his personal spiritual master, the disembodied eighteenth-century alchemist Count St. Germain. With the count as his guide, Ballard embarked on a visionary flight through the earth's prehistoric past, learning that one ancient civilization had used "airships" for transportation[7]

It was Ballard who elaborated on the Theosophical teachings to include physical ships, but the basic extraterrestrial contours are implicit in Blavatsky's original writings. For all intents and purposes, extraterrestrials play the role of God in Theosophical literature. Lunar and Venusian intelligences do what God did in the Book of Genesis, creating life and inaugurating humankind. They perform a Christological role in human history as well, watching over our doings on Earth. And they come again, like Christ, to usher in a new and spiritually purified era.

Everywhere is order, structure, and pattern. Blavatsky's works burst at the seams with data collected or, more precisely, plagiarized from the scholarly explosion of research in nineteenth-century natural and social sciences, but the essential plotline is simple enough. There is a Book of Genesis and a Book of Revelation, Theosophical style—a beginning, middle, and end to the human drama. When extraterrestrials appear, they are not particularly *alien*. They have been domesticated within Theosophy's master narrative.

The last time I saw Bev, she was escorting me back to my truck. "You know," she said thoughtfully, "you just might make it." "Make it to what?" I asked her. "Through the coming shift," she replied coolly, referring to the upcoming, extraterrestrial-orchestrated elevation of planetary consciousness.

Her manner was so matter of fact and confident, without a hint of the dread that suffuses twentieth-century tales of truly alien extraterrestrials. These latter stories have their roots in the cultural shockwaves that followed seismic shifts in early-twentieth-century science. The nineteenth-century map of Nature, based on Newton's laws, came to an abrupt end in 1905. Albert Einstein published his special theory of relativity, which demonstrated that time and space must behave differently—shrinking, compressing, expanding from one reference point to the next—if the laws of physics are to remain constant throughout the universe. The general theory of relativity, published 10 years later in 1915, demonstrated that gravity could be accounted for by the "curvature" of four-dimensional space-time. And in the 1920s, quantum physicists began to plumb the nature of subatomic reality, where energy and matter collapse into a single continuum, and demonstrated that the act of measurement affects what is measured, for reasons that are still debated among physicists.

Relativity and quantum physics together demolished the Enlightenment hope that a coherent map of the universe could be built up from empirical observation. The everyday world of the senses could no longer be counted on as a reliable source of information. What analogies can we find from the world of ordinary experience to comprehend post-Newtonian nature? As a body approaches the speed of light, time slows down relative to an outside observer. "Entangled" quantum particles are in instantaneous communication with each other, regardless of the distance separating them. One can mouth the words or even work through the mathematical equations. But relative to our day-to-day existence, where the sun is still "rising," statements like these are truly pointing to a weird and uncanny natural world.

Extraterrestrial beings (whether real or imagined remains to be pondered) creeping out of a post-Newtonian cosmos bear the strangeness of their native ground. Driving across the desert at night, I remember some of these darker tales, starting with the legend of Roswell. The so-called Roswell Incident has all the elements of a twentieth-century UFO story:

fear, confusion, and paranoia. According to eyewitnesses, it was a night just like this when aliens came hurtling down to Earth, overcome by a fierce storm. The exact day is still debated, but the month was either late June or early July 1947. Some accounts claim that there was but one UFO. The craft exploded some 70 miles north of Roswell, showering debris onto the Foster Ranch below, before eventually crashing in the plains of San Agustin, New Mexico, some 225 miles to the west. Another scenario has the craft exploding over the Foster Ranch but crashing onto the Bud Corn Ranch, just 25 miles north of Roswell, spilling its bleeding humanoid crew onto the earth there. Other accounts have two saucers colliding in midair—one meeting its doom north of Roswell, the other on the plains of San Agustin.

Eyewitnesses recall as well an orchestrated cover-up of the entire affair by the U.S. Army, which in 1947 staffed a major air base on the south side of Roswell. Mac Brazel, a foreman at the Foster Ranch, was the first to find anomalous debris strewn about the ground on the morning after the storm. Suspecting some military-related accident, he notified army officials. They quickly dispatched personnel, cordoned off the Foster Ranch, and sequestered the wreckage. A similar fracas allegedly followed at the Bud Corn Ranch. The contents were then transported via airplane to Kirtland Army Air Field in New Mexico, never to be seen again.

Newspaper accounts of a crash near Roswell further muddy the waters. On July 8, the Roswell army base issued a press release that it had captured a "flying saucer" at the Foster Ranch (there was no mention of alien bodies). But then the next day, it released another report that the wreckage was in fact the remains of a weather balloon. Whatever the actual event, the second press release effectively quashed public interest in the Roswell crash. Aside from the press releases, whatever the public now knows about the event did not become widely known until decades later, after two ufologists—William Moore and Stanton Friedman—collected the first round of interviews from various eyewitnesses to events surrounding the crash. In 1980, Moore and coauthor Charles Berlitz published *The Roswell Incident*, setting in motion one of the most widely discussed UFO legends of the century.[8]

Since 1980, the story of Roswell has taken on a life of its own. New witnesses and new details have emerged periodically. Today, the legend of the Roswell Incident includes accounts of nefarious government research on the remains of the crash at secret military bases and cabals within the Pentagon in league with extraterrestrials. In addition to its back-to-back and contradictory press releases of 1947, the U.S. Air Force (which took over the Roswell army base and monitored UFO reports during the mid-twentieth century) has now released an official report claiming that *both* of these accounts were part of a disinformation campaign. According to a 1994–1995 air force report on Roswell, the real object that crashed at the Foster Ranch was a *top-secret* weather balloon, a part of the classified Project Mogul established to monitor atomic tests by the Soviets.[9]

As for the humanoid bodies that eyewitnesses remembered seeing (eventually traced to Bud Corn's Ranch and never reported in the 1947 press releases), the air force has also felt compelled to address this issue. In a second 1997 report, it ventured that eyewitnesses had mistaken crash-test dummies for aliens.[10] Oddly, dummies were not attached to weather balloons, classified or not, until 1953.[11] The air force explained this discrepancy as a distortion of memory over the decades. Various sightings and time frames were confused, and bits of science fiction had crept into the recollection of real events.

The Roswell Incident evokes confusion at every turn. It begins with accounts of a physical cosmos more bizarre than science can or will admit, but it does not stop there. Representations of all kinds—eyewitness testimonies, media accounts, and expert pronouncements—are all partial, shifting, and untrustworthy. The realities they describe—natural phenomena, historical events, and political agendas—take on an unreal and illusory appearance. In the face of the *mysterium tremendum* that is post-Newtonian Nature, Nature's Nation comes undone. The faith that reason can or will map the many facets of the world into one coherent whole founders. Aliens come to unnerve us, riding on the shock waves of early twentieth-century science.

But why stop with the Roswell Incident? There are literally thousands of similar experiences, collected by both military and civilian agencies since the late 1940s, when the so-called waves of UFO sightings first began. I think about the Chiles-Whitted sighting, which stumped even the most skeptical military observers at the time. This occurred on July 24, 1948, as Captain Clarence S. Chiles and copilot John B. Whitted flew their Eastern Airlines DC-3 over Montgomery, Alabama. Suddenly, unbelievably, they saw a torpedo-shaped object approximately 100 feet long, flying alongside the plane. As the skies that night were clear, they could make out more precise details: the craft was brightly lit from within and had two rows of windows. From its back side trailed a 50-foot column of flame. All but one of the passengers were asleep at the time—it was 3:00 in the morning—but the passenger who was awake independently corroborated their report in a later interview. An object matching the pilots' description had also been reported an hour earlier by a maintenance worker at the Robins Air Force Base in Georgia.[12]

And then there was the strange story reported on April 24, 1964, by Lonnie Zamora, a highly respected law enforcement official from

Socorro, New Mexico. Zamora was distracted from a high-speed car chase that night by a loud explosion and a slowly descending, blue "cone of flame" heading in the general direction of a nearby dynamite shed. Fearing an explosion, Zamora sped off the main highway toward the light. Cresting over a hill, he came on what he thought at first was an overturned car in a ravine. Beside the vehicle stood two small men, wearing white coveralls. Zamora then realized that the car—about 50 feet away from where he stood—was actually an oval-shaped, metallic craft. While the rattled Zamora radioed in his report, the object proceeded to emit a deafening roar, shoot blue flames out its underside, and rise slowly off the ground before flying away. At the site where Zamora reported the incident, investigators found a number of impressions in the earth, including four trapezoidal indentations in the earth and what appeared to be small shoeprints. In the center of the imprints were discernible insignia marks, stylized with crescents and arrows.[13]

Closer to our times, I can still remember when thousands of eyewitnesses reported and recorded on camera and videotape a massive triangular object slowly moving through the skies of Phoenix, Arizona, on the night of March 13, 1997. Nine lights in a "V" formation were clearly visible from the ground. The object, which witnesses approximated to be the size of a football field, blocked out the stars and reflected the city lights of Phoenix on its underside. One eyewitness reported catching a close-up of the craft and seeing rows of windows with the silhouettes of humanoid figures within it. Six days after the sighting, Governor Fife Symington downplayed the event in a phony press conference, standing next to an aide dressed in an alien costume. But 10 years later, Symington went on record as having seen the object and admitted he had no idea what it was.[14]

How to evaluate the data these legends recount? First, we want to know something about the credibility of the witnesses, perhaps wishing that we could simply ignore their stories as hoaxes or lies. But in all three of the accounts I am now recalling, the integrity of the informants—licensed pilots, a police officer, and a former state governor—is difficult to dismiss out of hand. In the case of multiple-witness sightings, as in the event over Phoenix, the reliability of the reports increases, as does the credibility of accounts that include corroboration on radar or film.

If we choose to accept these stories as true testimonies, we are pressed to know how to make sense of the data—where to put them. For Theosophical ufologists like Bev, there are answers to this question because there are stable cosmologies that can account for the facts. But for baffled modern bystanders like myself, we are left face-to-face with this amorphous construct called Nature, asking questions about its depths, its possibilities, and its limitations.

It was the secular U.S. Air Force that coined the term "unidentified fly-ing object" in the early 1950s to signify a flying thing that has no name and no place in the modern scientific model of nature, pending further investigation. It was deemed preferable to the more popular designations at the time of "flying disc" or "flying saucer," both of which came laden with preformulated and unsubstantiated theories concerning extraterres-trial visitation. Based on its own studies, the air force concluded that about one-fifth of reported UFO sightings during the middle of the twentieth century constituted truly unidentified phenomena; the rest could be explained as misidentifications of known objects, such as airplanes, stars, the planet Venus, and refractions of earthbound lights.[15]

In order to grasp the truly awe-inspiring power of a UFO tale, all it takes is a few minutes dwelling on the unadorned details—two-rowed tiers of lights, tiny footprints in the sand, and football-field-long fuselages—while resisting the temptation to categorize them somewhere. Unfortunately for Rudolf Otto, who wrote in 1919, mass waves of UFO sightings had not yet begun sweeping the United States and other countries across the world. In secular terms, "UFO" is synonymous with incomprehensibility. In Otto's religious terminology, it constitutes the *mysterium*, the mind-blowing, totally Other. "Ufology"—literally the study of UFOs—is a mis-nomer since one can hardly be said to study incomprehensibility. In this field, one gazes on the anomalies in fascination and awe, and Nature itself becomes a dark wonder.

There is no going back to Lily Dale. Haunting has become a heavy thing.

II.

I cut off the interstate onto State Route 285, heading south, approxi-mately 50 miles north of Roswell. The sun has risen, as they say, over the Chihuahuan Desert, now to my left. Scattered in between the thousands of square miles of agave, mesquite, and yucca plants along this route are the Anglo-founded towns of southern New Mexico. This is the country where the "West was won." In contrast to the older Mexican settlements, with their central churches and plazas, the communities I drive through here are arranged along the typical grid pattern of mid- to late nineteenth-century American Western towns.

The perpendicular rows and columns of streets are slapped down uncer-emoniously atop the landscape. Once again, rational order, structure, and pattern are reflected in the very layout of the towns. The dream of settling other planets is an extension of this ideal of colonizing the earth's own, more punishing ecosystems. All we need is just a little water—discovered

Cowboy & Aliens.

in Roswell in 1890 in an aquifer connected to the Pecos River. On the moon, water was found in 2009 and inspired a brief but lively discussion about human settlements there.

Shopping centers, hundreds of them, are the first signs of civilization as I cruise into the northern edge of Roswell. Driven by the engines of alien-tourism, every year they encroach a few blocks farther into the desert. They make for a rather banal entrance into this famed citadel of ufology. I decide to drive farther south before taking a full plunge into the carnival. I want to reapproach Roswell from the other side of town, where the remains of the Roswell Army Air Force Base still stand.

Today, the former base serves as both the local airport and an industrial park—renamed the Roswell International Air Center—but the original hangars, buildings, and airstrips remain. During most of the years of its military operation, from 1941 to 1967, these bland beige buildings housed the "best in show" of America's nuclear attack dogs. Beginning in 1945, Roswell was home to the 509th Bombardment Group, an elite cadre of pilots formed from the squadron that dropped two atomic bombs on Japanese civilians. During the Cold War years, Roswell became the largest base of the U.S. Air Force Strategic Air Command—on call to deploy hydrogen bombs, with the renamed 509th Bombardment Group initially at its core.

It is true that I could have stayed in New York, simply listening to George Noory interview Roswell celebrities on the radio, but a pilgrimage into this desert really should be a mandatory initiation for all budding ufologists. Although Roswell's base has shut down, New Mexico is still the heart of America's nuclear homeland—a monument to the immense shifts in social life that the new physics of the early twentieth century came to effect. Two hundred and twenty-five miles to my north are the Los Alamos Laboratories, built during World War II to house the Manhattan Project and still in use today for military research and development. One hundred and twenty-five miles to my west is the White Sands Missile Range, where the first plutonium-implosion device was detonated in 1945, prior to the dropping of "Little Boy" on Hiroshima. It too is still in use as a site for testing weaponry. Against the backdrop of the grid-patterned settlements and nuclear-era bases of New Mexico, the Roswell Incident takes on an irony that can easily get lost on the airwaves.

The buck has stopped here on the western frontier, where the Anglo-American fantasy of colonizing Nature reached its climax. It is impossible to entertain the thought of aliens—here at Roswell or anywhere else—without relinquishing the idea that humans are the sovereign masters of the universe. On the one hand, we have the spawn of ancient stars mocking, taunting, and watching us. On the other, we have the ongoing and failed human attempts to understand exactly what is going on. The manifold networks of mass communication—journalistic, political, artistic, and scientific—all talk past and cancel each other out. As the sightings and encounters continue to pour in, growing ever more bizarre, we are mired in our own confusion, trying to untangle news from fiction, facts from hoaxes, transparency from disinformation. All signs point to system failure.

With the former Roswell Army Air Force Base behind me, I speed back to the carnival, a perfect setting to contemplate the dark wonders at hand.

III.

I would extract a single quote, attributed to an alien, from the tomes of ufological literature to sum up the entire state of the field. It was telepathically communicated to the legendary alien abductee Betty Hill on the night of September 19, 1961, after she and her husband had allegedly been abducted in the White Mountains of New Hampshire. Aboard the ship, one of the extraterrestrial crew showed Betty Hill a map of the stars used for navigation. Hill asked the alien to point to its home port. The moment could have been the ufological equivalent of discovering the Holy Grail—*we would know where to place them*. But instead, the alien asked her to point to her home star first. She could not.

"If you don't know where you are then there isn't any point of my telling where I am from," the alien responded.[16]

At UFO festivals like the one at Roswell, participants do not gather to behold the anomalies firsthand. They cannot. The aliens are in control of the game, revealing themselves in their own time and ways. A UFO festival is a second-order event, an open invitation to identify the unexplainable to the best of one's ability and in this way to bandage up the wounds of Nature's Nation. It is a fine vantage point from which to view the breakdown of popular faith in an inherently rational cosmos here in our post-Enlightenment world.

I drive back to the city to the International UFO Museum and Research Center in the older, statelier part of town. There they are in front of the old Plains Theater—crowds of tourists in khaki shorts and T-shirts waiting to pay their admission. A few even wear tinfoil hats, an always popular prop in the alien parade (foil allegedly thwarts the telepathic intrusions of alien life forms).

Once inside, this mixture of UFO buffs, conspiracy theorists, and idly curious vacationers will hobnob with leaders of the ufological field in a setting that combines elements of an academic conference, democratic town meeting, and religious tent revival. During the day, the full-time ufologists (with rare exceptions, they are all men) will be seated in front of various museum exhibits, autographing books and answering questions from the general public. They will also deliver presentations on various aspects of the UFO phenomenon in the conference rooms of the Research

Pulp Ufology.

Center. In the evening, panel discussions will pool together an array of experts on various aspects of the mystery (the Roswell Incident, alien abductions, and government secrecy).

In 2007, other speakers congregate at the Roswell Visitor Center, built courtesy of the Roswell Chamber of Commerce. As the festival continues to grow, so too does the number and range of ufologists. These include self-identified Christians and members of the Mutual UFO Network, the nation's largest civilian UFO research organization today. On my return to Roswell just two years later, the Christians have broken off from the festival and are now hosting their own conference over in a Best Western ballroom, while the Mutual UFO Network's speakers are now housed on the New Mexico Military Institute campus. The Visitor Center is still in use but now almost exclusively as a place of commerce.

I join the crowd outside the International UFO Museum and Research Center, located in the former Old Plains Theater on Main Street. We are shielded from the desert heat by the shadow of the marquis and slowly shuffle past the wrought-iron statue of "Mac Brazel & Debris Field." Brazel, the ranch foreman who allegedly discovered the remains of a downed spaceship outside Roswell, is now rendered as a silhouette of the archetypal western Cowboy, seated atop a horse and standing above a bunch of dead aliens.

The huge block letters "U," "F," and "O" above our heads blend in with the deco architecture of the old theater building. They are painted orange and white and topped by a flying saucer that looks like a donut. We are stepping into an enormous cartoon made of steel and concrete.

It is no accident that the facade resembles a comic book. Tales of extra-terrestrials were first popularized in America through pulp-fiction maga-zines, predecessors to the modern comic book, widely read throughout the 1920s and 1930s.[17] In journals like *Weird Tales*, *Amazing Stories*, *Thrill-ing Wonder Stories*, or *Marvel Tales*, short-story writers penned imaginative accounts of encounters with races from other planets, typically set in the future. The space-exploring swashbuckler Buck Rogers, to cite a famous example, made his debut in a 1928 issue of *Amazing Stories* as the main character in a short story about postapocalyptic America, set in the twenty-fifth century. In homage to ufology's pulp-fiction roots, volunteers at the 2007 festival hand out souvenir postcards for the "Amazing Roswell UFO Festival." They feature a pulp-fiction style of cartoon depicting an astonished Brazel and his horse, beholding the downed saucer near Roswell. "Amazing Roswell Mysteries," it reads: "Fifteen Cents."

As I edge closer to the ticket booth, I stare at my postcard, resisting the temptation to reduce the entire UFO phenomenon to an instance of "sci-ence fiction." Certainly, the Roswell Chamber of Commerce is playing with these associations. It mixes kitsch and irony into its marketing ploys, luring jaded postmoderns alongside die-hard UFO fans into the local UFO economy. It was in 1991, on the eve of the decade of the *X-Files*, that the city of Roswell began to reinvent itself as the UFO capital of the world.[18] Two eyewitnesses to the Roswell Incident—Lieutenant Walter Haut, who issued the first press release of a "flying saucer," and W. Glenn Dennis, a local mortician who fielded military inquiries about child-sized caskets—teamed up with a real estate agent to found the International UFO Museum and Research Center.

In 1996, the museum organized the first UFO Festival, inviting promi-nent Roswell investigators and other ufologists to share their findings with the public. But then the Roswell UFO Festival itself made for good press. In advance of the 1997 convention, scheduled for the fiftieth anni-versary of the crash, national media outlets stepped in to provide free advertising. Anticipating crowds as high as 50,000, the Roswell Chamber of Commerce quickly mobilized to coordinate its own event, embellishing the museum's speaker schedule with attractions that have since become stock fare: a UFO film festival, scheduled rock concerts, and an alien cos-tume contest. With an estimated 40,000 tourists eventually converging on the city, Roswell was transformed overnight into a Mecca of ufology and American pop culture.[19] Stylized heads of gray aliens (enlarged heads with oversized almond-shaped eyes) came to top the lampposts on Main Street, McDonald's built its local restaurant in the shape of a flying saucer, and local businesses gave themselves UFO-related names: Cover-Up Café, Not of This World Espresso & Gifts, and Roswell Landing, to name just a few.

But even as it entertains the masses and fills local Roswell coffers, pop science fiction is working through a serious social question. From the heyday of pulp to the present day, the genre has helped Americans come to grips with a physical universe whose immensity and complexity are ultimately beyond anyone's ability to fathom. We still yearn for a coherent representation of the physical world. Enter the parade of science-fiction pioneers, from the swashbuckling Buck Rogers to the inquisitive Agent Fox Mulder of the *X Files*, who gently lead the nation into the unfathomable abyss of space and reassure them that they still have some hope of finding some order. The twentieth-century obsession with understanding the extraterrestrial is part of this quest. We yearn to give our God a face and a name.

A new breed of extraterrestrials entered the popular imagination through the pages of pulp during the 1920s and 1930s. Of the many examples that could illustrate this new breed of imagined life form, the creatures of H. P. (Howard Phillips) Lovecraft are among the most graphic. A regular contributor to *Weird Tales* magazine during the interwar period, Lovecraft created his own bestiary of monsters whose age, scale, and sheer otherness bordered on the mythological. While some of these entities were supernatural, most inhabited our universe as either extraterrestrials or primordial things that had survived unnoticed on the face of this earth. Some went by generic designations: the Deep Ones, the Great Race, the Elder Things. Others had names: Shub-Niggurath, "the black goat of the woods with a thousand young"[20]; Tsathoggua, "molded . . . from a toad-like gargoyle to a sinuous line with hundreds of rudimentary feet"[21]; and Azathoth, "whose name no lips dare speak aloud, and who gnaws hungrily in inconceivable, unlighted chambers beyond time amidst the muffled, maddening beating of vile drums and the thin monotonous whine of accursed flutes."[22]

Lovecraft was explicit in making connections between his aliens and the nature of the physical cosmos opened up by the scientific breakthroughs of his day. In "The Call of Cthulhu," one of his most famous tales about a race of antediluvian creatures lying dormant beneath the earth's deep seas, Lovecraft put words to the modern zeitgeist:

> We live on a placid island of ignorance in the midst of black seas of infinity, and it was not meant that we should voyage far. The sciences, each straining in its own direction, have hitherto harmed us little; but some day the

piecing together of dissociated knowledge will open up such terrifying vistas of reality, and of our frightful position therein, that we shall either go mad from the revelation or flee from the deadly light into the peace and safety of a new dark age.[23]

This "terrifying vista of reality" was condensed in the creature of Cthulhu itself, described as a cross between an octopus, a dragon, and a human caricature, "whose face was a mass of feelers, a scaly, rubbery-looking body, prodigious claws on hind and fore feet, and long, narrow wings behind."[24]

Rather than asking his readers to believe in the reality of these beings, Lovecraft's fiction ultimately pointed beyond them to a universe whose vastness and quirkiness eluded any sensible representations whatsoever. He coined a term to describe the genre he was trying to create: cosmicism, or cosmic horror. "The Theosophists have guessed at the awesome grandeur of the cosmic cycle wherein our world and human race form transient incidents," Lovecraft wrote in "The Call of Cthulhu." "They have hinted at strange survivals in terms which would freeze the blood *if not masked by a bland optimism* [emphasis added]."[25]

Through lurid descriptions of his creatures' otherness and meditations on the vastness of cosmic space and time, Lovecraft's cosmic horror afforded modern readers an experience of catharsis. It gave them a way to manage the dread of living estranged in a natural world. In the process, he and his pulp colleagues transformed extraterrestrials from their metaphysical predecessors in many ways. First, humans encountered them, or they came to humans, in the extraordinarily ordinary fabric of space-time rather than through the visionary mode of channeling. Second, they were much stranger than we had previously imagined them, as befitted the inhabitants of distant and discontinuous space-time coordinates. And third, they embodied what literary critic Vladine Clemens calls "daemonic dread," a deep anxiety that the natural universe is utterly oblivious to the outcome of human affairs.[26]

The woman behind the ticket counter abruptly interrupts my reveries. "One adult?" she asks impatiently. She wears a furry black hair band, complete with eyes and adorned with tentacles. A young man beside her wears a *Star Trek* T-shirt. He is asking tourists for their zip codes. "13214—is that in this solar system?" he asks me.

I have now stepped completely inside the cartoonish world of the Roswell Museum. The main room gives the vague impression of a school gymnasium decorated for a Halloween party. There on the far wall is a gloomy mural of the downed saucer and bleeding extraterrestrials, done in browns and ocher. In the middle of the room stands a life-size plastic horse, pasted with newspaper clippings about the Roswell Incident, circa

1947, and shellacked. A replica of a flying saucer, maybe five feet in diameter, hangs from the high ceiling, covered in crinkled aluminum foil. The room is packed with hundreds of tourists, abuzz with conversation.

IV.

I spend the next hour or so ambling through the museum's exhibits, acoustic-board booths jammed with photographs, placards, and homemade dioramas of or about the UFO. I am trying to find my way out of this cartoon world, beyond the representations of the alien, and down to hard facts of the UFO phenomenon. I want to know the nature of this world.

The first display is of little help. It is titled "The Era of Modern Sightings Begins." This is mostly a series of placards documenting strange sightings throughout the world during the 1940s. We read about strange balls of light that American and German pilots during World War II spotted trailing their planes. They nicknamed them "Foo Fighters." We learn of unidentified projectiles, "Ghost Rockets," that rained down on the forests of Sweden in 1946. And we brush up on the details of the 1947 sighting by Kenneth Arnold that inaugurated the first wave of UFO sightings in the United States.

Kenneth Arnold was a businessman and private pilot who lived in Idaho. On June 24, 1947, he was flying his plane through clear blue afternoon skies over Mineral, Washington, when he made out an unusual sight. He saw what appeared to be a formation of nine shining discs, flying south at an estimated 1,700 miles per hour (an unthinkable speed for an aircraft in 1947) and swerving in and out of the mountain peaks around Mount Rainier.

In an interview with Oregon-based reporters shortly after his flight, Arnold struggled to describe the strange things he had seen in the sky. While his exact account is disputed to this day, one of the newsmen ended up writing down "saucer-like aircraft," a term that eventually metamorphosed into "flying saucers" as the story circulated from one media outlet to the next throughout the nation.[27]

Within a month, everyone, it seemed, was seeing flying saucers in America. The first wave of UFO activity lasted from 1947 until 1951. Three other waves followed: from 1958 to 1960, from 1970 to 1972, and from 1979 to 1981.[28]

And that is how the "modern era of sightings" begins.

But we still want to know, sightings of what?

In the 1940s, the interpretation of flying saucers was up for grabs. Kenneth Arnold at first thought he had sighted a military airplane. Toward the end of his life, however, he believed that he had encountered

Inside UFO Museum.

some form of as-yet-to-be-classified biological life that inhabits the skies. In 1948, the new pulp magazine *Fate*, launched in the wake of the Arnold sighting story by *Amazing Stories* editor Raymond Palmer, popularized its own theory that flying saucers were shooting up to the skies from underground caves, piloted by the survivors of an antediluvian civilization.

But curators of the Roswell Museum have showcased flying saucers (and Foo Fighters and Ghost Rockets) as the prelude to an *extraterrestrial* crash in the high deserts of New Mexico, as much of a forgone conclusion today as it was in the 1940s.

There are no hard facts here. I move on to the next three displays, which focus on the Roswell Incident itself. The first is a time line of the 1947 events at Roswell, reconstructed from newspaper reports and the interviews collected by Moore and Friedman. Then there is a large exhibit titled "The Roswell Dig." It tells us that in 2002, the Sci-Fi Channel sponsored an archaeological excavation at the Foster Ranch in search of the legendary debris left from the saucer. According to eyewitnesses, this was an amazing material. They nicknamed it "memory metal." Thinner than aluminum foil yet extraordinarily strong, memory metal would spring back to its original shape if crushed or folded, free of creases and wrinkles.

We read that the dig failed to find even a shard.

There is, however, a piece of metal on display, framed and hanging on the wall. It was pocketed at the Foster Ranch by an "unnamed soldier," passed on to artist Blake Larsen, and donated to the museum in 1996.

Laboratory tests classified it as a type of *mokume gane*—a stylized wood-grain metal used in Japanese jewelry.

I move on to "The Great Cover Up" display, complete with a collection of wooden crash-test dummies in the corner. Here at last I find a promising artifact: a reproduction of the so-called Ramey Memo. The memo was a 1948 telegram sent by General Roger M. Ramey to Lieutenant General Hoyt S. Vandenberg, acting chief of staff for the Army Air Force. No copies of the original document have ever been found. What we have is a photographic negative of Ramey, posing in his office for the second military press release about the Roswell crash that recounted the story of a downed weather balloon. The telegram is part of this larger photograph—clutched in the general's hand as he crouches over the pieces of a balloon in his Fort Worth, Texas, office.

A greatly enlarged copy of the memo hangs in the display, its many provocative phrases transferred onto placards. We read, "FWAAF [Fort Worth Army Air Force] acknowledges that a 'disk' is next new find west of the Cordon," "the victims of the wreck," "aviators in the 'disc,'" "misstate meaning of story," and "sent out pr [public relation reports] of weather balloons."

There is no doubt about it—the Ramey Memo is the most provocative exhibit in the museum. At the very least, it points to military disinformation, as the air force itself has conceded since 1994. But its exact syntactical meaning is ambiguous without some overarching narrative to guide the reader. If this were any other place, "victims of the wreck" and "aviators in the disc" would clearly suggest *human* pilots. But here at the UFO Festival, these words suggest other meanings that change kaleidoscopically, depending on which crowd of ufologists happens to surround you at the time.

Here in the museum itself, the forgone conclusion is the so-called extraterrestrial hypothesis (ETH). This is the working assumption that UFOs hail from other star systems somewhere within our galaxy. The reasoning behind this theory is as follows: factoring in for the large number of *mis*identified flying objects reported as UFOs (e.g., military aircraft, flairs, the planet Venus, or weather balloons), the truly unexplained things seen have an undeniable physical aspect; they really are flying *objects*. Sightings have been correlated with radar readings or after-the-fact material traces like the imprints in Lonnie Zamora's Socorro, New Mexico, account. They also appear to be of artificial rather than natural composition, in most cases made of a metallic material. And their flight patterns, most of which defy the present-day understanding of aerodynamics, also suggest intelligent design. UFOs accelerate to great speeds, decelerate abruptly, make 90- and 180-degree turns, and hover.

If the UFOs are the product of advanced scientific know-how and they are not from Earth, then they must be from some other planet. That is the ETH in a nutshell. But as with all other things in ufology, speculations on the extraterrestrial are not as straightforward as they might at first seem.

The first ufologist to popularize the ETH narrative was a one-time writer of pulp fiction. In 1949, the editor of *True* magazine, a popular men's journal, approached Donald Keyhoe about writing an article on the wave of UFO sightings that had been sweeping the nation since 1947. Keyhoe, a former marine naval pilot with contacts in the Pentagon and a former freelance writer to boot, was the perfect man for the assignment. He wasted no time contacting his military colleagues, mining government-collected information about the UFO wave. The result was his article "Flying Saucers Are Real," published in the January 1950 edition of *True*.

Keyhoe's article became the template for the ETH. Its claims were threefold. First, military researchers who had investigated the UFO wave were in agreement that the phenomena were of interplanetary origin. Second, the military was deliberately concealing this fact from the public. And third, UFOs were probably visiting the planet in wake of the relatively recent detonation of atomic bombs whose blasts had attracted their pilots' attention from outer space.

"Flying Saucers Are Real" catapulted Keyhoe into national fame. By the end of 1950, he had rewritten the article as a full-length book by the same title—the first of five on the subject—and was instantly recognized as a de facto expert. In 1956, he joined the board of governors for the newly formed National Investigations Committee on Aerial Phenomena, founded by American physicist Thomas Townsend Brown as one of the two largest and most prominent civilian UFO research bodies of the mid-twentieth century.

What most of the public did not know in 1950 was that Keyhoe's free-lance experience came from his premilitary career as a pulp magazine writer. Several of his stories, with titles like "The Master of Doom" and "Through the Vortex," had appeared in *Flying Aces* and *Weird Tales* magazines, but this was in another era, during the 1920s and 1930s. Perhaps some might have guessed from the style and cadence of his prose. *If it were a Soviet missile, I thought, God help us. They'd scooped up a lot of Nazi scientists and war secrets. And the Germans had been far ahead of us on guided missiles. By why would they give us a two-year warning, testing things openly over America? It didn't make sense.*[29] But few readers of Keyhoe were scrutinizing his text for literary style. What really mattered to most Americans at the time was that Keyhoe had contacts inside the Pentagon, and the assumption was that they would know something the public did not.

In fact, by 1950, the air force was already conducting its second full-scale investigation of the UFO phenomenon. The first effort, which had run from 1947 to 1948 as Project Sign, had ended in a split jury over the nature of UFOs. Researchers could explain about 80 percent of the 167 well-documented sightings collected for analysis as misidentified objects. The rest—approximately three dozen—were classified as "unknowns." These latter reports included Eastern Airlines pilot Clarence Chiles's and copilot John Whitted's account of their near collision with a flame-shooting, two-tiered ship in the skies over Montgomery, Alabama.[30] Project Sign had concluded that there was no evidence to either confirm or deny the existence of flying saucers.

According to the later testimony of military personnel, however, Project Sign researchers had drafted a preliminary report for Air Force General and Chief of Staff Hoyt Sanford Vandenberg. It was titled the "Estimate of the Situation" and concluded that the UFOs were of extra-terrestrial origin. Copies of the report have never been found, however, and certainly the air force never made such pronouncements to the public.[31] Whatever the truth of the estimate may be, air force researchers *had no idea what they were looking at.* Some ventured that they were space-ships: if they were not Soviet aircraft, what else could they be? Others simply assumed that witnesses had misidentified earthly objects, even though that conclusion flew in the face of the reports. Vandenburg, for one, fell into the latter category, dissolving Project Sign in late 1948 and starting the second program, Project Grudge, made up mostly of staff who found the ETH ridiculous on principle.

Keyhoe certainly had enough data to craft a coherent story about ETH theorists in the military and official disregard for their claims. But "Flying Saucers Are Real" too quickly passed over the debates and confusion within the military about the UFO wave. Skeptics eventually learned of Keyhoe's background as a pulp fiction writer and used this information to discredit both his work and the UFO phenomenon altogether. But this is not the only conclusion that can be drawn from the facts.

An alternate moral is that Keyhoe's identification of flying objects with extraterrestrial spaceships was a premature explanation, one that never really functioned as a "hypothesis" at all. It had no more predictive power than any other account. And the only way to disprove it is to visit the suspected planets, one by one, to establish that aliens do not in fact inhabit them. By the 1970s, in the wake of mounting reports of alien abductions, most ufologists would in fact abandon the ETH as an insufficient hypothesis, instead embracing a near-religious hypothesis of "ultraterrestrials" visiting from other dimensions of reality. In any case, the ETH had given Americans *some* way of wrapping their minds around the waves of sightings throughout the 1950s and 1960s, some way of holding at bay what Lovecraft called "terrifying vistas of reality, and of our frightful position therein."

With all its talk of metal debris, bleeding bodies, and sequestered saucers, the Roswell Incident has resuscitated the ETH in both ufological circles and popular culture. Here at the museum, sitting at tables and selling books, are the real-life Buck Rogerses and Fox Mulders, men who have ventured into the outermost regions of a weird, marvelous, and amazing nature and returned with reassurances of order. For all their contempt of professional skeptics, they too are ultimately convinced that Nature is a reasonable, orderly place and that their informants are fundamentally rational beings.

And it is undeniably Stanton Friedman who has the most clout here. There he sits, dressed in suit and tie, the godfather of the Roswell Incident. It was he who collected the initial eyewitness interviews back in the 1970s, together with William Moore, and launched this entire ufological phenomenon. Friedman is a large, bearded, bespectacled man, now in his seventies. Frequently featured on television talk shows and documentaries, he spends much of his time insisting that ufology is not the pseudoscience that skeptics have alleged. With a master's degree in physics from the University of Chicago, Friedman has bequeathed to ufology a precious gift these days: conventional credentials and therefore a certain degree of legitimacy. His fellow ufologist Bruce Maccabee also holds an advanced scientific degree in optical physics. He is signing books here at another table.

I wait in line to buy one of Friedman's autographed works. The tourists ahead of me finally drift off to another attraction, and I am left standing face-to-face with one of the giants of contemporary ufology. "Dr. Friedman," I ask him respectfully, "what does all of this *mean?*"

Friedman looks down at his table, furrowing his bushy eyebrows. "Well, I'm a scientist, not a philosopher," he begins, "but I tried to answer that question in my latest book." He hands me a copy of *Flying Saucers and Science*. I introduce myself and tell him about my road trip, but our conversation seems to have reached its end. I purchase a copy of his book, ask for an autograph, and let the people behind me get their turn to meet the University of Chicago celebrity.

I flip through *Flying Saucers and Science* to the chapter "The UFO 'Why' Questions" and begin to peruse. Friedman has listed a number of reasons why extraterrestrials would have begun visiting the earth in such large numbers, beginning in the mid-twentieth century. It is not exactly the question I am asking, but I read on. Friedman's main argument is that the detonation of the first atomic bombs attracted the attention of space creatures in the 1940s. Since that time, they have been buzzing around the earth, scrutinizing our military-industrial advances, making sure we do not eventually turn our weaponry toward them.[32]

But this, with a few name changes and flourishes of detail, is Donald Keyhoe's ETH. Friedman, for one, has become convinced that the star map in Betty Hill's abduction tale, which she remembered and sketched during a hypnosis session years after the initial experience, points to the binary star system of Zeta Reticuli as the aliens' homeland.[33] Working off this postulate, he has further speculated that intelligent beings living in a binary star system would have a natural incentive to develop the required technology to visit their own sun's neighbor.

What most interest me about Friedman's chapter are the other reasons he lists for the aliens' visits, ones that seem to undermine the otherwise urgent tone of the book. These include "specimen-gathering for an ET zoo," "participation in galactic chess competitions (recall Bobby Fisher and Boris Spassky meeting in Iceland)," and "punishment for space miscreants: two weeks near Earth is punishment enough for a lifetime."[34]

I cannot help but suspect, with Freud, that these wisecracks are giving vent to otherwise forbidden possibilities, tamped deep down in the ufological unconscious.[35] Through the words of Trekkie humor, I can hear the call of Cthulhu: *Nature is a dreadful thing. Nature's Nation is undone.*

And the mad laughter of Charles Fort seems to peal through the din of the crowd. A contemporary of Lovecraft, the reclusive writer from Albany, New York, spent decades scouring the professional journals of science, cataloging strange things and weird events. These included the very first collections of UFO reports. They also included observations of flying bipeds, exploding animals, rains of frogs, spontaneous combustion, phantom cats, telekinesis, and more. Between 1919 and 1932, Charles Fort published four encyclopedic collections of these "damned facts"— his own term for data that modern science has ignored, dismissed, or denied because they undermine a "natural order" that currently seems reasonable to us.[36]

Ufology began as damned facts, and unless you take the stories of pulp fiction at their face value, this is where it remains.

"If you don't know where you are, then there isn't any point of my telling where I am from," said the alien to Betty Hill.

4

Roswell (Cont'd): Behemoth

I.

We have listened to ufologists advancing this or that hypothesis and have pondered the evidence displayed before us in the Roswell Museum. But hypotheses and facts have yet to congeal into a coherent theory of UFOs, one that will satisfy most members of the ufological community and the incredulous skeptics at large. I am about to turn a corner where ufology departs with science altogether and veers off into the realms of the nonrational, the dwelling place of gods and monsters. But I am willing to give this scientific approach to the UFO phenomenon one last shot.

I am still ruminating on the details of Stanton Friedman's lecture "Star Travel? YES" as our bus heads to the alleged crash site of the extraterrestrials. The talk was held this afternoon in an overcrowded conference room in the UFO Research Center. There I sat, recovering from vertigo induced by the museum's funhouse displays. The eminently rational Friedman led us on a tour de force through the history of aviation, starting with the Wright Brothers' glider and ending with present-day research on plasma technology. His main point was that engineering in general—and aviation in particular—records a history of unexpected quantum leaps in know-how and understanding. In the 1940s, for example, the great astronomer John William Campbell "proved" the impossibility of sending a rocket to the moon because nobody had yet conceived of using gravity to aid its flight. What conventional science deems impossible one day is revealed to be well within our reach the next.

The moral of his story was clear: other civilizations in different solar systems could very well have mastered the science and engineering of interstellar flight. Most scientists currently reject this idea as highly improbable, but Friedman, with a lifetime of nuclear engineering behind him, does not. All considerations of pulp fiction aside, the extraterrestrial hypothesis (ETH) is a rational explanation for UFO sightings, particularly

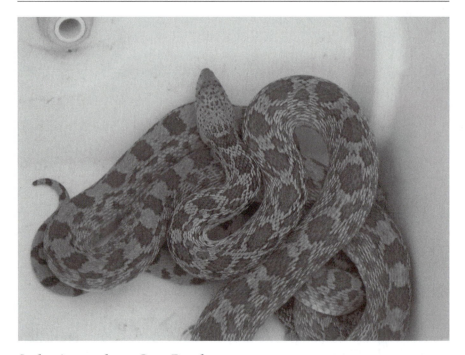

Snakes in a cooler at Corn Ranch.

if we take signs of their physicality at face value: the radar readings, the photographs and footage, and the material traces. Rationality compels Friedman to believe that there *must* be metallic discs from other planets flying through the skies and, more particularly, that one must have fallen to Earth outside Roswell. How else to explain so many eyewitness accounts of anomalous sightings, military disinformation, weird metal, and a claim of wounded extraterrestrials by the side of a saucer? Friedman has come to believe in the Roswell disc's existence through the sheer powers of deduction and his faith in the rationality of his informants.

Friedman and other ETH ufologists remind me of those famed romantic-era scientists who sailed off into unknown realms, confronted confusion and vanquished it through their wits, and then returned victorious to their homelands with new visions of order. This distinctive tale of scientific heroism has been told again and again since the late 1700s: as naturalist Joseph Banks's journeys with Captain Cook to Tahiti, as explorer Mungo Park's travels into the interior of Africa, and as biologist Charles Darwin's expeditions on board the *Beagle* to the southern seas.[1] This afternoon, Stanton Friedman himself stood in as a great discoverer, the pioneering thinker who dared—and dared us—to go where no man has gone before and to dispel the shadows of UFO confusion using good old-fashioned scientific reasoning. His challenge held out all the promise of a religious initiation, a transformative experience in and through finding an order, a Logos, to the cosmos. His faith in the powers of science inspired us.

The bus turns off the main highway onto the dirt road that leads to the Bud Corn Ranch. This is the place, according to one of the many contested sequels to *The Roswell Incident*, where a flying saucer came to its final resting place on that fateful night in July 1947, spewing dead and wounded aliens onto the ground. In Charles Berlitz's and William Moore's original version of events, an eyewitness claims that he spotted the bleeding extraterrestrials 150 miles west of Roswell, near the town of Socorro. But fortunately for participants at the UFO Festival, the later reconstruction of the Roswell Incident has relocated the final resting place of the aliens to just twenty-five-miles north of town.

Here we are, out in the desert, about to reenact the pivotal moment in the saga of the Roswell discovery: the finding of a real, honest-to-goodness artifact from a faraway civilization. Perhaps I too will see or learn about something in the desert that gives me a rational explanation for all this chaos. The bus rumbles over cattle guards and slowly rolls past creosote bushes. A lady who has been chatting with the bus driver turns around to face the rest of us. She wears a straw hat and Jackie-O sunglasses and a name tag that identifies her as a reporter from the still-extant *Fate* magazine, which once posited the subterranean origins of flying saucers. Other excited tourists are already snapping pictures of cacti through the windows. We are almost there.

The afternoon temperatures are soaring, but the dryness of the desert air has masked the intense heat. As I rise from my seat, the back of my shirt sticks to the green plastic covering. Filing off the school bus, none of us is quite ready for this afternoon's welcome to the ranch. A man is sitting underneath a canopy in the near distance beside a Thermos cooler. As we approach him, he reaches inside and pulls out what appears to be a long, fat, writhing rattlesnake.

"Welcome to the Corn Ranch," he says, rising from his folded chair. He extends his free arm, beefy and tattooed, to shake the *Fate* reporter's hand. She has stopped in her tracks. The rest of us, walking behind her, are transfixed by the serpent. "Bull snake," he says calmly and smiles, quietly amused by our alarm.

The crowd breathes a sigh of relief. "Yeah, I thought so," one man says. Other tourists take out their cameras and start clicking away. The *Fate* reporter asks one of us to take a photograph of her and the man who is apparently our guide, with one of the misidentified serpentine objects draped around her neck. The guide puts his arm around her. He is burly and early middle aged, sporting a goatee and a long black ponytail. He wears black sunglasses and a Harley-Davidson T-shirt, jeans, and black biker boots.

I peer down into the Thermos cooler. There are several of them, coiling, a dense brown mass of reptilian flesh. They are doing what they can to impart an air of dread and gravitas to this field trip.

We are ready for our vicarious encounter with the Mystery. The man with the ponytail escorts us to the entrance of the path that leads up to the legendary butte, now marked by red flags indicating where eyewitnesses say the extraterrestrials were lying. We make our way along the trail, which is bordered by two megaliths on each side. Our guide narrates the story of the Roswell Incident as we walk:

> They say that when the soldiers got here there was one of those aliens sitting up where that flag is, another guy sitting on that rock, and he was injured, really injured. He was *leakin'*, *bleedin'*—whatever stuff they do. They say that the skin was real white, white, white—*the color of white*—and the veins were like a purplish-black color, and you could really see a lot of the veins.

His brows are furrowed as he speaks, and his flailing for words, "white, white, white—the color of white," impresses on us all the sheer otherness of the things that lay on the rocks. They cannot be described or imagined easily.

When we reach the end of the path, the mood is solemn. Our guide stops talking momentarily to let us take it all in. There, a hundred feet or so ahead of us, is the crash site, or at least one of them. Beside us is a large boulder into which has been carved an ominous message in runic-style letters. The engraving reads,

WE DON'T KNOW WHO THEY WERE
WE DON'T KNOW WHY THEY CAME
WE ONLY KNOW
THEY CHANGED OUR VIEW
OF THE UNIVERSE
THIS UNIVERSAL SACRED SITE
IS DEDICATED JULY 1997
TO THE BEINGS
WHO MET THEIR DESTINIES
NEAR ROSWELL, NEW MEXICO
JULY 1947

On the fiftieth anniversary of the Roswell Incident, Pueblo Indian dancers were invited to dance here, blessing the grounds.

Back underneath the canopy, the bull snakes are still writhing in the Thermos cooler. The megaliths are casting shadows to the east. The stage has been exquisitely set for this afternoon's memorial service commemorating an encounter with Something Strange in the New Mexican wilderness. Our guide breaks the silence, continuing the narrative in the first person:

> And you know, it's hard to believe all of this, and I'm still learning from those who saw it. I was speaking with a gentleman just yesterday—he's *ninety* years old. He was asking the other guide about the kind of tour he gives and all of that, and he kept saying, "Yep, that's right, that's right." And so I go, "Did you know about it?" And he says, *"Yes, sir."* He was playing bridge with the Air Force general the night it happened. He said the soldiers brought back some debris in the back of a government truck back to the house so the general could see what it was, and then they all went out and looked at it. And when they got here, they saw the guy sitting there— *he points back to the butte*—whatever it was.

Something about this plaque looks familiar, and then I remember the numerous *descansos*—literally the "resting places" of victims of fatal automobile accidents—that I have driven past on my way to Roswell. These memorials are typically small wooden crosses bearing the names of the dead, part of the Mexican American landscape of the Southwest. But here at this *descanso*, on the crossroads of the cosmic highways, we do not even get the aliens' names.

Our guide continues with the narrative, as if he himself had been there:

> They blocked the highway off five miles in either direction. The military got here. There were tanks, and planes making sure nobody was coming over. It was unreal, just unreal. You know? They just shut everything down. And whatever it was they put on the flatbed of a trailer—they had a tarp over it—they say it was twenty- foot wide and fifteen-foot tall. They had floodlights up here, and there was one guy half-in and half-out of the ship, and there was one hanging out, and there was a pretty small one inside. And at the funeral home they said that they ordered three child-size caskets—some of them were for a four-to-five-foot person. So three of 'em were already dead, and one was laying alive.

He pauses again and smiles: "And it makes you wonder what they did with them, you know? Did they tend to the one that was still alive? I don't know. Did he die here? Or did they take him and then he died? You know? I don't know. You don't know that yet. It was all so hush-hush."

We are speechless. Everyone seems quite moved by this personal initiation into the secrets of Roswell. Our guide is a gifted storyteller, bringing the legendary events of yesteryear to life. As I take one last picture of the flags on the butte, it is a bit easier to envision the extraterrestrials sprawled out on the ledges, gasping for air like so many fish hauled out of the waters. But I cannot help but let go, once and for all, the hope of a scientific explanation for the Roswell Incident. Aside from a few pictures of snakes and megaliths, we are returning to civilization with absolutely nothing to show or say about the legendary event. To quote the plaque on the boulder, we have no idea who they were or why they came.

When Joseph Banks returned with Captain Cook to Britain, he published near-pornographic accounts of the Tahitians, having recorded their customs and sexual habits, even measuring their bodies and skull sizes. When Mungo Park returned to Scotland from his first expedition to Africa, he published *Travels in the Interior of Africa* for his countrymen, a swashbuckling memoir of adventures through the bush and near misses with bellicose tribes and chieftains. On his return to England, Charles Darwin penned his now classic *The Voyage of the Beagle*, sharing his meticulous observations of the flora, fauna, rocks, and exotic cultures of South America and the South Pacific.

Friedman and other ETH ufologists model themselves after these scientific explorers. They claim to have emerged from the chaos of ufology, shedding new light on who the visitors are and why they came. Several years ago, an ETH researcher claimed to have decoded the alien star map shown to Betty Hill during her 1961 abduction experience, pinpointing the extraterrestrials' origins to the binary star system Zeta Reticuli.[2] Stanton Friedman believes that this is where the aliens who crashed at Roswell came from, a point he embellished in today's lecture. Not only is Zeta Reticuli relatively close to our sun—a mere 39 light-years away— but inhabitants of a binary star solar system would have natural incentive to explore the planets of their sister star. As for the reasons why the aliens came here in the first place, Betty Hill remembers her alien guide explaining that the lines on the star map indicated trade routes and points of expedition. The extraterrestrials were perfect mirrors of our modern Western selves—capitalists and explorers.

But we who now board the bus back to Roswell have lost control of this narrative. American Nature has reverted into an incomprehensible wilderness. We are haunted by the silence of these beings in the desert who rob us of our peace.

II.

The sun is going down when I return to the museum. They have circled the wagons and are meeting inside: the alien abductees have gathered. Tonight is a special panel discussion titled "Meet the Abductees."

UFO Crash Site.

I have been talking with them as I circulate through the crowds. At the Roswell UFO Festival, abductees seem to be everywhere. I have met less than a handful of people who have actually *seen* a UFO but dozens who have related in terse terms their own experiences of being transported aboard an alien spacecraft. *It happened to me. I know because I've been abducted. You don't have to believe me, but I've had that experience.*

Abduction accounts lend a certain urgency to this gathering that neither the Roswell Incident nor secondhand reports of UFO sightings imparts. Abductees have been irreversibly, even visibly changed by a close encounter with the alien. Here in a supportive environment they testify to both the strangeness and the horror of it all. They exhort all of us—full-time ufologists and amateurish bystanders alike—*to please find out what is going on.*

This has been a pressing question in ufological circles for well over 40 years. It was first raised by the strange case of Betty and Barney Hill that captivated the American public during the 1960s. It resurfaced powerfully in the 1980s when hundred of reports reminiscent of the Hills's began streaming into civilian UFO research groups. No longer an isolated case from the White Mountains of New Hampshire, the abduction phenomenon demanded answers and since the 1980s has been a permanent feature of ufology.

Abduction accounts move the study of UFOs into even more confusing intellectual territory than the physical sightings. ETH ufology already blurs the boundaries between science fiction and the natural sciences. But since the 1980s, with psychologists, folklorists, and theologians weighing in on the UFO phenomenon, there is no longer consensus that we are even dealing with *objects* or extraterrestrials at all. Some abduction researchers do remain faithful to the ETH theory, emphasizing the physical traces attributed to alleged alien kidnappings: the "scoop marks" on the victims' skin, their unexplained burns, and sometimes even physical implants found underneath the skin. But there are many others who explain the experience as a rendezvous with an alternate universe altogether, akin to the visionary realms of religious experience.[3] A growing number of self-identified Christian abductees have identified the alien intruders even more particularly as the *nephilim* of the Old Testament, a class of beings they understand as "fallen angels."[4]

As I reenter the museum for tonight's "Meet the Abductees" panel, I recognize a few faces. I take my seat beside a woman named Angela, from Colorado, who shared part of her abduction story with me earlier in the festival in front of a booth over in the Convention Center. She is a thin, pale woman with slightly wild eyes, intensely clear and blue. She shared with me her stories of multiple abductions, all of which began with tales of her floating up off the bed at night and *through* the bedroom ceiling and into the underside of a hovering craft. She had forgotten much of what happened aboard but did recount the creatures there, loathsome reptilian things whose unblinking gazes left her speechless and frozen.

Staring past me into space, Angela insisted that these were different than dreams, far more vivid and intense. The things were *real*, she said, but they are not *from here*. The unsolicited visitations stopped after a period of several months, during which time she claimed to have twice seen an anomalous flying object in the skies above her house. Unlike many abductees, including Betty and Barney Hill, she had not yet sought out a hypnotherapist to plumb her memories. She did not want to relive them, but instead she had begun to attend UFO festivals like this one, looking for others who would understand her and who might help her to understand *them*.

In the midst of the 1980s wave, folklorist Thomas E. Bullard sifted through the then-1200 abduction accounts on record and found in 103 "high information cases" a recurring pattern of events. In his analysis, the full-blown narrative consists of eight discernible sections: the initial capture; a physical examination; a conference with the alien, usually via telepathy; a tour of the ship; an otherworldly journey; an encounter with a divine being; a return to the initial place of capture; and the aftermath.[5] Angela's truncated version of events left out the most uncanny, middling details but nevertheless left me somewhat dumbstruck. She is now clearly living out the "aftermath" phase, a haunted woman, irreversibly changed by whatever it was that happened to her.

Three abduction experts sit at a table before us, in front of the brown and ocher mural of the Roswell crash site. There is an aerospace engineer who specializes in the detection of UFOs by spy satellites, a certified hypnotherapist who treats traumatized alien abductees, and a man whose eclectic résumé defies easy classification. He too is a certified hypnotherapist, as well as a real estate agent, a former military police officer, a one-time employee of the CIA, a fourth-degree black-belt martial artist, an alien abductee. His name is Derrell Simms, but around these parts, he is better known as the Alien Hunter.

The panelists open the discussion with brief introductions of their background. The aerospace engineer is there simply to lend his support as an ETH researcher to the abduction phenomenon in general. Many of his colleagues are not so inclined, drawing the line between the genuine "nuts-and-bolts" ufology and the quasi-visionary stuff of abductions. During the mid-twentieth-century UFO heyday, ETH investigators used to make the same distinctions between their own research and the claims of UFO channelers, the so-called alien contactees who brought through benevolent messages to humankind. As far as the ETH crowd was concerned, the latter group was a bunch of "cranks."

That leaves the hypnotherapist and Derrell Simms as the real authorities on alien abductions. The hypnotherapist is soft spoken, but Simms, who introduces himself last, easily emerges as the star of this show. He is broad shouldered and wears a mustache. He wears a brown plaid Wrangler shirt and a shiny belt buckle shaped like Texas, his home state. He kicks off the evening by telling us he was abducted repeatedly as a child and adolescent. He has interviewed hundreds of abductees, in the United States, Puerto Rico, and Turkey. He has referred them to doctors for the removal of subcutaneous implants inserted during their physical examinations on board the ships. I saw some of these during my museum tour this morning, bits of tiny metal displayed in a red-felt-lined box.

"And I'll tell you something else," he says. "I'm not gonna rest until these aliens are brought to justice! These are crimes against humanity!" I look around the room. His first impression seems to have won over most of the crowd. They have edged forward in their seats, and some are nodding approvingly.

When the panelists are through with their introductions, almost all the questions are for Simms. Abductees in the audience want to know what he has learned about the aliens. There are different kinds, he tells us: pasty and gray, lithe and vampiric, tall and hairy, or slender and Aryan, although the most common are the so-called grays. When most Americans today imagine an alien, they are probably thinking of the grays: short, smooth-bodied humanoids with enlarged heads and huge, almond-shaped eyes that wrap around the sides of their faces.

A woman in the front row asks Simms, "What can we do to stop them?"

"Not much," he says. "They're gonna have their way with you until it's over. But you can learn just as much about them as they are about you."

The Alien Hunter talks slick and fast, making learned quips as he goes—"those grays, they're not as smart as people think"—and building a rapport with many people in the audience. A man in the row behind me opens up and shares his tale—"they came right through my living room walls"—but Simms has plenty of material to top him, filling out the details of the typical abduction narrative along the way. Since the middle of the 1980s, the examinations have turned sexual. Gray aliens (Simms calls them "drones") forcefully remove their victims' sperm and ova. The ETH ufologists who do take these reports at face value assume that the aliens are now involved in a hybridization experiment, breeding new human-alien life forms who currently dwell among us undetected.[6] Simms is not so sure. He has no overarching theory. His mission now is simply to understand and to help others to understand.

About 30 minutes into the discussion, Simms's descriptions begin to get gorier: "They shoot these needles into people brains. They're just doin' what their bosses tell 'em—they're in the back, the ones that look like vampires. But sometimes they mess up, bad. There was a case in Texas not too long ago. A child was found floating dead in a swimming pool. I know, it's horrific. But look how they can mess up! They forgot to put her back in her bed where they found her! Man!" I glance over at Angela. She has been scribbling notes furiously onto a small notepad, looking up at the Alien Hunter, transfixed. The fear in the room now is palpable and contagious. I am starting to feel uncomfortable. My breathing is short and tight. It feels hot in here.

There is no doubt about it: the fear itself is real. But beyond this, there is little consensus about what, if anything, lies beyond all the sound and fury. Since the 1980s, a number of skeptical explanations have been offered for the so-called abduction experience: hallucinations, epileptic seizures, sleep paralysis, and false memories implanted by hypnotists. Joining the theories of ETH hybridization, parallel universes, and the nephilim, these critiques have rendered ufology a hopeless quagmire of claims and counterclaims, accusations, and denials.

Abduction researchers across the board, skeptics and "true believers" alike, are trying to find a place for the fear: to name it, to tame it, to make it go away. But to me, this catharsis of terror in the Roswell Museum is

merely an exaggeration of the normal state of affairs in Nature's Nation. It
has been this way since the beginning, when the New World was a wilderness and the White Man lived in dread of his own ground. Since the
1980s, a large number of ufologists have abandoned hope in a reasonable
universe. They have followed the abductees back to America's original
condition, when strange and bloodthirsty savages surrounded us on all
sides. If the ETH researchers look forward optimistically to a day when
science will dispel all the mysteries of UFOs, abduction researchers concede to their radical alienation from the universe and the other-than-
human beings who inhabit it.

Religious studies scholar Jonathan Z. Smith has suggested that the
alien abduction narrative is in fact a graphic illustration of our culture's
unresolved encounter with cultural difference.[7] What strikes him as most
noteworthy about the accounts is not the sundry details about the aliens—
their ships, the hybrids, the weird physical exams—but the fact that neither they nor their captives learn anything whatsoever about the other.
"The aliens betray no interest in human culture, and impart nothing of
their own," he writes.[8] In return, we simply gaze upon them, confounded:

WE DON'T KNOW WHO THEY WERE
WE DON'T KNOW WHY THEY CAME
WE ONLY KNOW
THEY CHANGED OUR VIEW
OF THE UNIVERSE

The dumbstruck wonder of the alien abduction narratives differs from
the rich textual accounts of extraterrestrials found in science fiction, where
readers learn of their origins and motives concerning Earth. Unlike ETH
ufology, which owes a debt to the imaginations of pulp-fiction writers,
abduction tales point beyond science fiction to a different source. And
Smith has located it in the modern colonial accounts of human otherness.

From the very first European renditions of "Native Americans,"
"Indians," or "First Peoples" through twentieth-century anthropological
monographs of non-Western cultures, the ways of the others remain
veiled. At first this statement might seem counterintuitive. What are the
explorers' travelogues or the scholars' ethnographies if not attempts to
understand lifeways and worldviews that differ from the West's? As Smith
and other scholars have answered, these accounts typically represent various attempts to render other cultures insignificant or accidental variations
on *our own* customs and beliefs. The Others are not Others at all, they say;
underneath surface appearances, they are *just like us*. As one commentator
on Columbus's journals has summarized, the prototypical colonial

narrative presents the reader with one of two options: either the Others are just like us, or else they lack culture and language altogether.[9] On closer inspection, the tomes of colonial literature on non-Western cultures sidestep the challenge of acknowledging genuine difference and grappling with how to translate it back into familiar cultural categories.

The Others remain unknown, even as the narrator relates titillating details of their day-to-day life. And the abduction narrative, in Smith's reading, is precisely a variation of this genre. On the one hand, abductees return with thick descriptions of the surface of things, particularly the physical appearance of the aliens. The aliens, in return, examine the surfaces of human bodies. On the other hand, abductees are clueless about the captors' deeper motives and general background. The sheer otherness of the alien is reflected in the "silence that remains" between them and their abductees, "be it expressed in the lack of either the interrogative or the indicative with respect either to the aliens' culture or to ours, or in the lack of recognition of the problematics of communication, within and between cultures, let alone across phyla, expressed in the Reports as the aliens' too-ready use of English or extralinguistic mental telepathy."[10]

As Derrell Simms continues into the night, I begin to lose track of what or who the aliens are: extraterrestrials, phantoms, or Native Americans. The Alien Hunter is a cosmic Texas Ranger, bent on bringing the aliens to justice, just as the historical Rangers once hunted down Cherokees and Comanches. He explains to us that aliens have a special attraction to Native Americans. They covet and steal their genes, which they then use to become expert warriors, cosmic Indians. One European fantasy of cultural otherness informs the next. Indians are aliens, and aliens are Indians, and American alienation becomes cosmic alienation. We have never been so rooted in our own ground, which here in New Mexico lies over the lands of the Apache, Comanche, Jicarilla, Kiowa, Lipan, Navajo, Pecos, Pueblo, Ute, and Zuni. But these cultures do not figure in our understanding of where we are, apart from reminding us that this is where the West was won. We blow like tumbleweeds across the desert, encountering the entire world as strange.

I stare at a museum exhibit I visited earlier today, unable then to decipher its meaning. The display is titled "Ancient Cultures and Their Connection to Extraterrestrial Life" and features a 10-foot-high replica of a Mayan tomb lid from Palenque, Mexico. Buttressed by reproductions of Anasazi and Mogollon rock art, the huge bas-relief of the Mayan god is embroidered with elaborate pre-Columbian designs. An unidentified "Oswald Weiss" has explained that the Native American god is really an ancient alien astronaut. He has translated the decorative symbols of the Maya into such NASA-style terms and phrases as "oxygen system," "well-cushioned headrest," and "crossing into another galaxy." Only now am I beginning to grasp why the exhibit occupies such a prominent place in the museum. It is the counterpoint to the Mac Brazel statue outside, the memorial to the Indian that goes with the Cowboy, an icon of our utter estrangement from this place and its history before the mid-1800s.

Tales of being kidnapped and tortured by the Unknown Others are the legacy, at least in North America, of the Puritans. It was 1682 when the Massachusetts Puritan Mary Rowlandson penned her memoir, *The Narrative of the Captivity and the Restoration of Mrs. Mary Rowlandson*, bequeathing to posterity a new and immensely popular genre, the "Indian captivity" tale.[11] It was written and rewritten for hundreds of years, right down through the Indian Wars of the 1880s. Rowlandson wrote of her kidnapping at the hands of the Wampanoag Indians during King Philip's War but stylized it as a religious narrative. Her "captivity and restoration" took place in the New England "wilderness," a preternatural place, the devil's playground. There, she grew closer to God in the midst of her trials, enduring interrogation and torture by the Indians, the devil's children. The power of the story came from the radical difference between Europeans and Indians, the foreign and exotic quality of both indigenous Americans and their native ground. "I had often before this said that if the Indians should come, I should choose rather to be killed by them than taken alive," wrote Rowlandson, "but when it came to the trial my mind changed; their glittering weapons so daunted my spirit, that I chose rather to go along with those (as I may say) ravenous bears, than that moment to end my days; and that I may the better declare what happened to me during that grievous captivity."[12]

When John G. Fuller published the first full-length account of alien abduction in 1966, Americans were once again enthralled and horrified by the details of this Puritan-derived captivity narrative, reborn in a new guise, and set once again in New England. In *The Interrupted Journey*, a re-creation of the Betty and Barney Hill case, extraterrestrials stood in for Indians—who by now had long relocated to Canada—and a lurid description of northern New Hampshire sufficed to evoke powerful associations with the American wilderness:

> September in the White Mountains is the cruelest month. The gaunt hotels, vestiges of Victorian tradition, are shuttered, or getting ready to be; motels and overnight cabins flash their neon vacancy signs for only a few fitful hours before their owners give up and retire early. The New Hampshire ski slopes are barren of snow and skiers, the trails appearing as great, brownish gashes beside the silent tramways and chair-lifts. The Labor Day exodus has swept most of the roads clear of traffic; very few vacation trailers and roof-laden station wagons straggle toward Boston or the

New York throughways. Winter is already here on the chilled and ominous slopes of Mount Washington, its summit weather station clocking the highest wind velocities every recorded on any mountaintop in the world. Bears and red foxes roam freely.[13]

The Interrupted Journey set the eight-part sequence of abduction later noticed by Bullard the folklorist. It also cast alien abduction as a captivity and restoration in the wilderness. When former horror writer Whitney Strieber wrote his abduction memoir *Communion* in 1987, at the height of the alien kidnapping wave, he too fell back on the seventeenth-century motif. His account began in a "hidden" log cabin deep within the Adirondack Mountains, cast as a "secluded corner of upstate New York," and went on to relate his awful ordeals at the hands of the gray aliens.[14] The text, which remained on the *New York Times* best-seller *nonfiction* list for 25 weeks became a landmark of late twentieth-century ufology, but essentially it retold a very old American tale.

I wish I could conclude from all this that alien abductions are merely the product of overactive imaginations, the result of reading too many American tales of violence and horror. But I cannot. The chasm that yawns between America and its native ground is real enough. It is part and parcel of the dominant culture, preceding all the fabricated captivity narratives, Indian and alien alike.

III.

Surviving in the ufological wilderness hinges on finding the right guide, someone who can read all the maps.

This is why I have chosen to study more closely with the Alien Hunter at a hands-on workshop on witness interrogation. It is held upstairs in the Roswell Museum on a weekday afternoon during the festival. Simms's expertise as a former CIA employee and former military police officer will surely come in handy. So too will his know-how in neurolinguistic programming, the study of alleged correspondences between the eye movements of alleged UFO informants and their invisible cognitive processes.

I have already been exposed to this latter discipline at Lily Dale, though for a different purpose. There, Reverend Elaine Thomas helped us fine-tune messages from the spirits by nudging our brains into different modes with a simple roll of the eyes. If we wanted more visual information from the spirits, we were to glance upward. For auditory cues, we were to look sideways and for emotional ones downward. In the Spiritualist context, neurolinguistic programming helped guide us through the inner realms

Mayan-ET Tomb Lid.

of human nature. Relying on these easy techniques, we honed our mediumistic abilities in order to become reliable narrators of the spirit world.

But now in a drab room above the museum, we are facing off with our fellow citizens, scanning each other's eyes to uncover a con. The Alien

Hunter models the process for us first, calling for a volunteer. "Okay, folks, who wants to be the first guinea pig? Don't be afraid—I don't bite!" A middle-aged man, an auto mechanic from Bakersfield, California, raises his hand. "Alright! Come on down!" The man ambles to the front of the room and seats himself on the cold metal chair facing Simms and the rest of us. The Alien Hunter assumes an intimidating posture, leaning forward toward the victim. We can only see his back. "Okay, folks, lemme show you how it's done! Watch carefully!"

He begins by asking questions to things he already knows: the man's name, his profession, his place of residence. He tells us to watch the sideways movement of his subject's eyes. We detect a consistent pattern of glances to our left. He then instructs the man to respond falsely to a set of other simple questions. We detect an opposite pattern. "Now everybody's different," Simms informs us, "but usually when they're tryin' to pull one over you, they'll look to the right."

After a few more practice sessions, we are ready for the first real test. "Are you ready?" Simms begins and then proceeds to unleash a torrent of interrogations in rapid-fire style: "Where did you eat your dinner last night? Did you order a dessert? What was the name of your waitress? How long were you at the restaurant?" The man sputters back his answers, with Simms interrupting in turn: "Are you sure about that? Are you telling me the truth? You're not lying to me, are you? Is that your final answer?"

"He's lying!" a woman in the front row screams out. "He didn't order the strawberry shortcake! His eyes moved to the right!"

"Well?" Simms asks the Bakersfield mechanic. And sure enough, the man was lying. He didn't even order dessert.

It is our turn now to play Alien Hunter. We break up into small groups of three to ferret out the unreliable narrators among us, one liar at a time, as Simms circulates around the room. The exercise is part of our advanced training for reconnaissance missions in UFO territory, a terrain known since its first discovery for thorny overgrowths of deceit, unsubstantiated claims, and downright disinformation.

I am grateful for any clarity Simms can provide us. So far, the "simple facts" of UFOs and Roswell have led only to confusion. The army was lying both times in July 1947 with its back-to-back claims about flying saucers and weather balloons. Why should I believe its third claim about Project Mogul and top-secret weather balloons? The ETH was not a hypothesis at all but a legacy of pulp fiction. And yet, there are thousands of UFO reports collected over the decades that are not easily dismissible as sightings of terrestrial things. The skeptics assure us that all sightings can be explained, but they cannot explain them all. Abductees claim they have been taken aboard spaceships, but even within the ufological community, there are contradictory theories to account for this. The fact that there is a long tradition of captivity narratives in American culture suggests that there are literary influences afoot, but can literature induce strange scoop marks and burns on people's bodies or induce all the signs of posttraumatic stress disorder?

In 1964, at the height of the Cold War, Columbia University historian Richard Hofstadter published a now classic essay in *Harper's* magazine titled "The Paranoid Style in American Politics." It was an early contribution to the now well-defined field of social psychology, applying the psychological concept of paranoia, or irrational fear of the other, to political movements in American history. Hofstadter's immediate inspiration for the piece was the relatively recent Red Scare of his generation, the orchestrated hunt for alleged Communist sympathizers and agents in America just a decade earlier. His essay traced a recurring pattern of such "exaggeration, suspiciousness, and conspiratorial fantasy" in American politics from the late 1700s onward, rehearsing the nation's waves of collective fears aimed at phantasmagoric Illuminati, Freemasonic, Catholic, and Communist enemies.[15]

Ufology is the perfect breeding ground for this so-called paranoid style, but as the old saying goes, even paranoids have real enemies. Mired in the midst of so many contradictory accounts of the UFO—each one of which promises but fails to deliver clarity—are there not reasonable grounds for suspicion and anxiety? Inspired by the labyrinthine twists and turns of ufology, television's Fox network produced one of the most popular series of the 1990s. The *X-Files* took viewers through the rabbit hole of paranormal-related claims and counterintelligence, as seen through the eyes of two FBI agents. The motto of one agent, Fox Mulder, aptly summed up the social moral of legends like Roswell: "Trust no one." This is not "the paranoid style"; it is merely sound advice for how to bushwhack through the jungles of ufology without losing one's mind. And because we trust no one, we are now gathered at the feet of the intrepid Alien Hunter, attending his workshop on witness interrogation, learning the ins and outs of neurolinguistic programming. As I sit, watching the eyes of my fellow citizens, my country is well into the fourth year of the Iraq War—initially launched because scientific, military, and media experts had alleged that Saddam Hussein was stockpiling weapons of mass destruction. Videos circulate on the Internet alleging that unseen cabals within the U.S. government orchestrated the events of 9/11 to begin with, ushering in this new global era. Nature's Nation is now haunted by a new species of aliens, one that crawls out of "sleeper cells" instead of downed saucers. We trust no one. The line between sanity and insanity has grown thin indeed.

The Alien Hunter is calling me. It is time for a volunteer to sit in front of the class and allow himself to be grilled by the entire group. I rise to the challenge.

The crowd fires out questions: "What is your name?" "Where are you from?" "How old are you?" "What do you do?"

It is my answer to this last question that draws in the Alien Hunter himself. I have answered them truthfully that I study religion.

In an instant, Simms plants himself on a folding metal chair directly across from me. Later, I will learn from him that his father was a Baptist minister, and the subject of religion intrigues him. But at the moment I do not know this, and his powerful gaze, no doubt honed from years of practicing hypnotherapy, frightens me.

"You mean all of 'em? Or do you teach in a seminary?"

I answer, "All of them."

"So which one is true?"

I hesitate. In my small witness interrogation group, two friends had each asked the other if he was a Christian. In both cases, the answer had been a cool "Yes, sir," to which the response had been, "Well I know *that's* true." At the same time, I know Simms has broken with the Christian ufologists over the question of the aliens' demonic origins. Hoping to stave off a heated theological quarrel in this secular corner of Roswell, I manage to blurt out a vaguely Puritan response, something about human limitations and our inability to judge the matter definitively.

I am seated facing the room and can feel the collective gaze of the crowd riveted on my eyes. Simms eyes flicker, unblinking. He is not finished with me yet.

"If God Almighty were sitting in this chair right now, and He asked you to tell Him which one is true, then what would you tell Him?"

From my vantage point in Nature, I cannot say, but the Alien Hunter has me in his crosshairs. So I flip through my mental Rolodex of religious traditions. Perfect, I think: Christian enough but not too close to the national mainstream. I answer. Simms looks stunned.

"The Mormons?"

"Yes," I reply, "the Mormons."

"Are you aware that Joseph Smith was convicted for selling bad wheat?"

I confess that I am not.

"Bad wheat! He sold seeds to people that he said were wheat, but they weren't wheat!"

The Alien Hunter looks at me with suspicion. He seems unsure of my response. He whips around in his chair and asks the audience, "Is he telling me the truth?"

I wait for the verdict, nervously. There do not seem to be any Mormons in the room. The jury is hung: "Yep." "No way." "Uh-huh." "Yes, I think so." "Nope." "Nope." "Can't really say." "I think so." "Maybe." "Yeah."

Simms, the cosmic Texas Ranger, has just chased me across a stretch of southwestern desert, but I have managed to escape across the border. He lets go. "How about a hand for this guy?" The room applauds, and the Alien Hunter gives me a warm embrace.

As I return to my seat, my fellow ufologists are still eyeing me suspiciously. Their paranoia is contagious. It is high time to get out of Dodge, back to the wilderness cover of the East Coast.

By sunset that evening, I am back on I-40.

IV.

I am 30 miles north of my nation's capitol. The month is April, and the cherry blossoms are blooming outside the Hilton Hotel in Gaithersburg, Maryland. I am here for one last look at ufology, having signed up for the 2008 X Conference. This is a relatively high-culture version of the Roswell UFO Festival, a three-day lineup of high-ranking military and

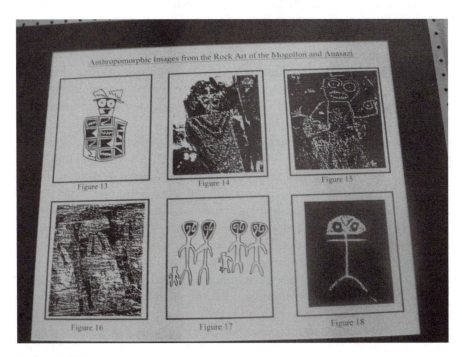

Indian ET Art.

government officials, many of them from Washington, D.C., who will speak out on all aspects of ufology. And they will make their demands for disclosure known.

In ufological circles, the term "disclosure" has many shades of meaning. First and most simply, it refers to the release of classified information pertaining to UFOs by governments around the world. In this sense, disclosure has already begun to happen. France was the first, in March 2007. Britain, Denmark, Canada, Sweden, Russia, New Zealand, Brazil, and Uruguay have since followed, and Wikileaks joined at the end of 2010. There are now thousands of previously inaccessible sightings and reports available to the public, many of them online, bolstering the perennial insistence by ufologists that something out of the ordinary has indeed been afoot for decades.

But disclosure has a stronger meaning. Virtually all the ufologists here in Gaithersburg are Roswell Incident literalists. They are quite certain that factions within the U.S. government have long been in possession of extraterrestrial technology and alien bodies since July 1947. And many believe that the U.S. government has long been in contact with extraterrestrial civilizations, an assertion that opens up the discussion about disclosure into an area called "exopolitics": speculations about how the United States has interacted with extraterrestrials in the past and how it *should* deal with such civilizations in the future.

There are no cowboy boots or tinfoil saucers in Gaithersburg. We are on the outskirts of Washington. People have come to the conference dressed in black and navy-blue suits. There will be PowerPoint presentations in the Hilton's drab ballrooms. There will be solemn deliberations. There will be urgent appeals to the people to take action, sign petitions, and contact representatives.

The man who has organized the X Conferences is a former business consultant named Stephen Bassett. Bassett quit his career back in 1995 to work with the late John Mack, MD, a professor of psychiatry at Harvard Medical School. Mack had just published his book *Abduction* to the delighted surprise of the UFO community and to the horror of Harvard.[16] Mack had been studying and in many cases treating victims of alien abduction for more than 10 years, and he announced that their experiences could not be reduced to conventional psychological categories. Like shamans or mystics, abductees were being initiated into the mysteries of other worlds, and they emerged as modern prophets.[17] Mack interpreted their experiences as dire warnings that the modern West had drifted too far away from Nature and faced destruction if it did not change its ways.[18]

Bassett has dedicated the 2008 X Conference to John Mack, his first mentor and a now legendary figure in UFO circles. But he did not study with Mack for very long. In 1996, Bassett took a turn away from research into politics, founding the Paradigm Research Group in Bethesda, Maryland. This was the nation's first—and to date the only—UFO- and extraterrestrial-related lobbying group. Bassett has pursued a number of strategies to pressure elected officials into making disclosure a reality. He has worked with local and national media outlets to defend the integrity of UFO researchers and mobilized electorates on both state and national levels to demand an end to what he calls the government's "truth embargo" on UFO-related information. In 2002, he made his own unsuccessful bid for national congress, running in the Eighth District of Maryland on the disclosure/exopolitial issue, and in 2008 organized the Million Fax on Washington, inundating the incoming Obama administration with thousands of phone calls, e-mails, and faxes demanding the release of UFO files *now*.

This is the Roswell Incident, Phase II. Bassett's goal is nothing less than to change our collective paradigm, to shift society's working model of reality. This goal he inherited from his mentor Mack, but his methods are pure Beltway.

Let it be said at the outset that UFO activism in and of itself is nothing new. Politics have been a part of ufology ever since Donald Keyhoe charged the air force with covering up the real extraterrestrial truth of UFOs. The flurry of debate that followed finally came to a head in the late 1960s, when the U.S. House Committee on Science and Astronautics heard cases from both ETH theorists and skeptics. A young Stanton Friedman faced off against the astronomer and astrophysicist Carl Sagan in Congress, and a panel of professional scientists, headed by the esteemed nuclear physicist Edward Condon of the University of Colorado, conducted an independent study for the air force.[19] With civil rights riots, hippie lovefests, and antiwar protests raging throughout the nation, Washington gave its official support to a rational universe. Following the recommendations of the Condon Committee's report, Congress decreed that there was less-than-sufficient evidence to merit public funding for UFO research. The scientific community had declared that the "damned facts" of ufology could *in principle* be explained away as misidentified common objects, even though the Condon Report had failed to explain nearly one-third of its case studies.[20]

The Condon Report and the subsequent discontinuation of official government studies of UFOs was a deathblow for ufology. By the end of the 1970s, the cultural craze for UFOs had gone the way of Spiritualism a century earlier, shrinking away into a marginalized subculture. But the war is not over yet, and Stephen Bassett is skillfully leading a new charge. Since 2004, the X Conferences have been assembling dream teams of high-profile Americans to testify to the reality of UFOs. Bassett has invited Apollo 14 astronaut Edgar Mitchell and Paul Hellyer, the one-time Canadian minister of defense and politician, to be keynote speakers at this event. Cheryll Jones, former CNN news anchor, will introduce lecturers and moderate discussions. Other ufologists speaking at the convention, while lesser known, have appeared on prime-time television shows and documentaries, or authored bestselling books.

As far as they are all concerned, the Roswell researchers have done their job. There is no need to rehearse the old arguments here about evidence and testimony—the downed spaceship and crew are a forgone conclusion. Our charge is simply to spread this Great Secret as far and wide as we can.

Pass it on: In 1987, William Moore, author of *The Roswell Incident*, said that he had long been in possession of top-secret documents pointing to the military's knowledge and possession of flying saucers. Back in 1984, his research assistant received an undeveloped roll of 35-mm film from an anonymous mailer, containing photos of briefings prepared for President Dwight D. Eisenhower. The briefings talked about a group called the Majestic 12 (MJ 12 for short), a group of scientists and military brass formed by Harry S. Truman after the Roswell Incident. MJ 12 oversaw and researched the remains of the saucer and extraterrestrial crew once they were removed to top-secret military bases, probably Wright Patterson Air Force Base in Ohio or Groom Lake in Nevada, the latter better known as Area 51.

Pass it on: In 1988, Moore said that soon after the publication of *The Roswell Incident*, a government intelligence agent named "Falcon" approached him to ask for help spying on the UFO community. Falcon promised Moore top-secret information on UFOs in exchange for his assistance. Moore said yes; the benefits outweighed the harm.

Pass it on: In 1989, Moore explained that he had actually been working for the U.S. Air Force Office of Special Investigations. Agent "Falcon" was part of a larger group called "The Aviary," so named because its members all have secret bird code names. The Aviary allegedly consists of high-ranking scientists and military officials from various government agencies who want to break the information monopoly held by MJ 12 and its successors.

Out by the watercooler in the Hilton lobby are three men in wingtip shoes, talking business. Pay close attention to them. Bassett has billed them as members of the Aviary. The man in the gray suit is retired Army Colonel John Alexander (also known as "Penguin"). He holds a doctorate in death sciences and directs the Non-Lethal Weapons Department at Los Alamos National Laboratory. The man in the pinstripes is former naval intelligence officer C. B. "Scott" Jones (also known as "Chickadee").

He has worked extensively in research and development for the Defense Nuclear Agency, the Defense Intelligence Agency, and the Defense Advanced Research Projects Agency. The thin man in the white pants and blazer is optical physicist Bruce Maccabee, PhD (also known as "Sea Gull"), a retired air force colonel. He has helped develop laser weaponry at the U.S. Naval Surface Weapons Lab in Maryland.

This is disclosure in the making. *Pass it on.*

I follow Penguin into the Grand Ballroom on Saturday morning after a breakfast of black coffee and bagels. The title of the colonel's talk is "UFOs: Good News and Bad News." He drones on for an hour with details of some of the twentieth century's top unsolved cases. He suggests that we are no closer to identifying unidentified objects than we were when Donald Keyhoe wrote *The Flying Saucers Are Real*. He reminds us that the presence here of public officials who happen to be interested in the UFO phenomenon does not in any way prove the existence of an *institution* within the government with either interest or knowledge of aliens.

This is clearly the bad news, but the good news is much more subtle. It was slipped in at the very beginning of the talk when Penguin asked us *not to record or videotape his lecture*. We all knew what he meant. This is a public venue. Members of the MJ 12 might be watching. We scribbled down notes on our paper pads, gratis from the Paradigm Research Group, knowing that the Secret had just been proclaimed, covertly if not explicitly. Brilliant.

Chickadee is more forthcoming, although he too makes no explicit mention of the Aviary. Jones's talk is titled "Plan C: A Global Program Preparing for Disclosure." His concern is to make sure the Secret does not capsize humanity. He also wants to send a clear message right now to the "Visiting Others" that we are doing our best to disseminate news of their presence among us. Chilling.

Finally, Sea Gull is the most overt. Maccabee's talk is titled "Tales of the Hawk" and relates his own insights into the Secret as related to him more than 20 years ago by another inside informant, an air force officer code-named Hawk. Sea Gull tells us that Hawk was in charge of an advanced physics division at Wright Patterson Air Force Base and learned there of ongoing plans to reverse engineer an extraterrestrial flying saucer. Unbelievable.

The rest of the weekend is in and out of the Grand Ballroom. We hear speakers elaborate on the implications of the Secret. There is extraterrestrial-derived science in the making that will revolutionize the world. Soon there will be unlimited energy for all. We hear former military personnel speak eloquently on the psychic phenomena of remote viewing and telepathy, already mastered by the aliens. This too is being studied at the Wright Patterson Base, or Area 51. When disclosure finally happens, it will unleash a new era in our collective understanding of human nature. We will know ourselves to be united with one another and with all other life forms throughout the universe.

Pass it on.

There is excitement, even jubilation, in the air. Disclosure is another name for apocalypse—literally an *unveiling*—and in faith we wait expectantly for Nature to be revealed once more, in all its benevolent coherence. On Saturday afternoon, George Noory himself leads a celebration of America in the Grand Ballroom. The host of *Coast-to-Coast AM* listens to the people cheer for the Aviary and the aliens and boo the bureaucrats who stand in their way. This wondrous world of free energy and love is our birthright, our national inheritance. "You people are the last best hope for a genuine democracy, and I mean that sincerely," the talk show guru says. "Don't ever stop asking your questions! Don't ever stop questioning the lies!" A woman seizes the microphone from one of Noory's assistants: "Have you ever thought of running for president?" The ballroom erupts into applause.

By the time the closing banquet comes on Sunday, we know as much as the keynote speakers. After dinner has been served, Apollo 14 astronaut Edgar Mitchell and former Canadian Defense Minister Paul Hellyer testify that they, too, have heard the good news from their own informants.[21] The extraterrestrials walk among us, and the flying saucers are real.

We go forth into the world on our separate ways, empowered now to spread the message.

As I drive north the next morning, the sun is shining, and the fragrant smells of spring waft through the truck's windows. Roswell seems so far away now, with all its dread and doubt and alienation. I wonder if it really matters that the MJ 12 documents were hoaxes or that William Moore admitted to waging psychological warfare against a fellow UFO researcher, with the help of air force counterintelligence.

Apparently not. Truth is no match for pulp fiction. Nature's Nation shall not perish from the earth.

Pass it on.

5

The Dowsers's Convention: In Arcadia

I.

It is early August when the northern light of New England starts again to change its hue, the white glare of midsummer tinged with a hint of gold, awakening memories of autumn. The days are still warm, but the leaves of trees are just beginning to turn in the chill of the night air. I have made a nostalgic detour on my way to the American Society of Dowsers (ASD) convention, cutting east for a stretch through New Hampshire for a visit to my parents' grave sites. Standing in front of their headstones, I remember the faint wet-sand smell of the state's rocky soil, and memories of my ancestors come flooding back.

Suddenly, my cell phone rings. It is my medium friend from Lily Dale. She has brought through a message from my father, from the Other Side, which she delivers to me long distance.

It is not the content of the reading (he wants to know how the book is coming along) that catches me off guard. Standing in Wilmot Flat's Pine Hill Cemetery, I am rooted in a specific place and particular genealogy. I would like to imagine my parents within this more intimate world, but the phone call rudely disrupts such fantasies, even as it adds yet another layer of uncanniness to my travels.

After a few minutes' reflection, I drive north along the old New Hampshire Turnpike. Crossing over the Connecticut River, I arrive in Vermont, the unofficial dowsing capital of America. For the past 50 years, the ASD headquarters have been based in Danville, a small town in Vermont's so-called Northeast Kingdom, and the annual dowsing conventions have always been held somewhere within the state. In its most basic form, dowsing (also known as divining, or sometimes rhabdomancy) is a method for finding lost or hidden objects, or determining answers to questions, using such simple tools as metal rods or pendulums.[1] The ASD was born in 1960 during a resurgence of interest in "water witching,"

Indago Felix.

the term for dowsing when it is used to search for underground water. The nascent ASD chose for its emblem a picture of two hands holding onto a forked branch (a traditional tool used in finding the right spot for a well) encircled by the Latin motto *indago felix*, or "joyful search."[2]

As I enter the Green Mountain State, the roadside billboards suddenly disappear. The highway department takes care to keep its main thoroughfares as pristine as possible, and the hills and pastures are unadorned. In this season, they are covered only by dandelions and black-eyed Susans. From higher ground, I see fields of corn growing tall along the winding rivers in the distance. Red barns and silos spot the cleared sides of wooded hills. The smell of sweet hay wafts through the windows. Dairy cows roam. Vermont needs no billboards because the entire state *is* a billboard for a particular way of life.

For at least a century and a half, Vermont has proudly identified itself with a quintessentially American ideal known as pastoralism.[3] This is a collective vision of culture as rooted in the life-sustaining powers of Nature.[4] Thomas Jefferson famously touted pastoralism in his *Notes on the State of Virginia*, a paean to small-scale agrarian life. Here is a book on American society that begins with five chapters on the beauty of the landscape—its rivers and mountains and cascades. To own and cultivate one's own land in such a setting was for Jefferson not merely an economic ideal but a spiritual one as well. The life of the farmer, poised perfectly between overly refined culture and raw wilderness, embodied for Jefferson a particular kind of character. The farmer was the bulwark of democracy, and the natural world the bedrock of the new republic.[5]

During the 1890s, pastoralism helped Vermont launch one of the first experiments in "geotourism," the marketing of a place by projecting an image of its distinctive natural and cultural offerings. The masterminds behind this strategy were not the Vermont farmers but rather coalitions of artisans, craftsmen, and professionals who searched for a practical solution to the state's stagnant population growth and economic trouble. Pastoralism found expression in several venues. Real estate agents marketed farmhouses to prospective buyers from beyond state borders as shelters from the modern storm. Local towns organized Old Home Days for Vermont emigrants to return to their homeland and reconnect with the life-giving spirit of place. Agricultural boards adopted and advertised the "Made in Vermont" seal as a little piece of the Good Life for export.[6]

Northern New England as a whole has featured in various literary and artistic renditions of Arcadian America throughout the twentieth century. My home state of New Hampshire, for example, has made guest appearances in the poems of Robert Frost and the movie *On Golden Pond*, as a powerful symbol of simplicity, integrity, and authenticity. But Vermont holds the lead. It was in 1968 that it became a state with no billboards, thanks to the work of a state congressman who had immigrated from New York, and it has continued to conjure up new and ever-innovative expressions of pastoral goodness: organic food cooperatives, Ben and Jerry's Ice Cream, and the band called Phish (the de facto successor to the Grateful Dead).

There are few from outside Vermont who can resist the allure of the Green Mountain State. Consider the case of the reporter from *The Baltimore Sun* who traveled north to cover the 2006 foliage season. She ended up writing an article called "The View from Vermont Foliage: In the Northeast Kingdom, the Autumn Festival Is Not Simply about Leaves but about Taking the Beautiful Back Roads to a Simpler Time." She was smitten by the state:

6 A.M. Sleep late . . . by Vermont standards. Dairy farmers and their herds have already been up for hours before you manage to roll out of bed. Lace up a pair of hiking boots, grab your camera and fleece pullover and set off on a roadside ramble in search of peak foliage and deer. Wonder why you don't live here.

6:30 A.M. Return to guest house for a traditional Vermont breakfast of apple pie with Cabot Cheddar, Chubby Hubby ice cream and crullers slathered with maple cream all procured at nearby country store. . . .

1:30 P.M. After a morning of visiting churches and historic houses, you plop down on the village green to watch the entire town parade by. Wonder again why you don't live here. . . .

4 P.M. Awaken to the late afternoon sunlight warming the russet leaves on the sugar maple tree outside your window. Shoot three rolls of film, telling yourself you should have been a *Vermont Life* photographer.[7]

There is hardly a better time to wax pastoral than when the hardwoods of the North Country blaze in reds and yellows. Foliage season is when the ASD conventions used to be held. Today the conventions are held in the late summer. No matter. Vermont will succeed in enchanting us nonetheless.

As I turn off the interstate onto Route 4, I am a little more than an hour from my destination. This year's ASD convention will be held at the Killington ski resort, nestled in the Green Mountains east of Rutland. The dowsing convention is a variation on Old Home Day, a chance for those who love the state to gather in the Appalachians to dowse. It was to provide entertainment at the Danville Foliage Festival that organizer Hank Balivet first assembled a group of local dowsers in 1958 to show off their feats of water witching.[8] Visitors were intrigued by the men walking through pastures with whalebones, iron spikes, and forked sticks in their hands.[9] In 1960 a small group of Vermonters and out-of-staters founded the ASD to promote, publicize, and explore the mysteries of their joyful search.[10]

Vermont Life wrote an article on the first ASD "convention" of 1960 in its autumn 1961 edition, appearing alongside articles on antiques, apples, and horseback riding. "Science may scoff, but confirmed water-witchers pursue age-old methods in their search of water," the article summarized:

> Several dozen real or would-be dowsers walked in a straight line from one part of the field to another. When they felt a strong tug, one of the officials made a note of the location. At the point where they felt water was most likely to be found a stake was placed, and the dowser was asked to name the depth at which the water would be found, and the number of gallons a minute in flow.
>
> At the end of the contest officials picked the point agreed upon by most of the dowsers. The consensus was twelve feet at five gallons a minute.
>
> A backhoe tractor then was used to check on their accuracy. Members gathered around, watching anxiously as the hole grew deeper. The backhoe could dig no deeper than eleven feet, so a volunteer with shovel dug away for several minutes, while others inspected samples of the hard-packed subsoil. It was dry. There wasn't any water. "We didn't dig deep enough," one said. "It's probably just a foot or two lower down."
>
> The failure was especially disappointing because the dowsers had predicted accurately the depth and flow the year before.[11]

News of dowsing spread through other venues besides *Vermont Life*, helping to renew interest in the "age-old" practice of water witching beyond state borders. In the fall of 1961, a Boston television station interviewed the ASD's president and one of its trustees, and the national magazine *Look* featured a one-page story on the fall gathering.[12] In the meantime, many registered ASD members returning to their homes throughout the country sent in letters and essays on dowsing to local newspapers, with one ASD member submitting a short statement to the paranormal journal *Fate* magazine.[13] No less than the first leaf peepers who had traveled to Danville, viewers and readers were fascinated. They learned of New England farmers using sticks to intuit hydrological details of underground water, its depth and rate of flow, and its mineral content as well. They wanted to know more about the causes of dowsing and how reliable it really was.

Many traveled to Vermont to find out. For its part, the ASD began inviting new speakers, starting in 1963, to explain how and why dowsing worked.[14] From then on, the annual convention transformed into a gathering that was as much educational and theoretical as it was practical. Over the next five decades, the questions continued, but definitive answers were in short supply. Indeed, the 2008 conference to which I am now driving is titled "What the Bleep Is Dowsing?"

Instead of unidentified flying objects, we come to grapple with an unidentified connection between the earth and ourselves. Make no doubt about it: the sticks (or rods or pendulums) will move, seemingly of their own accord, if only you "ask them." Make no doubt either about the fact that oil and water wells have been dug, objects have been found, and questions have been answered by such means, for reasons that are debated both among dowsers themselves and—more fiercely—between dowsers and skeptics.[15] "What the Bleep is Dowsing?" is in fact a 500-year-old conversation, dating back to a sixteenth-century German tract on mining.[16]

Enigmas abound in the world of the dowser, but in Vermont, Nature itself is often indistinguishable from what theologians call "the ground of being," the ontological bedrock of reality, the body of God. Finally, through dowsing, we are afforded a sustained and close-up look at what this actually is. The sticks bring us face-to-face with a wonder that has eluded us at Lily Dale and Roswell. It is as if the Spiritualists had captured a ghost in one of their cabinets or Stanton Friedman had towed a flying saucer out of Area 51 into his garage. We are here to do "science" in the nineteenth-century sense, relying on our own five senses and reason to plumb the depths of the ground of being right beneath our feet.

I drive toward the slopes of Mount Killington for a closer look, speeding past the extraordinary beauty of the rivers and trees.

II.

On Saturday, the Killington Grande lobby is abuzz with dowsers. Participants are walking excitedly to their first lecture of the weekend. There will be hundreds to choose from. The convention looks and feels like a trade show. Some dowsers carry metal rods by their sides. Others stand in corners of the lobby, twirling their brass and crystal pendulums. They are talking excitedly among themselves, exchanging practical information and also entering into more philosophical debates. Why does dowsing work at all? Is it an uncanny demonstration of some as-yet-to-be-identified natural law? Or is it suggestive of a new dimension of the cosmos as yet to be discovered?

I have already checked in at the registration table and picked up my name tag and complimentary ASD satchel, a red and black shoulder bag embossed with the *indago felix* logo with its picture of two hands grasping a forked branch. I find a chair in the lobby and leaf through the program booklet. The weekend schedule reflects the loose division within these conventions between practical and speculative concerns—between the *art* of dowsing and the *philosophy* of dowsing. Of interest to the more practical dowsers are the lectures on finding water and locating missing or lost objects. For the more metaphysically inclined, there are workshops on

Dowsed Labyrinth.

"personal well-being," "wisdom/spirituality," and "earth/earth mysteries," to quote the language of the program.

Judging from the number of lectures devoted to each of these topics, practical dowsing is on its way out at the convention: there are only eight talks out of a total of 90 devoted to water or missing objects. The vast majority of the remaining lectures span a dizzying array of applications that at first glance do not seem to have much to do with dowsing at all. They have titles like "Healing with the Energy of Angels: Introduction to Integrated Energy Therapy," "Archetype of the Vampire and Psychic Energy," and "The Acupressure Facelift: Chinese Beauty Secrets for Skin Balancing and Rejuvenation."

I look up from my program and watch the various dowsers milling by. Most of the attendants here are dressed for an indoor conference, wearing khakis and casual shirts or pantsuits and blouses. A mix of men and women, they appear to be in their early to mid-sixties—members of the aging baby-boomer generation, architects of the New Age. Then there are a handful of more elderly clientele who stand out from the others. They are men, dressed in working clothes: overalls, flannel shirts and suspenders, and work caps; one sports a leather belt and holster, his dowsing rods ready for a quick draw.

This last group makes up the dwindling number of Old Timers, as they are known around here, dowsers who have been with the ASD since the beginning. It is they who have passed on the actual practice of dowsing to their boomer heirs and as a rule seem to be better versed in technique. These are dowsers who scrutinize the properties of the flowing water and the rocks that come up from the wells they have dug. They debate theories of groundwater origination with mainstream hydrology, arguing—contrary to scientific consensus—that at least some groundwater is created within the earth itself, pooling in "domes" and running through "veins." They talk about drill bits and offer tips about subterranean clay and boreholes to anyone interested to learn.

Despite their differences, however, both baby boomers and Old Timers share a love for talking *about* dowsing. When the ASD was formed in 1960, many of the elected trustees were newcomers to the practice. They had come to the 1958 Fall Foliage Festival in Danville from Massachusetts, Connecticut, and Virginia. They wanted both to learn the technique of water witching and to discuss *why* it worked. At the 1961 meeting in Danville, one of the first orders of business was to establish a newsletter, which continues today as the society's quarterly journal, catering to the interests of both practitioners and dowser-philosophers.

Today, the ASD has approximately 3,000 members, with local chapters throughout the country. Arkansas dowsers now have their own local center, the Ozark Research Institute in Fayetteville. In California, the West Coast Dowsers have been holding their own annual conventions since 1979. Meanwhile, back in Vermont, the ASD has been growing steadily. By 1994, the yearly convention had become too big for the townsfolk of Danville to accommodate and was moved to Lyndon State College. In 2006, even larger ski resorts, like the one here in Killington, became the preferred venue. Throughout the country, a modern tradition of dowsing is presently taking shape in and through this grassroots network of organizations and meetings.

Over the past half century, American dowsing has unfolded as a technology in search of a science—or at least a metaphysic. The ASD journal and its yearly conventions have created the space for this conversation to unfold. In 1961, ASD president Robert Plimpton announced to the readers of the first newsletter, "We in this country have but a small idea of the great variety of uses to which the dowsing talent can be put. Perhaps some of our members have put the ability to unusual uses. . . . Personally, we had no idea how vast the subject we were studying was until we made the visit to England."[17] Plimpton was referring to the visit he and his wife had paid the previous summer to British Society of Dowsers, founded in 1933. More experienced American dowsers responded in droves to this confession of ignorance by a relative newcomer, writing in with their own stories about the rod and pendulum. In and through the process, the modern discourse of American dowsing was born.

In addition to using the tools for finding physical objects, dowsers who wrote in to the ASD also revealed their familiarity with informational dowsing: asking the rods or pendulums simple yes-or-no questions. In offering theories as to *why* such divination should work at all, American dowsers availed themselves of many different theories. A few betrayed at least a passing knowledge of the European sources to which Plimpton had alluded. They made reference to twentieth-century French theories of "radiesthesia"—literally "extended perception"—that posited precise energetic correspondences between the dowsers' tool and the things he or she sought out in nature.[18] Others spoke in more general parapsychological terms about dowsing as a sixth sense.

Spurred on by these early conversations, ASD founders made their own inquiries into parapsychology. In May 1962, they informed readers of a recent field trip to the Association for Research and Enlightenment in Virginia Beach, a school founded by the famed American psychic Edgar Cayce, where they learned from "the principal members of the association ... that various specific glands within the physical body of man ... control the dowsing ability."[19] By the end of the year, the founders announced that the society was exchanging publications with the Parapsychology Foundation, Inc., and the American Society for Psychical Research. Inquiry was under way into a possible link between dowsing and the untapped powers of the human mind.

In the meantime, other American dowsers found answers in the Bible. An article titled "Aaronites" appeared in the August 1963 issue of the journal, the first claim on ASD record that dowsing continued an age-old art:

> Aaron, older brother of Moses, and son of Levi, was the water dowser commissioned by Moses to provide water from a stone with his "wand." This story of the Bible, condoning and abetting dowsing as a fact, seems to have been considered with reserve and caution down through the following centuries. Anyone discovering in himself the talent to follow in Aaron's footsteps is viewed with suspicion by others. People who would not be heard questioning Bible teachings otherwise state flatly that dowsing is a fake without basis in truth.
>
> Is it an indication of the separation of church and today's generation that this generation is predicting water famine in the near future—because of the population explosion—and pushing research for the provision of a water supply by some artificial means? Have they lost faith that water can be brought from the earth as in Bible times, or only that we lack an ability to find that water? That we have forgotten our heritage since the time of Aaron?[20]

Other like-minded members echoed these sentiments. One described dowsing as "a gift from almighty God and . . . a talent which should be used, as every talent should be used, or it will die," adding supernatural to parapsychological explanations.[21] This early flurry of correspondence records how today's Old Timers once thought about dowsing, if and when they had occasion to theorize about it at all. They thought of it as an innate ability, inherited at birth or granted by God, but as yet had developed no overarching context that might connect dowsing to other spiritual affairs.

Times have certainly changed since then. Despite the title of the 2008 convention, there is an emerging consensus about what dowsing is and why it works. As I am about to find out, dowsers find an underlying unity in water and angels and acupressure and more. I begin my own foray into dowsing by asking an Old Timer for directions. In the plush lobby of the Killington Grande sits a silver-haired man in work clothes, relaxing on a burgundy leather couch. I guess correctly that he has been coming to these conventions for years. He tells me his name is Leroy Bull. Leroy is a kind, soft-spoken man and invites me to sit down next to him. I ask him to tell me about his craft.

Leroy tells me he learned dowsing as a child from his grandfather, who was a farmer in upstate New York. There's nothing to it except practice, he says. His neighbors in Pennsylvania ask him where to dig a well, and he shows up at their property with his two metal dowsing rods. He walks across the land until the rods swing open; here, he tells them, is where you will find freshwater flowing at a particular rate and at a particular depth. Occasionally, Leroy gets a phone call about a missing person, and for this he uses a pendulum—a deceptively technical term for any weight suspended on a piece of string or chain. Leroy asks a series of yes-or-no questions about the situation and comes to his answer from the ways the weight swings. I ask him about his success rate. "About 90 percent of the time," he replies nonchalantly.

Harking back to the Roswell Alien Hunter's seminar on witness interrogation, I try to discern first if this man is telling the truth. Like UFO sightings, stories of dowsing, particularly those concerning wells and lost objects, travel primarily by word of mouth. "There was this man, his name was Paul Oakes, and he was looking to dig a well at his new home near St. Johnsbury." Most often these stories end with a successful discovery. In contrast, data from the most extensive scientific study of water dowsing ever undertaken, the so-called *Scheunen* experiments conducted in Munich during the mid-1980s, suggest that the method is no more reliable than random guessing.[22] I realize, however, that both Leroy's professional and personal reputation rest on getting good results. He can claim whatever he wants, but at the end of the day, the revealed water or found objects do the talking for him.

"So why do you think it works?" I ask him.

After a long pause, Leroy says, "The easiest way to explain it is this. There was this *National Geographic* documentary on TV one time. It was on some African country. There was this old, old elephant there that everyone knew about, and scientists used to follow it around with their cameras. So there's this one film of the elephant leading its herd up to the watering holes during the dry season, and suddenly it stops dead in its tracks. The other elephants are looking pretty surprised, like *what's going on?* And then the elephant takes a few steps backward and starts digging in the dirt with its tusks—and suddenly, there's water."

I repeat the story back to make sure I follow him. "So you're saying the elephant dowsed for water?"

"Dowsers do what animals do all the time," Leroy affirms, adding that dogs can sense an impending storm or earthquake long before human beings know about it.

"It's that simple?" I ask.

"It's that simple," Leroy says.

"So what about the finding-of-missing-persons-over-the-telephone-thing?" I ask, somewhat more incredulously. "Elephants can't do that."

He smiles. "There are stages to all of this."

"Stages?"

"Yes, stages—stages of development." And then he asks me if I have read a book called *The Divining Mind*, by Terry Ross, which I have not.

"Well, that's the book I'd recommend to you if you really want to learn more about this," he says. "Terry's been with us for a long time, and his book will tell you all the ins and outs. There's a lot more to this than finding water." A faraway look comes over his face. "It's really about a connection . . . with the universe."

I wait for him to elaborate on this last point, but Leroy is done. "You're just at the beginning of your path," he says. "More will be revealed to you." And then he changes the subject to cars. When the time for pleasantries has run its course, I thank Leroy for his time. "Remember," he says as I rise from the couch, "it's a natural ability. Anyone can do it."

He reminds me again: "I think Terry Ross will give you what you're looking for."

This is, apparently, an important book. I approach the volunteer at the registration table and ask her for directions to the bookstore. It is located in a large ballroom at the other end of the Grande, she tells me. I mention *The Divining Mind*. She smiles knowingly. "Oh, by Terry Ross! Have you read it?"

I proceed along the carpeted hallway to the ballroom. The lectures are now in session, and the halls are nearly empty. As I walk, I muse on the nitty-gritty origins of dowsing. In the mid-1500s, the German mineralogist and physician Georg Bauer, better known as Georgius Agricola (Latin for "George the farmer"), compiled and published the various techniques and lore of local miners. These included the use of what Agricola was the first to call the *virgula divinatoria*, or "divining rod": a forked stick cut fresh from a tree that certain adepts could allegedly use to locate underground veins of ore. In *De Re Metallica* (*On Metals*), we read that these miners practiced their divination with reference to the medieval theory of the four "humors" or elements (heat, cold, wetness, and dryness) said to constitute all physical things. Since ore was classified "hot" and "dry," surveyors narrowed their quest by searching during the winter months for frost-free patches of vegetation, supposedly thawed out by the underground metal, or during the temperate months for streams bubbling up from beneath the ground, sweated out, as it were, from the heated earth. Then they would take out their rods and walk over the ground until their hands jerked involuntarily up or down, just as Leroy related. Agricola recorded that some miners swore by rods made from hazel wood, while others used different kinds of wood to divine different metals, adding in his own conclusion that divination was a skill of the miner and not an intrinsic property of the tree.[23]

The actual term "dowsing" appears in another allusion to mining by the political philosopher John Locke.[24] Locke mentions the "deusing rod" and its ability to "discover mines of gold and silver" in his 1692 monograph *Some Considerations of the Consequences of the Lowering of Interest*. In the United States, the term "dowsing" first appears in an 1831 article on techniques of metal surveying in *The Quarterly Mining Review* and since that time has been used interchangeably with "divination" to signify the practical search for underground ore or water.[25] The etymology of the word is unclear. One historian has suggested the German *deuten*, "to indicate"; the Middle English *duschen*, "to strike"; or even the Cornish *dewsys*, "goddess," referring to the earth, as three possibilities.[26]

My reveries are interrupted as I turn a corner and enter into the space of the bookstore. Felt boards propped on tables line both sides of the hallway, displaying colorful photos of the developing world. This is a record of the good work that Water for Humanity has been doing, helping villagers in Africa, Latin America, and Asia dig and equip their own wells. My eyes light on a photo of six men standing outdoors with their dowsing rods, tall mountains in the background. The caption tells me that three are from Honduras and three from El Salvador. Water for Humanity has supplied a summary of its 2002 Central America project: "presented a five-day dowsing and drilling course to six students," "successfully completed the drilling of a well begun during the course at Lake Yojoa," and "researched non-electric pump technologies." Summaries of similar projects continue down the hallway. Water for Humanity, founded in 1991, reflects the coming-of-age for the ASD's more practical explorations of dowsing. We may not know why it works, but for people who need water, this really does not matter.

Before I walk into the ballroom, I stop a stranger and ask him if he has ever heard of a book called *The Divining Mind*. He laughs. "You mean by Terry Ross? Of course!" I ask him where I can find a copy, and he directs me to the ASD vending booth.

The Grail is within reach. I walk into the bookstore.

III.

The convention's "bookstore" is a misnomer. This is indeed a trade show, and there are tools for sale alongside the books. I walk into the ballroom: thousands of square feet set aside for gadgets and gizmos peddled by an array of private vendors. I head straight for the ASD booth, mesmerized by its own variety of homespun wares, the more conventional devices of the dowsing trade. There are rods made of various materials: plastic, metal, and metal-and-wood combinations. The plastic variety are the so-called Y-rods, replications of the old forked branch. When the dowser passes over or near a hidden object, the rod jerks up or down involuntarily. Alternately, a dowser might choose to hold an L-rod, a thin wire bent at a right angle, in each hand. On approaching the desired object, these swing together or apart, seemingly of their own accord. Others prefer the metal-and-wood "bobbers," so named because their supple metal wires, mounted on handles, bob wildly up and down as the dowsers near their target.

Then there are the pendulums, also sold by the ASD bookstore. Weights made of metal, wood, or crystals are lathed into various shapes: plain and stylized cones, cylinders, pyramids, and spheres. Dangling from a wooden rack, strung on silver and golden chains, they could easily be mistaken for jewelry. Water dowsers use pendulums for "map dowsing," suspending the weights over charts of distant sites and waiting for their telltale spin to indicate where water may be found at the site. Other dowsers simply ask a pendulum any question they may have and wait patiently for its yes-or-no movements. As oral tradition has it, dowsers should begin by asking three general questions—"May I ask?," "Can I ask?,"

Tools of the Trade.

and "Should I ask?"—so that humility, practicality, and ethics bind their quest for knowledge.[27]

After a few minutes of playing with rods and weights, I explore the tables of dowsing literature and find *The Divining Mind: A Guide to Dowsing and Self-Awareness*. I flip through its pages in search of the secrets that inform Leroy's work. The authors of *The Divining Mind*, Vermont dowsers Terry Ross and Richard Wright, are neither parapsychologists nor Christian apologists. They are spokesmen for Nature. I find myself returning once again to an uncanny native ground, dwelling place of spirits and home to extraterrestrials. Suddenly, the solidities of technology, of drill bits and boreholes, disappear.

I read that the entire physical cosmos is nothing more or less than pure consciousness. All the discrete particulars of the universe are specific oscillations of this One Sentient Source.[28] Dowsing, according to Ross and Wright, is the art of synchronizing one's own brain-mind waves with the frequencies of the desired object-mind wave. The dowser *resonates* with his target, and the motion of his tools, be they rods or pendulums, indicates a successful merging of subject and object. The terminology of "rods" suddenly sounds rather lumpish. What *The Divining Mind* really seems to be describing is something more akin to *gauge lights*; the dowsers' tools are indicators of the mind's invisible back-and-forth rapport with Nature's other wave-emitting and -receiving forms.

I read on, intrigued. Just as Leroy has told me, *The Divining Mind* presents dowsing as a progression through seven distinct stages of awareness. During the first three, the dowser perfects his or her abilities to find oil, water, or lost objects by availing him- or herself of various tools. But by stage 4, deviceless dowsing, the dowser has now honed the ability to access pure information with his or her mind alone. At stage 5, the dowser gains telekinetic powers, "as in moving underground streams in a totally mental act."[29] Ross and Wright describe this phase as "cooperation with nature." In stage 6, the dowser masters an ability to heal humans, animals, and even plants from a distance, the authors describing such marvelous feats as "co-creation with nature." And at stage 7, they experience moments of "total *conscious union with Creative Forces*," becoming one with Nature itself, which is now described ambiguously as somewhere in between materiality and mind.[30]

This metaphysical cosmology may not be what the Danville farmers taught the 1958 leaf peepers or what the Water for Humanity folks teach the villagers of the developing world, but as I am beginning to suspect, *The Divining Mind* has become something of a scripture for ASD convention-goers. Outside the air-conditioned rooms of the Killington Grande, dowsing continues as a technology—with or without a science—but in here it is a way of life.

The full-fledged paradigm of dowsing developed by Ross and Wright is in large part a European import, the legacy of a 400-year-old debate over dowsing that followed in the wake of Agricola's treatise on metals. By 1949, the Dutch geologist Solco Walie Tromp had cataloged just under 1,500 studies of the topic, conducted by both individual researchers and university- or government-funded programs.[31] The lion's share of these studies was written during the Enlightenment, as modern science came to eclipse the medieval cosmology of humors. During the 1700s, the reigning hypothesis was that the rods and pendulums of dowsers allegedly tapped into the earth's naturally occurring electromagnetic fields.

But electromagnetism failed to explain the informational side of dowsing, its alleged ability to access pure information, most strikingly in applications of the pendulum. Starting in the 1800s, romantic models of Nature took over. New theorists seized on the idea that dowsers interacted with Nature as a Cosmic Mind, using their own minds to link into the Source.[32] In essence, this was the first formulation of what Terry Ross and Richard Wright call "deviceless dowsing" and the subsequent merging of the dowser with Nature.

When the first ASD president, Robert Plimpton, traveled to England and met with British dowsers, he unwittingly crossed paths with the European tradition. But it took nearly two decades for America to reconnect with its Old World roots. In 1979, a British dowser by the name of Paul Devereux came to Vermont. At the time, he was a leading exponent of the so-called Earth Mysteries—the study of anomalous natural energies allegedly known to and harnessed by the world's prehistoric and premodern civilizations. For Devereux, dowsing was more all-encompassing than a sixth sense and more prosaic than a divine gift. It was immediate and tangible evidence that all minds connected to the One Mind, the Universe-as-God or God-as-the-Universe. The ASD journals of the 1980s were awash with articles on Earth Mysteries, and in 1990 Ross and Wright summarized its main principles in *The Divining Mind*.

A little piece of the European tradition piques the curiosity of convention-goers here in the ballroom. The Reverend Alicja Aratyn, born and raised in Poland, is initiating an American audience into the French tradition of radiesthesia. This method of dowsing works with the subtle vibrations allegedly coursing through the natural world, which can manifest into such discernible forms as colors, shapes, and sounds. It is a highly technical system of dowsing, requiring sustained study and practice. She has brought her own collection of tools with her from Canada, a stupendous array of more than 40 kinds of pendulums, each one sensitive to a particular vibration and designed for a specific function. To cite just a few by their names, there are basic, UFO, neutral, Osiris, Karnak double, universal, left-turn, and color pendulums.

There are also special gadgets here not found in other booths: the Nikram, "a device for generating energy and sending it long distances to a living body"; the Radiation Neutralizer MA 1506, which "disperses harmful radiation within an area of 150 square meters, 25 meters above and 3.5 meters below itself"; and the H40 Colour Energy Generator, "used to supply the body with energy of a specific wavelength as determined by colour according to the reading of the [color] chart." Also on display are a multitude of amulets and talismans, each with a unique design, used to attract, repel, and neutralize energies around the human body or the home.

Nikram generators and esoteric talismans certainly add to the overall color of the convention, but they are not an accurate reflection of the *Americanized* version of European dowsing, which is now Vermont's own. The majority of vendors here are self-taught mystics like Leroy Bull, down-to-earth and unpretentious. They peddle human-scale tools, promising the Common Woman and Man a closer connection to the earth. A white shaman sells Native American rattles and drums. A man from Syracuse sells machine-tooled crystal skulls. A hypnotherapist from Boston markets resonance-tuning colored cards. There is also a small army of vendors selling elixirs and tonics infused with healing powers: restorative salts, blue vials containing energy-infused water, pearl extracts for youthfulness and vitality, and antioxidants made from Siberian mushrooms. There is even a company from Colorado selling a range of wireless contraptions that in form and design are indistinguishable from abstract, modern-art sculptures but purport to heal the body, increase agricultural yields, and even divert hurricanes.

I walk outside to the Water for Humanity display and listen in on a group of men who have traveled to the convention from Danville. After a while, I remark that dowsing has come a long way since the 1960s. There is a pregnant pause. One of the men looks me in the eye. "You know the best way to find water?" he asks. "With a drill!" They all laugh.

The Vermont native then tells me that back at the ASD headquarters in Danville, most of the calls are still queries for wells and missing objects. "Nothing too fancy about that," he summarizes wryly. Another man adds that the dowsing conventions no longer reflect the goal of the Dowsing Society, which is to help people find water. He asks if I've noticed the small number of lectures here devoted to water dowsing, and I tell him that I have.

But the men are powerless over the spell that their own state has cast on the rest of the nation. The allure of a simpler life has brought most of us here. I leave the luxuries of living in a solid world to the men from Danville and make my way deeper into the convention, venturing farther into this corner of Vermont's compelling dreamscape.

IV.

I am yearning to step outside into the fresh air of northern New England but have decided to sample one of the indoor lectures first. After purchasing a cup of coffee at the hotel's convenience store, I skim through the convention program. "Dowsing When Technology Fails" catches my eye, its title evoking pleasant scenes of simple, rural life—hand-dug wells and vegetable gardens, fresh laundry drying in the sun on a clothesline.

I hurry down the stairs to the specified conference room just in time to catch the beginning of talk. Taking care not to spill too much coffee, I slip into the back row of seats. The speaker is an attractive woman in her mid-sixties. Her name is Sandee Mac, and she hails from Texas. As I will learn later, she happens to be one of the few women recognized as an Old Timer by ASD members. She is talking now about something on the mind of many dowsers—"the Grid," a term used here as shorthand for global industrial society.

The word is not completely the dowsers' own invention. According to the *Oxford English Dictionary*, 1926 was the first year that "grid" appeared in print as a reference to "a network of high-voltage transmission lines and connections that supply electricity from a number of generating stations

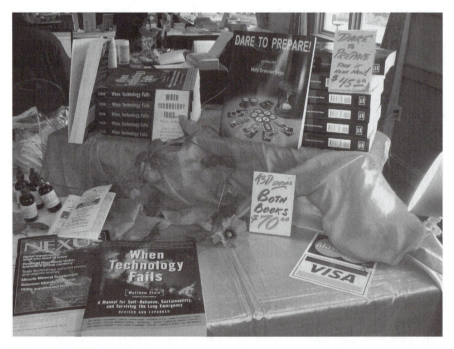

The Grid Will Go Down.

to various distribution centers in a country or a region, so that no consumer is dependent on a single station." In dowsing circles, however, the grid has come to connote the entire infrastructure of modern society, its telecommunications networks, transnational cash flows, military-industrial complexes, and more.

Her talk starts off disarmingly enough. "I'm here this morning to talk to you about some . . . impending changes . . . some problems with the grid you can expect to see over the next few years." She says this with a smile. Her makeup is carefully applied, and her hair is freshly styled. Standing in her crisp white blouse and black slacks, Sandee is the picture of middle-class normalcy, defying my earlier expectations of meeting a homesteader. Her tone is pleasant and calm.

"As you know, dowsing has so many applications," she says, "and as dowsers you all know how to think and do things for yourselves. Please do not accept what I am about to tell you at face value. Please do your own research. Please check out the facts. I know you will." This nod to scientific method is even more reassuring. The comforting smell of coffee wafts through the conference room.

And then, just a hint of foreboding: "And you all know too that dowsing will be there for you when the grid no longer works." Perhaps an overstatement, I think to myself, taking a sip of hot coffee. Perhaps she will give us tips for enduring power outages. Very helpful.

Sandee tells us about her childhood in the early 1950s. Her parents worked in the food concession business, traveling from one state fair to another. It was an exciting way to grow up, she says, quite a way to discover America. She has just one dark memory. When she was quite young, she watched a documentary on Nazi Germany at a state fair in northern Michigan. She was "morbidly mesmerized" by the scenes of death that flickered before her: the blitzkriegs, the bombs, the concentration camps.

The movie has haunted her ever since. I am not sure now where this is going.

"Are any of you here familiar with neurolinguistic programming?" she suddenly asks. A few of us raise our hands. This was Elaine Thomas's technique for teaching mediumship, and the Alien Hunter's method for ferreting out the ubiquitous liars at Roswell. Now Sandee is giving us yet another application: "Well, in N.L.P. there is something that they call a metaposition. That's your stable point of observation, the place where you watch and evaluate the world. I've known since the time I was a little child that there is something wrong with this world, something very, very wrong, and nothing I ever learned in school got down to the bottom of it."

Starting in her twenties, Sandee set out on a quest for spiritual wisdom that took her all around the world, looking for this "metaposition."

Suddenly, there are nods of recognition throughout the audience. She is speaking about their collective experience. These are the baby boomers, a generation made up of a disproportional number of spiritual seekers.[33] Clearly, Sandee is not the only person in this room who questioned deeply the religious and cultural mores of her upbringing, who looked for some way to transform this unnamable corruption lurking in her society's midst. Sandee goes on to tell us that she became a nomad, for many years. She traveled around the world, from Peru to India to China to Tibet and then back again to Texas. She studied shamanism with the Quechua Indians, but this was not her metaposition. She studied the Vedas and yoga in India, Taoism in China, and Vajrayana Buddhism in Nepal—but none of these traditions gave her the stable, timeless place from which to evaluate reality that she was looking for.

Then, finally, she found it. Here, in Vermont. Sandee became a dowser, in Terry Ross's *Divining-Mind* sense of the term.

There are further nods of understanding. At this point in her narrative, Sandee has positioned herself right in the pastoral middle. By "civilization," we understand that she is referring to something global, having made reference to four of the seven continents already. She has extricated herself from them all and now speaks in the name of Nature, the universal reference point.

We are poised for a great revelation. She takes a sip of water. She mentions the Kali Yuga, the Hindu term for the fourth and final age in the infinitely repeating cycle of time. And then she drops the bomb:

"The grid is going down!"

It is clear that she does not mean temporarily.

The grid is going down, once and for all. The grid is going down at some unknown but particular moment in the future, in an instant, in the twinkling of an eye.

Airplanes will fall out of the sky. Automobiles will fail to start. Water will stop running. The heat will not work. People will starve. Wars will erupt. Blood will flow. Pestilence and plague will spread death.

I burn my mouth on my coffee.

The grid is so vulnerable. The grid is open to a number of threats. The detonation of an electromagnetic pulse weapon or a simple nuclear device can bring it down. The eruption of a solar flare could fry our infrastructure in a heartbeat.

And then, there are the Nazis. Did we know, she asks us, that the Bush family had a hand in the cleanup of the Oklahoma City bombing? Most likely this was part of a cover-up to hide its own role in destroying the federal building. A secret cabal within the world government could deliberately bring the whole grid down and plunge the world into death.

A man in the audience shoots up his hand. Did we know that in 1859, solar flares actually did erupt, shorting out telegraph wires in the United States and Europe, igniting fires, and momentarily bringing the industrial world to a communications standstill? Another man chimes in: "Has anyone here heard of the Georgia Guidestones?" Only a few people raise their hands, so he elaborates: "There are these stones down in Georgia—nobody knows who built 'em, really. They've got these sayings written on 'em in different languages—one of them says to keep the population down to 500 million! A lot of people think the Illuminati are behind all of this, or maybe the Freemasons."

Where is George Noory when you need him? I have heard of these megaliths before, on *Coast-to-Coast AM*, but I do not raise my hand. The stones are real enough, a cluster of six 20-ton granite slabs inscribed in eight different languages with principles for a sustainable civilization. The man who orchestrated and funded their construction identified himself only as "Robert C. Christian," a cryptic allusion to the Rosicrucians.[34]

Sandee does not miss a beat. "Some folks like to call these things conspiracy theories—but how about conspiracy realities?" She comes back with an even weirder story she once heard on *Coast-to-Coast AM*. A government cabal is presently perfecting a plan to force lethal vaccinations on the population in the form of mandatory vaccines. "It's like Schindler's List! We think that if we just stick together, everything will be alright. But there's nowhere to run. When the grid goes down, we're talking 90 percent of the population dead. Ninety percent!"

I have conjured up the spirits of the dead on the shores of Cassadaga. I have toured the swamp-infested lairs of the Mothman. I have looked into the eyes of victims snatched by alien grays. But none of these has prepared me for Sandee Mac's preview of the hell-on-earth yet to come.

She is reaching into her satchel for something as she speaks and pulls out a stack of papers. "I've got some handouts for you." The papers circulate around the room. I look down at my survival-and-preparedness packet, the first page of which lists 24 varieties of potential natural, technological, and universal emergencies—including avalanches, earthquakes, dam failures, and civic disturbances. Recommended items include a heavy-duty flashlight and batteries, plastic garbage bags, iodine tablets, and a shortwave radio, to name just a few mass-manufactured items. For floods, an inflatable raft is suggested as well. Sandee emphasizes the importance of buying a healthy supply of potassium iodate in the case of a nuclear strike. Few people know that these tablets help protect the body against radiation poisoning.

"Luckily I kept these handouts after Y2K," she says.

Perhaps there is hope after all. Maybe we will stave off the Angel of Death, the next time He comes.

Much of what I have heard reminds me of the conversation surrounding "peak oil," the point at which the world's oil's reserves begin to decline and the world descends, according to some, into a nightmare of famine, war, and death. This, too, is a dire warning of the imminent collapse of our global technological infrastructure. On the one hand, there is ample scientific data to suggest that the world as we know it must change in order to continue. Endlessly rising rates of consumption are simply not ecologically sustainable, and a civilization—or a "grid"—that relies on such an ideal is doomed to fail eventually. But Sandee's lecture is not really about change. It is about The End. Prophets have been announcing the Apocalypse for 3,500 years, and here we sit, listening to a similar story.

This is not the Christian version of the Last Days. "Dowsing When Technology Fails" is American pastoralism in its gothic mode. Is it a coincidence that one of the first Americans to tell this story was a native Vermonter? George Perkins Marsh, the man hailed as America's first environmentalist, was born and raised in Woodstock, a charming and affluent hamlet on the eastern base of Mount Killington. In 1864, Marsh penned his now classic *Man and Nature*, later retitled *Physical Geography as Modified by Human Action*. On the one hand, it was an eminently rational analysis of deforestation during the days of the late Roman Empire. On the other hand, it was an Arcadian morality tale.

Marsh wanted his readers to understand the Fall of Rome as a Fall from Nature. When the Romans lost sight of the sublime dimension of the environment, their civilization collapsed. "It was only in the infancy of lands where all the earth was fair, that Greek and Roman humanity had sympathy enough with the inanimate world to be alive to the charms of rural and of mountain scenery," he wrote:

> In later generations, when the glories of the landscape had been heightened by plantation, and decorative architecture, and other forms of picturesque improvement, the poets of Greece and Rome were blinded by excess of light, and became, at last, almost insensible to beauties that now, even in their degraded state, enchant every eye, except, too often, those which a life-long familiarity has dulled to their attractions.[35]

And unless it changed its course, industrializing America was next in line. The two sides of George Perkins Marsh—one prosaic, the other poetic—are today memorialized in two separate monuments. In Woodstock, his original home now stands as the Marsh-Briggs-Rockefeller

National Park, where levelheaded foresters practice sustainable husbandry and rangers strategize practical ways to preserve the ecosystems of America's national parks. In the meantime, Marsh's body is interred in the Protestant Cemetery of Rome, alongside the romantic bards Percy Bysshe Shelley and John Keats, memorializing Marsh's indebtedness to a more mystical vision of the cosmos. Similarly at the Killington Grande, dowsing lingers in the ambiguous space between science and literature, along the blurred boundaries separating fact and fiction.

After Sandee's lecture is over, I file out of the room with the rest of the crowd. A woman from New Hampshire walks with me. She relates to me her prolonged bout of sickness caused by the carrier waves from cell phone towers located near her home. Conventional doctors were unable to help her. After years of seeking out a cure, she discovered the ASD and learned about "geopathic zones." These are regions of excess electromagnetic energy, toxic to human beings. Some are natural, but many more are caused by the various wave-emitting gadgets of modern technology, including computer screens and television sets. After studying with American dowsers and European masters of radiesthesia, she learned how to divert and neutralize the rays and has been healthy ever since.

Modern technology is literally making people here sick. I am not sure how to take the warning of the grid's collapse: as a dire prophecy or an expression of hope. Presumably, the dowsers see themselves as surviving the End Times and inheriting the earth. They have already taken the necessary steps of disentangling themselves from the doomed web of toxic machinery. Let Rome fall as it will then. Vermont will be left standing.

The assumption here seems to be that we are standing on solid ground indeed. When the Apocalypse comes, Mount Killington might just be the best place to be.

But that is only because we have not ventured outside the hotel to take a closer look.

6

The Dowsers's Convention (Cont'd): *Et in Arcadia Ego*

I.

Joseph Smith Jr., the founder of the Mormons, is the forgotten dowser of Vermont. I hear him mentioned only once during my two visits to the American Society of Dowsers (ASD) convention. Joe Sullivan, a Spiritualist minister from western Massachusetts, alludes in passing to the Mormon founder during his lecture on "Dowsing, Dreams, and Spirituality" in 2009, reminding some of us and enlightening others that Smith, born in Sharon, Vermont, worked for many years as a dowser and treasure-seeker-for-hire in upstate New York before translating the *Book of Mormon*. And indeed, Sullivan explains dowsing in much the way that Joseph Smith would have thought about it, as a particular form of guidance from the spirit world.

Joseph Smith's life as a religious prophet began when he was just 15 years old. As a boy, he had been perplexed as to which one of the many Protestant sects he should follow. One fateful day in 1820, a prayerful Smith retired into the woods of Palmyra, New York, beseeching God for an answer. According to Smith, God the Father and Jesus Christ themselves appeared to give him a reply directly: follow none. Three years after that visitation, an angel named Moroni paid the first of many visits to Smith's Palmyra home, informing him of the location of a cache of golden plates, buried on the slopes of the nearby Hill Cumorah. On these tablets, Moroni explained, the true, long-lost teachings of Christ were inscribed, as well as the hitherto unknown history of America before Columbus. In 1827, the angel finally gave Smith permission to unearth the plates and begin his translation. The resulting text was the *Book of Mormon*, published in 1830.

I am delighted to finally hear Joseph Smith's name mentioned at the ASD convention and am not surprised that it should come from the lips

Author at Joseph Smith Birthplace Memorial.

of a Spiritualist. Both Mormonism and Spiritualism were products of the Great Awakening, that great period of turmoil when Protestant Christianity was forced to readapt itself to survive in a modernizing nation. In the first case, a new revelation was required; in the second, an unprecedented ease of communication between the visible and invisible worlds. Joe Sullivan, a jolly Bostonian Spiritualist, relates some of the seldom-discussed facts of Smith's religious biography. The Mormon prophet had an intimate familiarity with dowsing, but this, along with his early career as a treasure hunter, generally go unmentioned outside academic circles. They are certainly not included in any public portrayal of Smith by the Church of Jesus Christ of Latter-Day Saints (LDS) itself.

But Sullivan's knowledge of Mormonism has something to do with his whole approach to dowsing, which by ASD standards is eccentric. Sullivan is more interested in haunted houses than he is in Nature. It was only a few years ago that he took up the practice of dowsing when a contractor friend handed him a pair of bent metal coat hangers as they walked across a lot. The Spiritualist minister was at first surprised when the rods swiveled as they walked across a water main but quickly came to recognize the anomaly as yet another way the spirits communicated with him. The audience is visibly disturbed when Sullivan stops his talk on water witching to instead play us tape recordings of Native American spirit guides mumbling audibly during séances. I cannot tell if they are frightened or annoyed that Sullivan has ventured so far afield, as far as they are concerned, from the topic of the convention.

I am intrigued, however, by Sullivan's segue out of modern dowsing and decide to leave the convention temporarily to get a closer look at Joseph Smith for myself. The Joseph Smith Birthplace Memorial, an hour's drive east of Killington, is located right on the border between the Vermont towns of Sharon and Royalton. The farmhouse where Smith was born no longer stands, but the LDS maintains the grounds surrounding the site and has erected a 38and-a-half-foot-tall obelisk close to where the house once stood, each foot commemorating a year in the life of its founder.

The sun is shining as I drive up Dairy Hill Road in Royalton to the Memorial, past white colonial farmhouses, stripped of shutters. A small sign indicates the turnoff onto LDS property, and suddenly I am on a promenade lined by stately old-growth maple trees. Expecting to soon behold something like a southern plantation, I am surprised to arrive at what looks like a national park information center, a plain, one-story building. It is the pillar here that is showcased. To my left I see it, rising up from a perfectly manicured lawn and surrounded by rows of yellow, white, and purple flowers. I park facing the obelisk and walk into the visitors' center, where an older man named Elder Stephen Mitchell greets me.

Elder Mitchell is working here as part of a two-year mission. He is broad shouldered and very tall, standing at about six and a half feet, and dressed in a black pinstripe suit. Even in this summer weather, he wears a tie. We begin with the customary introductions. I learn that he is a native of Utah, the father of eight children and the grandfather of 28 grandchildren. He learns that I am a professor of religion and compliments me on having persisted along my professional path. After he learns that I am not a Mormon, he invites me aside for a solo tour. It is his opportunity, perchance, to win a convert. Together, we enter a separate room in the visitors' center, lined with portraits of the first four LDS presidents and paintings of the events surrounding Joseph Smith's discovery of the golden plates. Mitchell recounts the history of early Mormonism as we walk past them.

He begins by elaborating on the artist's depiction of Smith's first encounter with Moroni in 1823. Moroni, Elder Mitchell clarifies, was an actual historical figure before being transformed into an angel in the afterlife. During his life on Earth, Moroni was a Nephite, the name given in the *Book of Mormon* to one of the major pre-Columbian American Indian tribes.

We stand beneath a painting of Joseph Smith unearthing a stone box housing the golden plates, from beneath the soil on Hill Cumorah. Elder Mitchell elaborates that Moroni had first shown Smith where they lay in 1823, but it took four years of meetings until the angel deemed Smith ready for the task of translation. Moroni had himself had buried the plates on Hill Cumorah, during his time on Earth as a Nephite. Moroni's father, a historian and scribe named Mormon, had done the actual engraving on the plates, and so the *Book of Mormon* is named after him.

Elder Mitchell explains that Mormon inscribed the plates in a strange alphabet, resembling Egyptian hieroglyphics. Smith translated the tablets using special "seer stones," smooth rocks he collected in the streambeds of upstate New York. When held up to or pressed against the eyes, the seer stones revealed the meaning of the foreign script.

Finally, Elder Mitchell leads me past artistic renditions of scenes from the *Book of Mormon* itself, with its sacred history of America: the coming of the ancient Israelites to its shores centuries before Columbus, the appearance of Jesus Christ in America after his resurrection, and the endless wars between the fair-skinned Nephites and the dark-skinned Lamanites. Elder Mitchell clarifies that it was the Lamanites who were the Indians first beheld by European colonizers in 1492. By that time, the Nephites had long since perished from the face of the earth.

There is no painting of the America-soon-to-come, when Jesus Christ returns to Earth—but this is what the Latter-Day Saints are preparing for, and this is what Elder Mitchell most tries to impress on me. Joseph Smith did not reveal a *new* interpretation of Christianity, Mitchell emphasizes several times; he *restored* the *original* teachings of Christ. We are currently living in the midst of the true church's restoration. This era will culminate with Christ's return to America during the End Times and the establishment of Christ's Kingdom on Earth after the Apocalypse.

Not surprisingly, Elder Mitchell does not mention a word about the links between Smith's dowsing career and the legends he has so patiently narrated in our tour through the center. Any suggestion of such a connection, which was first raised by former LDS historian D. Michael Quinn, is tantamount to heresy in the Mormon church.[1] Quinn's meticulous research, enriched by his access to LDS historical archives, paints a very different picture of Joseph Smith than that recounted by church elders. According to Quinn, Smith was a man deeply influenced by the Renaissance "magic worldview" imported from Europe and kept alive in America through the folkways of British and German immigrants.

Quinn, who has since been excommunicated from the LDS, argued that the legend of Smith's discovery of the golden plates reflected the practices and lore of early American dowsers. Had he, rather than Elder Mitchell, escorted me through the visitors' center this afternoon, the golden plates would have been likened to buried treasure, with Moroni as their spiritual guardian. Smith's visions would be seen as standard episodes in any dowser's magical hunt for lost or hidden objects. As for the seer stones, these would have been explained as typical tools of the dowsing trade in the early nineteenth century, magical devices through which the seeker received ongoing visionary information about the object of his quest.

As for Smith's particular version of the Apocalypse, this too bears for Quinn a striking resemblance to the teachings of an obscure band of religious dowsers from Middletown, Vermont, whom local newspapers dubbed the Fraternity of Rodsmen.[2] The Rodsmen believed that ancient Israelites had settled in America and that members of the fraternity were their true spiritual heirs, divinely ordained to build a temple. When the Apocalypse—predicted by the Rodsmen to occur in 1802—finally came, the fraternity believed they would inherit America. Rumors in fact circulated in Vermont at the time that Joseph Smith Sr., the father of the Mormon prophet, was a member of the fraternity.[3] Whether or not there were such actual connections, substitute "Mormons" for "Rodsmen," and the rough outline of Smith's prophecies concerning the end of things comes into focus.

Joseph Smith's world could not have been any further away from the pastoral America I crossed into a few days ago. The Mormon prophet certainly did not see himself as communing with Nature. In the early 1800s, he and most other Americans still thought of themselves living in God's Creation. As a consequence, the beings, things, and places of the natural world had a fixed place in the divine ordering of things.

Something of this premodern attitude is reflected in the Mormons' own showcasing of the obelisk at Smith's birthplace memorial. The obelisk is not simply a place marker but an object infused with supernatural significance. My tour with Elder Mitchell ends here, at the foot of the pillar. The missionary explains to me that God Himself was watching as the Mormons hauled the 40-ton granite slab up Dairy Hill Road in 1905. Halfway up the hill, the team of men and horses encountered a massive mud hole. There was no way around it. The foreman in charge of building the memorial prayed to God, and overnight the temperature dropped 30 degrees. The soft ground was frozen solid the next morning.

The natural world of the Mormons seems a little more stable in this corner of Royalton than it does in the rest of Vermont. We are actually *somewhere* in the bounded cosmos that is God's Creation as elaborated here in Mormon scriptures, with Joseph Smith's birthplace featuring as America's Bethlehem. Elder Mitchell invites me to pray for my friends and family at this sacred site. I bow my head respectfully for a half a minute or so and afterward tell the missionary I must be on my way. I have more dowsing to do.

As I drive back down Dairy Hill Road into the White River Valley, I understand now why modern dowsers have passed right over Smith in their historical reconstructions of the practice—even though he is a native of Vermont. By 1958, when the Danville farmers organized the first convention, the magic worldview had long since disappeared from the state's culture. Exactly when is not clear. In the meantime, Joe Sullivan, the Bostonian Spiritualist, has yet to win many converts at the ASD convention with his own spirit-derived theories of dowsing. Dowsing today has come of age as part and parcel of American pastoralism; other theories take a backseat.

And yet how odd it is that dowsers have retained a perennial obsession with the end of the world, at least as far back as Smith's time and continuing through today. What the Fraternity of Rodsmen and ASD members share in common is the desire to find stable cosmological ground in modern America and the conviction that at the present time, this is an impossible quest. Either Christ must come again to restore the church, or the grid must go down to clear the way for Nature's restoration.

As Sandee Mac would say, something in America is very, very wrong. And for dowsers, this message is coming up from the ground itself.

When the young Joseph Smith unearthed the secrets of ancient America in Palmyra, he learned that the land here is nothing less than a massive graveyard, the site of bloody warfare between the Nephites and the Lamanites. For Smith and his early followers, the news turned out to be prophetic. Their Protestant neighbors hunted and chased them all the way from New York to Utah, with Smith gunned down by a Missouri mob along the way.

The earth has been whispering through the dowsing rods: the nation has blood on its hands.

Clouds are gathering in the sunny skies of Vermont. As I ascend the wooded slopes of Mount Killington once again, I muse on the famous paintings by Nicolas Poussin, *The Shepherds of Arcadia*. The French artist created two versions of the same pastoral scene: four ancient shepherds, donned in tunics, gathered round a tomb. On the face of the sarcophagus are inscribed the Latin words *Et in Arcadia Ego*, "Even in Arcadia, I am there."

I am no less surprised than the Arcadian shepherds to find these thoughts of death intruding into this pastoral Vermont countryside. But the dowsing rods, pointing to the ground beneath our feet, do not lie.

II.

All that remains are the ruins.

I have returned to the Killington Grande just in time to sign up for a special archaeological field trip to one of the curious stone chambers of Vermont. The leader, a seasoned dowser named Ivan MacBeth, has restricted the size of the group to 20-or-so convention participants, and I am the last person to get my name on his waiting list. After stashing away a few souvenirs from my visit to Royalton in my hotel room, I meet up with my fellow dowsers in the parking lot, and soon we are caravanning down the mountain to a secret spot, well off the grid, hidden somewhere between bucolic Woodstock and Hartland. We drive off pavement onto a dirt road, passing by stone walls and pastures for miles until we see it.

And strange it is indeed: a stone room built from indigenous granite and set into the side of a hill. Its roof is fashioned from solid slabs of rock 10 feet long and several feet wide, then covered with earth. A rectangular smoke hole peeks through to the top of the bank. The entrance, an upright opening, faces south, toward that point on the horizon where the sun rises on the winter solstice.

The so-called Calendar II site is an anomaly in Vermont's pastoral landscape, although some have tried to make it fit. One theory is that this chamber—and the many others like it—was once a colonial root cellar.[4] The foundations of a colonial dwelling do sit less than a hundred feet away from the site—it seems plausible that the stone vault could have been an addition to some farmer's backyard. But it is impossible to say which structure came first, and it is equally plausible that a colonial family would

Dowsing for Vermont.

choose to build their house next to a preexisting structure. The root cellar
hypothesis also has a major engineering detail working against it; the
structures in question are all made of stone. Surviving literature on
colonial root cellars records that farmers used wood and mortar rather
than rock in constructing such buildings.[5]

We take turns entering, proceeding in groups of twos and threes. The
interior is cool and damp and smells like musty earth. We turn around
to face the entrance, imagining a shaft of sunlight piercing in, illuminating
the back wall on the solstice. Calendar II seems to be but a nexus within a
much more extensive complex: about 200 feet to the east, a stone platform
rises a few feet above the earth, now cracked and overgrown with moss
and grasses. Large rocks resembling megalithic standing stones have been
incorporated into the ubiquitous Vermont stone walls that crisscross the
surrounding fields.[6]

One is hard pressed *not* to group the Calendar II site together with
other megalithic remains more commonly associated with Europe: the
henges, barrows, and cairns of the British Isles, for example. But who
needs to cross the Atlantic? The New England landscape is peppered
with *hundreds* of these chambers as well as with its own standing stones

and underground tunnels.[7] The most magnificent of these is in North Salem, New Hampshire, where tiers of tunnels, wells, and platforms made of stone envelop an entire hill. A grooved granite altar standing near the summit is the centerpiece of what is now dubbed "America's Stonehenge." Carefully placed standing stones mark cardinal directions, as well as the spots where the sun rises on winter and summer solstice and the equinoxes. One non–peer-reviewed radiocarbon test provocatively suggests that the site may be approximately 3,000 years old.[8]

Since 1964, the New England Antiquities Research Association (NEARA) has been cataloging these sites and mobilizing support for their protection as national monuments. In this part of the country especially, they are the only physical remains of an America before Columbus, the solitary ruins of a civilization unknown to us, hidden among the trees.

Ivan MacBeth, our ASD guide, leads us toward this abyss of historical memory, playing his pennywhistle. He sports a black top hat, adorned around its base with a band of green and red plastic oak leaves. A long piece of pink ribbon trails off one of the sides, running down the back of his head. Ivan is a Druid, born and raised in England, but presently living in Vermont. He has instructed us to roam as we will through the pastures, letting our rods and pendulums lead us into the mysteries.

We are dowsing for America, that state of mind that shimmers between fact and fancy. Where in the world are we? Europeans and their descendants in America have delighted in asking themselves this question since 1492, never content to simply ask the natives. Our culture is bent instead on *discovering* things—and there is nothing like a heap of ruins to fan the flames of curiosity about our cultural origins. In Joseph Smith's day, pioneers spreading out into the Ohio and Mississippi River valleys encountered huge earthen *mounds*, some shaped into the form of snakes and squirrels, others into domes and pyramids, seemingly abandoned by their former builders. In the absence of native informants, cleared away by disease and warfare, speculations about who built the mounds abounded. Fantastic stories arose of ancient Welshmen, seafaring Egyptians, survivors from Atlantis, and the Ten Lost Tribes of Israel settling into the New World, centuries before Columbus.

The *Book of Mormon* elevated this last theory to the status of divine revelation, but for non-Mormons, the questions remain unanswered. As recently as the 1970s, Harvard marine biologist Barry Fell set out on a quest to discover America anew, visiting the Calendar II site and other New England megaliths. Fell's landmark work, *America, B.C.*, resurrected the old sagas of ancient Welshmen and seafaring Egyptians, to which the author added his own signature theories. Fell argued that the unidentified markings at some of these sites were nothing less than Celtic Ogham script, making clear references to ancient Phoenician fertility gods.[9]

Harvard colleagues responded to Fell with all the affection they later showered on alien abduction researcher John Mack. They dismissed his arguments as a classic example of pseudoscience, too hasty a leap into theoretical certitude from only a handful of data. But it was too late. Readers of the NEARA journal seized on the ideas of *America B.C.* and made them their own. Since many NEARA members were also dowsers, Fell's theories made their way via this back door into the ASD circles as well. Nearly 200 years after the demise of the Rodsmen, a band of Vermont dowsers were once again espousing theories of pre-Columbian American civilizations.

Ivan MacBeth has come to the Calendar II site on a sort of hajj to the center of his imagined homeland. Druids in particular have figured prominently in the meditations on New England ruins. Fell muses on them in *America B.C.* Children's author Madeleine L'Engle wrote them into the plot of her novel *An Acceptable Time*, turning Connecticut's standing stones into magical time machines linking modern America with ancient Britain.[10]

Indeed, MacBeth looks like he has stepped through a time machine to be with us today. I take a closer look at the buttons on his top hat: on the front, a colorful butterfly and the all-seeing Eye of Providence, the symbol featured on the backside of a United States one-dollar bill, above the pyramid, and on the back, a pin that simply reads, "I Believe." He wears a black T-shirt adorned with a familiar design: a white ray of light, passing through a triangular prism and dispersing into the colors of the rainbow. It is the image from Pink Floyd's classic rock album *The Dark Side of the Moon*, released in 1973.

Where in the world am I? I back away from the Druid, clutching onto the metal dowsing rods in my hand. They swing open and shut, uncannily of their own accord. Perhaps I am treading over water veins or nearing Golden Plates. I am lost in Nature's Nation, doomed by my own ancestors, who never bothered to ask the natives for directions.

The Druid calls out to us now—"Come, my friends! It is time to gather! Come!"—and from all directions we amble in like zombies, arms outstretched, holding our rods, meeting at the raised stone platform east of the chamber to share the fruits of our "joyful search."

We position ourselves into a circle and join hands. "Welcome, ladies and gentlemen, to a place of many theories and few facts," Ivan begins. "Before we share our findings, let us start with a simple prayer." For several minutes we chant the sacred Hindu syllable *Om* and then sit down. The only sound is the wind, rushing through the late summer trees.

Ivan's eyes twinkle as he rubs his gray beard. "There are many secrets of this place being disclosed to us today, and they are all true," he says merrily. "Who would like to begin?"

One woman, who wandered away into a far pasture, informs us that Native American spirits are clustered very densely around this place. She felt called to commune with one of them at the top of the hill.

A dowser from Massachusetts tells us he dowsed a "time window," which opens up four times a year for 20 hours and is located directly above the stone chamber.

Ivan joins in and tells us that a long time ago, the Druids had a university here, its buildings sprawling over the countryside. It was absolutely beautiful, he says, one of the finest the world had ever seen.

As they talk, I am having my own sort of negative epiphany, the opposite of T. S. Eliot's proclamation that the end of all journeying is to "know the place for the first time."[11] Having been born and raised in New England, I am forced to concede, at the end of all my journeys through paranormal America, that I have no idea where I am from. The realization is accompanied by a slight feeling of nausea. I offer up my own reflections to the group.

This place feels dark and desolate, I say.

There is a long silence, and then a woman says, "I am glad you said that. I have been afraid to say this. I cannot get the image of sacrifice out of my head. I really think this was a place of sacrifice." She furrows her brows, searching for the right image. "I see women and children being sacrificed here."

Another woman chimes in, "The power here has become polluted."

The Vermont coordinator for NEARA, who has come here with our group, weighs in to share that researchers did find a stone here with beveled edges—perhaps to drain off the blood of the victims—much like the grooved altar slab at America's Stonehenge.

A thin man dressed in jeans and a green flannel shirt takes a pendulum out of his pocket and watches it swing. "Some of us were victims here, in our former lives," he says, not taking his eyes off the weight.

The group falls back into silence. The wind blows again. Absence has presence here, and we are trying to describe its sound. Our thoughts have turned toward death.

After hundreds of hours spent communing with spirits, pondering UFOs, and poring over metaphysical tomes, I seem to have found the key to the "occult," that term derived from the Latin word for "secret," right here beneath my feet. America is a burial ground, covering up crimes that bleed through the soil, coagulating into spirits and extraterrestrials and Golden Plates. A haunted ground, and the paranormal only the ordinary state of affairs.

There are no Abenakis with us today at the Calendar II site, and nobody mentions their centuries-long presence in Vermont. A few of the region's indigenous peoples still live within the borders of the state, but many more fled to Quebec and northern Maine hundreds of years ago. In the past few decades, the Abenakis have joined other tribal members of the United South and Eastern tribes in reclaiming the lithic structures as the sacred ceremonial landscapes of their ancestors, together with the old earthen mounds of the Mississippi and Ohio River watersheds. In the latter case, conventional archaeology backs up the assertion of Native American origin with evidence from countless and meticulous digs. Inexplicably, here in New England, science has yet to delve into the ruins, but many accept the tribes' claim as the most plausible explanation in the meantime.

None of which detracts from the fact that all of us, non-Native and Native alike, must live and move and have our being atop this expansive grave, stretching from sea to shining sea.

The playful Druid looks somewhat more subdued now. "Well," Ivan says wistfully, "our time here has almost come to its end. I think it is appropriate that we close with a gesture of thanks to this place for its beauty, its spirit, and its permission to let us be here today."

We shape-shift into Hindus again, chanting *Om* a second time. This time our prayer rises up, an elegy drifting into the oaks and birches.

We file back, a sobered band of pagans, to our caravan of cars. Calendar II watches us as we pile into our automobiles, fasten seat belts, and pull out of the property back onto the dirt road. The stones have cast a spell on all of us.

We drive back to Mount Killington through the meticulously charming town of Woodstock, passing through carefully zoned streets of brick houses, quaint storefronts, and handsome churches. I am again reminded of the *descanso* in the desert near Roswell:

WE DON'T KNOW WHO THEY WERE
WE DON'T KNOW WHY THEY CAME
WE ONLY KNOW
THEY CHANGED OUR VIEW
OF THE UNIVERSE

All that remains are the ruins.

III.

Aho!

Our small group lets up its prayer to the spirits of the mountain. We have just finished our three-day medicine wheel ceremony, officiated by Peter Champoux, a dowser and writer from western Massachusetts. We have constructed our own sacred spaces, large circles of stones, inspired by a Great Plains Indian custom, on the slopes and on the summit of Mount Killington.

In the Lakota dialect of the Siouan language group, still spoken some 1,800 miles west of Vermont, *ho* is an adverb of affirmation, akin to the archaic English word "verily."[12] But in Native-style ceremonies conducted by non-Native Americans, the word typically mutates into *a-ho*, seemingly a substitute for "amen." I first heard the word uttered many years ago, back when I worked briefly at a retreat center in California. More recently during my paranormal road trips, I noticed that Bev, the alien channeler of Sedona, concluded our breathwork session with the same supplication. None of these interlocutors seemed bothered by the fact that in the Lakota language, *aho* means "to stand up."[13]

Making the Wheel/Machine.

"Aho," we now cry out to the Green Mountains, attempting to bring our intricate ritual to an auspicious close. Over the past three days, Champoux has led us through his own introduction to the so-called Earth Mysteries.[14] The origins of this discourse date back almost a century, to the writings of an amateur British archaeologist named Sir Alfred Watkins. Although Watkins never used the term "Earth Mysteries," he did coin the all-important concept of "leys" in a 1925 book titled *The Old Straight Track*. In this extended meditation on the landscape of his native Herefordshire County, Watkins drew attention to an intricate series of lines crisscrossing the countryside. These leys were nothing other than piles of ruins—megaliths, crumbling Roman forts, and former Catholic churches—all lined up in a row. They seemed to hold answers to how various ancient civilizations had interacted with their native landscapes; Watkins's leys were a key to unlocking the secrets of the past.

Not too surprisingly, it was the preponderance of anomalous stone structures dotting the New England landscape that first awakened Vermont dowsers' own interest in the study of leys. In 1979, ASD members invited Paul Devereux to explore with them the Calendar II site in Hartland. Devereux was himself an amateur British archaeologist and one of the men who helped popularize the term "Earth Mysteries." In his own elaboration of Watkins's writings, Devereux taught Vermonters that an intricate web of "ley lines" encircled the earth, conducting powerful currents of invisible Earth energy. He explained how British dowsers had long been using their rods to find them. And he elaborated how prehistoric civilizations—Welsh, Egyptian, Druid, and Native American all—had built their sacred architectural sites at points where the leys crossed or converged in order to harness the earth's currents for their own ends.

After returning to England, Devereux wrote to his New England friends that he had included Calendar II as one of the case studies in his then-extant Dragon Project, a scientific study intended to record Earth energies in and around prehistoric ruins throughout the world. ASD officials published his letter in the journal, setting American dowsers on a new course.[15] Over the next 10 years, members wrote in, relating their own explorations of ley lines, and reflections on Earth energies. And in 1990, Terry Ross and Richard Wright published *The Divining Mind*. In this streamlined adaptation of Devereux's original lessons, the earth is a field of conscious energy that dowsers can locate, harness, and direct toward new ends—just as members of ancient civilizations allegedly once did.

Peter Champoux's medicine wheel workshop is based on his own unique synthesis of Devereux-style Earth Mysteries and Native American ceremonialism. Like everything else related to dowsing, wielding Nature's power is a technique, a craft, and Champoux strikes us all as a competent guide.

Before turning to the mysteries of dowsing he worked as a professional mason, studying the properties and uses of stone. Now in the last years of his midlife, the burly Massachusetts native still retains the countercultural ideals of the 1960s, seeking through the Earth Mysteries to ground an overly rational and machine-driven society in the life-giving powers of Nature.

Day 1 of Champoux's workshop is an intensive introduction to the basic ideas of the Earth Mysteries lineage. Dressed in a flannel shirt, he inundates us with PowerPoint images in a Killington Grande conference room. We gaze on colorful slides of sacred mountains from around the world (Mount Kailash in Tibet, Mount Fuji in Japan, and Machu Picchu in Peru), ancient architectural wonders (the Great Pyramid of Giza and Stonehenge in Britain), and cosmological maps from medieval Hindu, Buddhist, and Catholic monasteries. Finally, there are the medicine wheels from the American Great Plains and the plains of the Canadian provinces of Alberta and Saskatchewan. Champoux pauses on a photograph of the Bighorn Medicine Wheel in Wyoming, 75 feet in diameter. Its 28 spokes radiate out from the center, aligned toward particular constellations as well as places on the horizon where the sun rises during solstices and equinoxes.

"How many of you know what a medicine wheel is?" Peter asks us. Almost everybody in the room raises their hands. I have read in an anthropological journal somewhere that their precise meanings have been lost to us, unknowable when separated from the original cultures that made them. I keep my hands by my sides.

"Yes, Stone Tree." Peter points to a man in the back row. He wears overalls and a green plaid cotton shirt. A black leather hat, adorned with feathers, is pulled down over his long, flowing blond hair.

The man declares in a thick Vermont accent that these wheels are energy accumulators. Peter affirms his answer, elaborating that the stone circles are places where the energies of the earth are superconcentrated, spots where human beings can plug into the planet's own "grid."

The other dowsers put their hands down. Our group is small, made up mostly of women. One woman from Michigan left her white-collar job years ago to raise horses in the country; another hails from Arkansas, a member of the Ozark Mountain Research Institute. The rest of the group is from New England, with two from Vermont. A woman from Rutland inherited her interest in things metaphysical from her father, a Silva Mind Control teacher. Stone Tree traveled here from the Northeast Kingdom. Now middle aged, he is the eldest of 17 children, raised on a chicken farm in Cabot, Vermont. He already knows our instructor. They have met before at former ASD conventions and various transtribal powwows held throughout New England.

Peter takes his cue from Stone Tree and elaborates on his own interpretation of the Earth Mysteries. He begins by discussing how the Great
Plains Medicine Wheel is but one example of an ancient science and technology based on the knowledge of a natural grid of power. Peter's choice
of the term "grid" seems deliberate, used as a counterpoint to our own
notion of humanly fabricated power bent on dominating the earth.

But the term is misleading. There is nothing rectilinear about
Champoux's grid. The coursing of the earth's natural power weaves
organic patterns and shapes over the landscape. Peter now returns to the
PowerPoint and clicks onto a topographic map of northern New England.
With a laser pointer, he shows us how Vermont's Mount Mansfield and
Ascutney, together with New Hampshire's Mount Washington, are
arranged in a triangular pattern. In turn, three nearby lakes form an
inverse triangle. "Do you see it? Do you see the Star of David?" he asks.
There are murmurs of recognition in the audience. "There it is, right
there—a naturally occurring hexagram," he confirms.

Champoux has in fact written extensively about his own system of
Earth-based geometry, inspired by an intimate knowledge of rocks and
minerals, in his book *The Gaia Matrix*.[16] What Champoux now teaches
as "Arkhom" geometry entails the study of the orderly crystalline and biological forms that run as the common thread through the natural landscapes, works of sacred art, and ancient architectural monuments that he
has shown us. As I stare at the topographical map of Vermont, straining
to make out the forms that Peter can see so clearly, I am reminded of the
skeptical explanation for synchronicity, or meaningful coincidences. As
the skeptics' argument goes, whatever coherent patterns we seem to find
in the world are ultimately a projection of our own subjective needs for
coherence rather than a feature of a coherent reality "out there." Nevertheless, at least for the duration of the workshop, we trust that Arkhom
has some correlation with the greater natural world around us.

After a lunch break, we return to the conference room, where Peter
dumps shopping bags of rocks onto the synthetic carpeting. We practice
making a medicine wheel on the floor, discovering a practical application
of Arkhom geometry and assembling what seems to be an archaic battery.
The dowsers take out their pendulums or rods to search for the choicest
stones, carefully arranging them in line with the points of a compass.

When we are finished and Peter has said a few more words about
Arkhom, we join hands and chant *Om* for several minutes, ending with a
collective *Aho!*

Our introduction to the real power of the Earth Mysteries must wait,
however, until the next afternoon. As Earth Mystery experts from the
1960s emphasized, their theories were meant to be put into practice. In

his 1969 book *The View over Atlantis*, Devereux's colleague John Michell developed the idea of a prehistoric network of "sacred engineers" who built and maintained a global network of ley lines that sustained human settlements.[17]

Taking this idea of sacred engineering to heart, we ride the electric gondolas to Killington's peak on day 2, intending to build a medicine wheel on the summit as a kind of *machine*. We trust that our careful alignment of the stones and their precise placement within the earth's grid will tap into an unlimited source of natural power. Flick the right switch, and the medicine wheel should run.

We drag our rocks and assorted ritual accoutrements along with us. When the gondolas reach the summit, we disembark and clamber up toward the last feet of the summit. Stone Tree hauls a 50-pound bag of feed corn over his shoulder. A few hundred feet away from the summit, Peter and two assistants dowse out the best spot for the wheel. We unload our baggage onto a patch of cool, mossy earth surrounded by scrubby pine trees and begin to reassemble our medicine wheel. We plunge our hands into the bag of corn and sprinkle it liberally around the center stone and the wheel's perimeter.

Stone Tree produces a stick of sage that he lights after several tries, and Peter picks up a drum. After a few clockwise circumambulations around the wheel, he breaks into a singsong, improvised prayer, his words crooning in time with the beat:

"Circle around, circle aro-o-und, wearing the long feathers as I fly, wearing the long feathers as I fly-y . . ."

Stone Tree falls into step behind him, carrying the smoldering bundle of sage.

"Circle around, circle around, the boundaries of the earth, the boundaries of the ea-arth . . ."

Somebody hands me a lit pipe of tobacco. I take a few drags and pass it on. Peter cries,

"Let this place be forever connected! City to the north—Quebec—know that you are part of this circle of our life! Great city of Montreal, know that you are part of this sacred circle. . . ."

He calls out to the cities of Boston to the east, Cleveland to the west, and New York to the south, as well as to the distant volcano of Cotopaxi in Ecuador, acknowledged as a sacred mountain by indigenous groups there since pre-Incan times. Summoning the Earth energies of these places to flow into our wheel, Peter cries out to the skies,

"May our prayers be carried on these carrier waves as they bounce through our atmosphere, and link the people of Killington to the rest of the world!"

His voice trails off, leaving just the beat of the drum to lull us. A curious hiker walks past our gathering, making his way to the summit. After he has passed, Peter begins to sing again, releasing the "great ones of light" who have come to help us light up the mountain, chanting the names of the ancient Indo-Iranian water goddess Anahita and the Zoroastrian high god Ahura Mazda.

The rhythmic beats stop with a final loud thud. And a round of *Aho!*s spontaneously erupts. The great transformation has finally arrived.

I wait for thunder, lightning, smoke, or sparks. There is only silence. The wind blows through the scrubby pines atop Killington's summit.

Whooooosh. Whoooooooooooosh.

We stand reverentially, eyes closed. As the scents of sage and tobacco waft through the thin mountain air, it occurs to me that this is probably the first time in American history that a medicine wheel ceremony has been performed in these parts. The Abenaki ceremonial cycle, still observed in parts of New England and Canada today, is based on the harvest and hunting cycles. The medicine wheels are a legacy of the Great Plains people.

As for energy accumulators and carrier waves, these do not figure in the sacred stories of any indigenous culture, in the Americas or elsewhere. The Abenaki, for example, speak of their first ancestors as fashioned from the red earth of this place or, in another version, the ash trees. All things are related, by way of a shared lineage and mutual exchanges among kin, rather than through energetic connections.

But our sacred engineering is not over yet. We leave the medicine wheel behind us to gather power from the grid and regroup on day 3 of the workshop. On a grassy stretch of lawn beside the Killington Grande parking lot, we build a second medicine wheel generator. This time we seem to be constructing a kind of ancient radio tower. The idea is that the main medicine wheel will beam down the earth's energy from the summit, where the reception is presumably better, and that the second wheel will in turn receive and disperse the rays to the people gathered at the base of the mountain.

Peter, master of ceremonies, successfully lures other ASD members into our rite. For nearly a half an hour, he walks around the circle spinning a homemade whirling string, a heavy object tied to the end of a cord, above his head. Then he lights a bundle of sage and carries it around the perimeter of the medicine wheel to bless the space. Passersby stop to watch the action. They notice our creation, an outer and inner ring of 14 rocks apiece, with a single stone in the center and, fascinated, end up staying for the main event.

Peter smudges them all with the sage. A hush descends. Then he prays aloud for the unity of the world. He prays for the end of war in Iraq and for the healing of our political leaders. He addresses Mount Killington directly, reminding it of its connection to Machu Picchu, Mount Kailash, and Cotopaxi. He leads us in the chanting of the five English vowels and the Hindu syllable *Om*. He renames Mount Killington "Mount Birth-ington," and the crowd is visibly moved.

"Aho!" the crowd spontaneously exclaims. They know what Peter has just done. In this one little corner of Vermont, pastoral balance had just been restored. Mount Birth-ington now beams healing energy down on all of us, just as it will on the skiers traversing its trails in the future.

A woman wearing a red kaftan speaks first. "I just want to say that this sends chills down my spine," she says.

An old Vermonter with a long white beard takes a step into the circle, testifying that peace has been restored to Killington: "It feels real good to be here today," he says. "I live on the other side of the hill, and I know for a fact that there was a lot of uproar around here when they started construction on this place, years ago. But I really think that our being here today, and your saying what you said, marks an end to that whole phase. We're in a different place now."

Another dowser shares that while Peter was praying, she could see the Nature People coming down from the mountain and gathering in the midst of our circle. When we began chanting, she said, they began to dance with delight until they fell down, exhausted. Somebody else gives news of Nature's approval: he saw a dark object flying across the moon last night and believes it was a spaceship. These are beings from the Pleiades star cluster, he informs us, who are coming back to Earth where they once lived, long ago, on the continent of Atlantis.

A young man wearing a Phish T-shirt says, "I never use the word 'aliens.' That's an insult. I call them Star People 'cause that's where they're from."

"If you've ever seen a Mayan, or a Navajo, or a Hopi, then you've seen a descendent of the Star People," a woman agrees with him.

There is seemingly no limit to the lengths we will go to speak on the Others' behalf. But I do not hear a single Indian speaking here and when I pause to listen to the earth myself, I hear only the same ominous sound that Alfred Watkins—the man who started this whole conversation about Earth Mysteries—also once heard.

Whooooooosh. Whoooooooooooooosh.

There is only silence, punctuated by the sound of wind blowing across the parking lot.

For Sir Watkins, leys had nothing to do with energies or even "the earth" in the abstract. They had rather to do with an unsurpassable limit to our cultural memories. Watkins's *The Old Straight Track* opened dolefully with a reflection on the forgotten dead of prehistory in his own native land:

> We sometimes feel (wrote W. H. Hudson in "Hampshire Days") a kinship with, and are strangely drawn to the dead, the long long dead, the men who knew not life in towns, and felt no strangeness in sun and wind and rain. In such a mood on that evening I went to one of those lonely barrows.
> In such mood we crave to know more of the life and doings of the people who lived in Britain before the Romans came. The knowledge is not attained by the same type of evidence which builds up the history of the period after written language commenced in this land.[18]

Rows of ruins gave Watkins a literal place to start writing about loss. But if the conversation about leys began as a response to the ineffable, that is not how it ended up. Nazi historians borrowed it for a time, searching for connection with indigenous Aryans, before Devereux and his colleagues adapted it to their own pastoral hopes of reversing the course of modern civilization.[19]

And Devereux in fact ended up abandoning his theory of ley lines long ago. His Dragon Project failed to record any measurable energies at the Calendar II site or at any other prehistoric site. He has since set straight the real import of *The Old Straight Track* and like Watkins has returned to a meditation on loss. Devereux now sees prehistoric ruins as "spirit lines," indigenous monuments to departed shamans believed to travel along them, journeyers in between the worlds of the living and the dead.[20]

But we who gather at the base of Mount Killington are still invoking ley lines to lay our claim to Vermont. We invoke them in the same breath we speak of Indian electricians and Mayan extraterrestrials.

Let the land return to silence, and let the mourning begin.

We are lost in America.

Aho.

IV.

Two back-to-back ASD conventions in 2008 and 2009 have effectively destroyed everything I once took for granted about my native New England ground. Puritan church spires marking village centers once conjured up for me the time of American beginnings. Now they join the ranks of more recent housing developments and strip malls: usurpers of the

Reich's Tomb.

landscape, all, impenetrable veils between the present and a pre-Columbian past. I leave Vermont to tour New England's ruins, undiscovering America one mile at a time.

I skim across the surface of the earth in my truck. My mind is loosened from its nested state, and like Andrew Jackson Davis, I fly through the continental vastness, connecting various dots along my travels. I start by recalling how in the woods of Lily Dale, we edged up close to the place where the wilderness begins, keeping close to each other so as not to get lost. Mediumship staved off the vertigo we felt as modern wanderers. We celebrated a shared sense of connection with both strangers and loved ones, a bond strong enough to overcome the separations of death. Parapsychology, the stepchild of Spiritualism, has yet to find this unifying force in the natural world, but at the Dale, human community was enough to console us in the meantime.

At Lily Dale, we played in an enchanted wilderness, but at Roswell, nature overwhelmed us. Extraterrestrial hypothesis researchers like Stanton Friedman, versed in the language of twentieth-century science, forced us to dwell on nature's fathomless depths. Vertigo returned, unabated. Alien abductees added ultraterrestrial beings and parallel universes to the list of dark wonders. Parapsychologists like John Keel only contributed to the sense of dread, sharing tales of winged beasts flying through the woods of West Virginia. Even the skeptics, with their denials of UFO sightings, failed to console us—yes, they concurred, humans are but specks in the cosmos.

And yet it was fear that bound us all together in Roswell. Without it, the UFO Festival would have simply been a chaotic mob of ufologists, each drifting off into his or her own interpretation of a natural world that unnerved them. At the ASD conventions, where there is no fear, participants have in fact worked up various and sundry descriptions of Nature, no longer bound by either the de rigueur of Spiritualist culture or the scientific rigor of serious ufology. In their drift away from the practical applications of dowsing used by the Old Timers, a new generation of dowsers have inadvertently revealed that nature—with or without the uppercase "n"—is both an illusion and a ruse, whether or not they recognize it. Nature is not only a metaphor open to a number of interpretations. It is also a myth that has perennially deflected our collective attention away from the tragic dimension of American history. It is our cultural shorthand for the denial of death, which is why the ASD conventions ended up circling around dim memories of violence, failing to find solid ground.[21] For all their pastoral pleasantries, these gatherings have unnerved me more profoundly than stories of rapping spirits or malevolent aliens.

Spiritualists, ufologists, and dowsers alike seem to have been pointing indirectly to this public secret, but they have never uttered it directly. I want to end my own paranormal road trip with a pilgrimage to one of the few monuments to tragedy in the entire history of these cultural movements. I am driving now through Maine, near the Canadian border, toward a town called Rangeley. I am closer to Quebec than I am to any major American metropolis. The northern Maine leaves are already beginning to turn, ever so slightly. Deep greens have shifted to lighter hues. Winter comes sooner here.

Water surrounds me. The Androscoggin River watershed now glistens like a sapphire. Mooselookmeguntic Lake is azure. Cupsuptic Lake is a cool cobalt.

I drive up a winding dirt road to the top of a hill. My destination is a place called Orgonon, which was once the home and workplace of Wilhelm Reich. Reich was a dowser of sorts, a man who understood Nature to be both the ground of being and the source of life. He invented his own kind of machines, considerably more sophisticated than rods and pendulums but designed as they also are to measure, harness, and direct natural energies.

Orgonon sits on the very top of a hill, overlooking Rangeley Lake and the distant Saddleback Mountain. It is a rectilinear, three-story building built of stones hewn from the surrounding area. The rocks here are volcanic, over 450 million years old, composed of Redington pluton.

Orgonon's flat roof was once used as an observation post. Reich would climb up there and peer through his telescope, pondering the Mystery that surrounded him. He could find no more grandiose display of beauty than this pristine New England wilderness, the power of the cosmos coursing like blood through Maine's unspoiled landscape, taking form and shape in the mountains and the rivers and the trees, and flowing through our own bodies, flooding us with sexual desires.

"Orgonon" is so named after orgasm, as is everything else associated with Reich's philosophy: Orgone energy, his term for the Cosmic Force; Orgone accumulators, the contraptions he built to harness It; and Orgonomy, the name for his entire philosophy.

For Reich, human beings and the Universe are drawn to each other like lovers, reciprocally bound by the cords of desire. The color of Orgone energy was blue, and so here in Reich's domain, Mooselookmeguntic Lake is alive with desire; Cupsuptic Lake is alive with desire. When human beings are healthy, they radiate not pheromones but the blue Orgone energy that gives rise to all things.

When I meet Adam, my tour guide, I explain that my visit here is part of a larger research project on dowsing and wait to see if he might make the connections more explicit for me. His immediate response: "Well, they do say that Wilhelm Reich was one of the original Hippies." I ask him what he means. He tells me that Reich was a "back-to-Nature kind of guy."

Adam is a college student. He sports a bushy mop of curly hair, a pierced tongue, and aviator sunglasses. He has heard of the ASD, although he has never been to an ASD convention. As we walk to our first stop on the Orgonon tour, we chat casually about his interests, which happen to focus on music. Adam was born too late to be a follower of the Grateful Dead, but he has been to several Phish concerts—huge outdoor-venue events lasting several days.

We are now standing outside Orgonon's lower-level basement, at the rear of the house. An open door beckons me to step through the outer wall, a mosaic of gray and brown stones, into a darkened interior. Adam says he has brought me here to watch a 20-minute film about Reich. He will be back when it is over. I step into the quiet darkness, the sole visitor to the theater this afternoon. When my eyes adjust to the lack of light, I spot a chair and sit down.

The documentary begins with Reich's tortuous childhood in Austria. He was born in 1897, the eldest of two sons. His father was a prosperous farmer, his mother a housekeeper. Both parents were Jewish. When Reich was 12 years old, his mother committed suicide after her husband learned she was having an affair with Reich's tutor. Reich, who had known about the affair but had done nothing to stop it, blamed himself for her death. In 1914, his father died. The same year, World War I erupted, and Reich joined the Austrian army to fight against the Russians.

The narrator's voice relates the facts coolly, as black-and-white stills of the era flash by. Suddenly, there appears the iconic profile of Sigmund Freud, dressed in a full suit, holding a cigar delicately in his right hand. The narrator continues:

Reich's career began took shape after the War. His chosen field was the new science of psychoanalysis. In 1918, he enrolled in the University of Vienna, and the following year, he met Freud. Reich was a brilliant student. He intuitively grasped Freud's then-emerging notion of the id—the psychic field of unconscious sexual cravings—and the psychoanalytic analysis of mental illness as the consequence of repressed or thwarted desires. After just a year, Freud gave Reich permission to see his own patients. In 1922, after graduating from the University of Vienna, Reich opened a practice in the city and made several of his own contributions to Freud's basic theory: the notion of "body armoring," or muscular tensions resulting from unfulfilled desires, and empirical verification of electrical changes in the male body during orgasm.

The images now shift from scenes of Vienna to stills of Germany, followed by communist and Nazi flags:

In 1930, Reich moved to Berlin. There he joined the Communist Party, and his interests in psychoanalysis began to merge with political interests. He spoke out against monogamy as a tool of bourgeois oppression and opened clinics in working-class neighborhoods. Through them, he taught classes in sex education and advocated for a proletariat-driven sexual revolution. These ideas proved to be too radical, however, even for the communists, and the party expelled him in 1933. The Nazi Party came to power the same year, and Reich fled to Oslo, where his greatest breakthrough would soon occur.

Now there are scenes of laboratories and black-and-white footage of protozoa:

From 1934 to 1937, Reich's interests took yet another turn. His fascination with the id deepened to a broader search for the Natural Force coursing through all living things. In his Oslo laboratories, Reich prepared cultures of inorganic matter—beach sand, grass, and coal—and studied the resultant vesicles under a microscope. He was amazed to see them pulsating with a bluish-tinged light. Reich termed these "bions" and believed he had stumbled on an intermediate form of protolife, midway between inorganic matter and organic life. When Reich added these bions to nutrient-rich Petri dishes, he observed something even more incredible: the spontaneous generation, or so it seemed, of various bacteria and amoebae. Reich was astonished. He sterilized the dishes and heated the bion cultures beyond the temperature living things could endure, but he obtained the same results.

Reich, the narrator tells us, had discovered the origins of life.

Amidst jeers and ridicule from his academic colleagues, Reich fled the Nazis a second time, leaving Europe for America in 1939. He joined the faculty of the New School in Manhattan, but during a vacation to Maine in the early 1940s, he decided to continue his research into the Life Force in the beautiful Androscoggin River watershed of southern Maine. Reich left New York City for northern New England and spent the rest of his days inventing an assortment of measuring devices and contraptions to record, capture, and harness the Life Force for the good of humanity.

The film winds to an end. I sit in the dark room, thinking. It was Goethe's essay on Nature (written, in fact, by Georg Cristoph Tobler, a Swiss pietist) that inspired Freud to study medicine, and in Freud's own writings, Nature reemerges in the guise of innate drives, the key to understanding human behavior and, by extension, history.[22] Reich seems to have taken the quest one step further, looking for connections between Nature in its interior, psychoanalytical sense and Nature in its exterior, objective guise.

Some say Reich was mad, but who can easily free himself completely from the power of this metaphor? In 1930, Freud was awarded the Goethe prize—reserved for those "whose creative activity served to honor the memory of Goethe" in both science and literature.

I walk outside into the sunlight, and Adam is there to greet me. Together we walk around to the blocky stone front of Orgonon, through the laboratory entrance.

Reich's wood-paneled laboratory has been lovingly reconstructed to appear as it might have in the early 1950s. In one corner sits an Orgone accumulator large enough for a person to sit inside and soak up the healing life rays. On a table in another corner rests a "Pantostat," a microscope connected to a small generator, used to observe the effects of electric current on cells. There is a field meter used to measure Orgone energy in outdoor settings, a microscope-cum-camera for time-lapse photography on tissues healed by cosmic energy, an "Orgonoscope," a Geiger counter, a "Vacor" (a vacuum device used to harness Orgone), and an Orgone accumulator for mice.

And against a back wall stands the most visually impressive of Reich's machines, the Cloud Buster. This is an assemblage of metal tubing mounted on a wooden frame. Visually similar to a cannon, this device consists of an assemblage of metal tubes—each one about eight feet in length—pointed slightly upward and mounted on a wooden frame. Designed for outdoor use, the Orgone cannon was used to blast clouds with Life Force energy in attempts to manipulate the weather. In 1953, Reich demonstrated its use before a gathering of local blueberry farmers. There were no explosions, no flashing lights. But after just a few hours of pointing the metal tubes up toward the sky, it began to rain, and the long drought that had been threatening the berry crop of southern Maine that summer was finally over. Reich claimed the change in weather as a victory for Orgonomy.

These various gizmos and gadgets no longer strike me as strange. I have seen them before, on display in the bookstore at the ASD convention. Particularly in their imitation of conventional scientific equipment, Reich's machines most closely resemble the tools of the Polish-born dowser Alicia Aratyn, who was selling UFO and universal pendulums, Nikram machines, and H40 Colour Energy Generators back at Killington. Exotic when compared to American rods and pendulums, these instruments are the stock-in-trade of the romantic tradition in Europe, which tries to base a science on the idea of a conscious, animate Nature. This quest includes but is not confined by American-style dowsing. Franz Anton Mesmer's studies of "animal magnetism," Karl von Reichenbach's alleged discovery of a unifying "Odic force" (named after the Norse god Odin), and Abbe Alexis Mermet's invention of radiesthesia are but three of the more famous chapters in this saga, similar to dowsing in their general goal and differing only in their experimental technologies.

Reich's obsession with human sexuality, however, struck many contemporaries in both Europe and America as particularly scandalous. The former outcast of the Communist Party lived to see the U.S. Food and Drug Administration (FDA) ban the sale of his Orgone accumulators across state lines. Reich defied the order and subsequently refused to go to court when the FDA pressed charges. In 1956, a federal judge sentenced him to prison for obstructing justice, ignoring his pleas that science should not be put on trial. The judge also ordered all of Reich's equipment and writings to be seized and destroyed. Here on this very hilltop in Rangeley, FDA officials stood over a state-sanctioned book burning. In 1957, Reich died a martyr for his work, perishing of heart failure in a New Jersey penitentiary. His body is buried in the woods behind Orgonon; a Cloud Buster stands next to his tomb.

Copies of Reich's banned books are displayed in the first-floor laboratory. "Pretty ironic, huh?" Adam says from the back of the room. I nod my head.

He escorts me up to Reich's private office, which covers most of Orgonon's second floor. Here in an airy time capsule of the 1950s, we stand before the sources of Reich's inspiration. Windows cover most of two of the walls, facing out toward the blue lakes below. A well-worn upholstered armchair sits across from a record player, an LP of Marian Anderson's *Beloved Schubert Songs* propped up against the cabinet. Bookshelves adorn the other walls, filled with the literature of American high culture, including works by Walt Whitman, John Steinbeck, and William Carlos Williams. A signed portrait of Sigmund Freud hangs in one corner, and an African walking stick—a gift from the great anthropologist Bronislaw Malinowski—is propped up against another.

We continue up one last flight of stairs to the flat-topped roof, Orgonon's observatory. Here we stand face-to-face with the Great Mystery at last: there is Lake Rangeley in the far valley. Saddleback Mountain towers behind it, and the White Mountains rise to the south. The late afternoon sun is golden, and crows caw from the tops of trees.

I imagine Wilhelm Reich peering through his telescope, quite literally lusting after this landscape. How fitting, I think, that he ended up here in America, the original object of Europe's desire. And how tragic that he, an Austrian Jewish émigré, lived to see his books burned by American authorities, dying in prison for his unorthodox beliefs.

It is not difficult to understand why Reich's communist leanings would have been as alarming to Cold War officials or why his constant talk about orgasms would have shocked and disturbed his contemporaries in those decades before the sexual revolution. But I suspect that Reich's offense against American sensibilities was even deeper than these. Orgonon is a mirror of our nation, driven mad by its own haunted ground. How scandalous to see a lettered man like Reich dowsing for secrets in the deep woods of Maine. There is indeed a mystery associated with Nature, but neither mainstream nor romantic science has been able to ascertain what it is. The enigma lies buried deeper than the Nature we both study or desire.

Look out one last time at the Androscoggin River watershed. The only thing missing here in this land of Indian names is the Indians themselves.

They hold no place in our pastoral landscapes, so beautiful, so sublime, and so wondrous.

But in the red glow of the sunset, Mooselookmeguntic Lake is the color of blood. Cupsuptic Lake is the color of blood.

And Wilhelm Reich's body lies in the ground.

Et in Arcadia ego.

Epilogue: The Damned Facts

Months have now passed since the last late-summer visit to Lily Dale. Snow is falling without reprieve on upstate New York, bringing with it an uncanny stillness. Even the spirits, a medium once told me, go into hibernation now. The Dale will wake up again, like Brigadoon, when the catalpa trees start to blossom.

There are months to go before the roads will be clear of snow. But as I begin to realize, there is really no further need to leave home. Down my street in Syracuse, a dilapidated city in the Rust Belt, a psychic hangs out her shingle. She is open for business throughout the year. My dentist, installing a filling, mentions a local dowser he thinks I should meet. From time to time, a UFO floats over New York.

They are everywhere, these damned facts—not damned in the Christian sense of the term, condemned to God's eternal wrath, but damned in the sense that Charles Fort used it: having no place in our extant cosmologies. Things and events that are so riveting, so seemingly miraculous when experienced, and yet so quickly forgotten or denied, dwelling in the shadowlands between the real world and unreality. Fort's 1919 *Book of the Damned* was the prototypical guide to a weird America, a compendium of entries on subjects like phantom cats, UFOs, and rains of fish and frogs. All other paranormal maps of the nation are modeled on this work.

In January, contractors come to save my old house, a Craftsman, from disrepair. I open the front door for Chad, an electrician. He will spend a part of the week in my house, rewiring. From time to time we pass in the hallway, exchanging small talk. On the first day, I learn he was schooled in an upstate Bible college, married young, and is now a father of three. On the second day, he learns of my recent time out on our country's highways, chasing down ephemera. He grows pensive, and I wait for a biblical

The Damned Trees.

warning. But instead he asks me, solemnly, "Have you been to Whiskey Hollow Road?" I have, I tell him. "Now there's some serious haunting going on down there, don't you think?"

I do. On a warm October morning, I went out looking for the legendary grove of local lore in the farm country west of the city. It is unclear what happened there, but rumors of violence now abound: secret Ku Klux Klan meetings, conspiring a lynching; the wife of a man unjustly accused of murder, hanging herself from a tree. My British GPS guide failed me that day—Whiskey Hollow Road is well off the grid, empty of houses or habitation. It is a mile-long gravel lane, studded with potholes, twisting through the woods in a forgotten corner of upstate New York. Patches of leaves not yet fallen off the trees shimmered in yellows and red-orange hues in the sun high above, but the earth below was shadowed and cool. Hundreds of starlings perched in the branches, drowning out all other sounds with their din of raucous screeching. Occasionally, the pale half-full moon peaked down at me through the colorful canopy.

"The trees there are damned," I say to Chad.

"That's right." It is something on which we both agree.

"And the birds are damned as well."

"Mm-hmm."

How do you get to Whiskey Hollow Road? It is not on the GPS and barely discernible on a road map. You need a map inspired by Charles Fort to get there—a copy of *Weird New York* or directions given to you by a wonder-struck native.

You might want to try to find it though. Go there yourself and stand on haunted ground. Breathe in the uncanny air of a paranormal America.

Whiskey Hollow Road is just a bunch of damned trees, growing and rotting and dropping their leaves. The starlings shriek in unison.

But it is unclear, exactly, where we are.

Hear the words of paranormal poet, William Carlos Williams:

so much depends
upon

a red wheel
barrow

glazed with rain
water

beside the white
chickens.[1]

How ordinary and yet how extraordinary. How marvelous it all is, and yet how damned.

Notes

PROLOGUE

1. "Axis mundi" is a term invented by the historian of religion Mircea Eliade to signify a place in the physical landscape where, for religious believers, the visible and invisible worlds of supernatural beings intersect. It has become part of the lexicon of the academic study of religion. See Mircea Eliade, *The Myth of the Eternal Return, or, Cosmos and History* (Princeton, NJ: Princeton University Press, 1954), 12–13.

2. See, for example, Mark Moran, *Weird U.S.: Your Travel Guide to America's Local Legends and Best Kept Secrets* (New York: Sterling, 2009).

3. Renee L. Bergland, *The National Uncanny: Indian Ghosts and American Subjects* (Hanover, NH: University Press of New England, 2000).

4. Peter Martyr, in *De Orbe Novo* in *New World Metaphysics: Readings on the Religious Meaning of the American Experience*, ed. Giles Gunn (New York: Oxford University Press, 1981), 12.

5. Ibid., 11.

6. Scholars from a number of fields have returned to the narratives of New World explorers to discuss and analyze the contours of present-day American cultural mythology. These studies focus on the subordination of European-Native American interactions to wonder-filled descriptions of the physical environs. Where American Indians are discussed, they are portrayed as "children" of this sublime natural setting. Wonder thus becomes a veil or screen hiding the historical dimension of the initial contact between European and non-European civilizations. See Stephen Greenblatt, *Marvelous Possessions: The Wonder of the New World* (Chicago: University of Chicago Press, 1991); Charles H. Long, *Significations: Signs, Symbols, and Images in the Interpretation of Religion* (Philadelphia: Fortress Press, 1986); Bernard McGrane, *Beyond Anthropology* (New York: Columbia University Press, 1989); and Tzvetan Todorov, *The Conquest of America: The Question of the Other* (Norman: University of Oklahoma Press, 1982).

7. Gunn, *New World Metaphysics*, xx.

8. Greenblatt, *Marvelous Possessions*, 135.

9. See Philip J. Deloria, *Playing Indian* (New Haven, CT: Yale University Press, 1999).

10. See chapter 6, "Metaphysical Asia," in Catherine Albanese, *A Republic of Mind and Spirit: A Cultural History of American Metaphysical Religion* (New Haven, CT: Yale University Press, 2008), 330–93.

INTRODUCTION

1. From Walt Whitman, "Song of the Open Road," in *Leaves of Grass: The First (1855) Edition* (New York: Classic Books), 91.

2. The subject matter of this book overlaps with a number of different discourses within the academic study of religion. Spiritualism, ufology, and dowsing intersect at various points and ways with what Catherine L. Albanese has termed the American "metaphysical" tradition in *A Republic of Mind and Spirit: A Cultural History of American Metaphysical Religion* (New Haven, CT: Yale University Press, 2008). Albanese delineates a fourfold set of concepts that constitute a metaphysical worldview: first, it posits the universe as a unified field of consciousness; second, it describes the cosmos primarily in terms of energy and transformation; third, it teaches that any and all discrete particulars embody the structure and patterns of the whole; fourth, it prioritizes gnosis—a direct awareness of one's own mind as contiguous with the One Mind—as the central purpose of the religious life. It is impossible to discuss Spiritualism and dowsing in particular without recourse to these central metaphysical concepts.

As an ethnographer, however, I am less interested in reconstructing a history of ideas than I am in understanding the role and function of religious movements to their followers. In and through the ethnographic approach, I have encountered many of the central issues that shape the study of New Religious Movements (NRMs). These issues include the insufficiency of received religious traditions to find meaning amidst many of the unprecedented developments of modernity; the reliance instead on "new"—which is to say, post–eighteenth-century— cosmologies and rituals, typically ones that have been revealed through prophetic founders; and ensuing conflicts between the NRM in question and self-appointed spokespersons for churches and institutionalized science. For an example of a scholarly work analyzing Spiritualism and ufology (though not dowsing) as NRMs in America, see Philip Jenkins, *Mystics and Messiahs: Cults and New Religions in American History* (New York: Oxford University Press, 2001).

And yet there is a limit to the usefulness of this model when approaching culturewide interest in such ideas as spirits, aliens, and Earth energies. Even Lily Dale, which is affiliated with an established religious denomination, lacks the social cohesion of an NRM. Michael Barkun, in his study of UFO-related conspiracy theories, has used the concept of "stigmatized knowledge" to describe ideas circulating through the venues of modern mass media that nevertheless deviate radically from the normative rationalized worldview of modern societies. See chapter 2, "Millennialism, Conspiracy and Stigmatized Knowledge," in Barkun's *A Culture of Conspiracy: Apocalyptic Visions in Contemporary America* (Berkeley: University of California Press, 2004).

Modern-day Spiritualism, ufology, and dowsing circulate freely in public venues; they are by no means confined to discrete religious movements. However, for reasons to be developed throughout the course of this book, I do not see them as particularly deviant. On the contrary, I have come to understand the "paranormal" as a veiled discourse about the so-called normative dimensions of modern American society.

3. The lack of any overarching taxonomy is particularly acute in scholarship focused on the kinds of movements in this study. The concepts of "magic" and "occultism" are subsumed within the discourse of metaphysical religiosity. Within the broad cosmological contours discussed by Albanese, all parts of a sentient universe affect the other parts, allowing for the "magical" manipulation of the world by mediums, the aliens of abduction accounts, and dowsers. "Occultism" is a term alluding to the initiatory dimension of metaphysical movements within their European milieu—although, as Albanese points out, the formerly esoteric knowledge of Europe's secret societies has become an exoteric or public discourse in America. As for "pseudoscience" and the "paranormal," both of these labels presuppose a scholarly focus on the observable phenomena of Spiritualism, ufology, and dowsing as possible features of the natural world—completely shorn of any interest in their religious and cultural significance.

4. For Kristeva, language is comprised of both "symbolic" and "semiotic" elements. The first term denotes the grammatical and syntactical devices through which human beings signify and thus make sense of their worlds. The semiotic refers to language's presymbolic dimension—its cadences, rhythms, and tones. It is the "first language" the child learns in the body of its mother, continuing as the nonverbal "speech" of the body—the music of speech as it were. See Julia Kristeva, *Powers of Horror: An Essay on Abjection*, trans. Leon S. Roudiez (New York: Columbia University Press, 1982).

5. A hierophany is a particular person, place, thing, or event through which the supernatural realities or a religion break through to the natural world. "If we observe the general behavior of archaic man, we are struck by the following fact: neither the objects of the external world nor human acts, properly speaking, have any autonomous value. Objects or acts acquire a value, and in so doing become real, because they participate, in one fashion or another, in a reality that transcends them. Among countless stones, one stone becomes sacred—and hence instantly becomes saturated with being—because it constitutes a hierophany." Mircea Eliade, *The Myth of Eternal Return, or, Cosmos and History* (Princeton, NJ: Princeton University Press, 1954), 3–4.

6. Otto reflects on the valences of religious experience engendered by an encounter with "an overpowering, absolute might of some kind," designated by the Latin word *mysterium* for "mystery." He argues that such an experience is comparable to other emotional states and yet constitutes its own distinctive kind: a feeling of one's own nothingness conjoined with a paradoxical mixture of dread (*tremendum*) and fascination (*fascinans*) directed toward the *mysterium*. The *mysterium tremendum et fascinans* constitutes the origin of any religion, preceding all theology or metaphysics. In his attempt to convey the texture of religious experience to the reader, Otto offers his own extensive comments on the fear and fascination evoked by ghosts and ghost stories: "It is the mark which really characterizes the so-called 'religion of primitive man,' and there it appears as 'daemonic dread,'...

That this is so is shown by the potent attraction again and again exercised by the element of horror and 'shudder' in ghost stories, even among persons of high all-round education. . . . The ghost's real attraction rather consists in this, that of itself and in an uncommon degree it entices the imagination, awakening strong interest and curiosity; it is the weird thing itself that allures the fancy." *The Idea of the Holy; An Inquiry into the Non-Rational Factor in the Idea of the Divine and Its Relation to the Rational* (New York: Oxford University Press, 1923), 10–28.

7. In his "Final Impressions of a Psychical Researcher," published in 1909, James wrote, "I began this article by confessing myself baffled. I *am* baffled, as to spirit-return, and as to many other special problems. I am also constantly baffled as to what to think of this or that particular story, for the sources of error in any one observation are seldom fully knowable. But weak sticks make strong faggots; and when the stories fall into consistent sorts that point each in a definite direction, one gets a sense of being in presence of genuinely natural types of phenomena." James alludes to his experience as a researcher for the American Society of Psychical Research, founded in Boston in 1885 to investigate the various phenomena of Spiritualist séances. See William James, "Final Impressions of a Psychical Researcher" in *The Writings of William James*, ed. John J. McDermott (Chicago: University of Chicago Press, 1977), 796.

8. James McClenon has employed a similar concept of wonder in his socio-logical analysis of religion. In the rationalized world of modernity, anomalies, or "phenomena thought to exceed scientific explanation," play a critical role in the development and maintenance of religious belief. It is cognitive dissonance, rather than a mind-shattering encounter with a mighty *mysterium*, that leads peo-ple to reconsider the various claims of suprarational realities found across the world's religious traditions. See McClenon, *Wondrous Events: Foundations of Reli-gious Beliefs* (Philadelphia: University of Pennsylvania Press, 1994).

9. Richard T. Hughes discusses the "Myth of Nature's Nation" in *Myths America Lives By* (Urbana: University of Illinois Press, 2004). Hughes employs the understanding of "myth" as developed within the field of religious studies as a collective "story that speaks of meaning and purpose, and for that reason . . . speaks truth to those who take it seriously." Insofar as this myth has become insti-tutionalized, particularly in the nation's political and scientific establishments, it is generally not recognized as a fictive construct—one does not so much "take it seriously" as accept its validity prior to thought and action. In the modern era, Nature is synonymous with "that which is so."

10. Following Hughes, I use the expression "Nature's Nation" as shorthand for the "myth of Nature's Nation." The term comes from the title of Perry Mill-er's *Nature's Nation* (Cambridge, MA: Harvard University Press, 1967)—a study of the symbolic function of "nature" in the literature of both Puritan New England and the American Renaissance.

11. For a discussion of the notions of embodied place and disembodied space, see Edward Casey, *The Fate of Place: A Philosophical History* (Berkeley: University of California Press, 1998). Casey explores the emergence of the quest for universal, placeless constants during the age of the Enlightenment and the subsequent mar-ginalization of discourses about place in the annals of Western philosophy.

12. See Anthony Grafton, *New Worlds, Ancient Texts: The Power of Tradition and the Shock of Discovery* (Cambridge: Belknap Press, 1995), and Edmundo

O'Gorman, *The Invention of America: An Inquiry into the Historical Nature of the New World and the Meaning of Its History* (Bloomington: Indiana University Press, 1961).

CHAPTER 1

1. See chapter 4, "Communion of Spirits," in Catherine L. Albanese, *A Republic of Mind and Spirit: A Cultural History of American Metaphysical Religion* (New Haven, CT: Yale University Press, 2008); Ann Braude, *Radical Spirits: Spiritualism and Women's Rights in Nineteenth-Century America* (Boston: Beacon Press, 1989); and Todd Jay Leonard, *Talking to the Other Side: A History of Modern Spiritualism and Mediumship* (Lincoln, NE: iUniverse Inc., 2005). For a discussion of *Espiritismo* and its relationship to Spiritualism in America, see chapter 7, "*Espiritismo:* Creole Spiritism in Cuba, Puerto Rico, and the United States," in Lizabeth Paravisini-Gebert and Margarite Fernandez Olmos, *Creole Religions of the Caribbean: An Introduction from Vodou and Santeria to Obeah and Espiritismo* (New York: New York University Press, 2003).

2. The emergence of Spiritualist camps and the rise of "physical mediumship" unfolded simultaneously beginning in the 1870s. Braude observes that the "triumph of the camp meetings ... marked a triumph for mediumship. At the core of the carnival atmosphere lay the appeal of spirit manifestations, without which the event could not have occurred" (*Radical Spirits*, 175).

3. Christine Wicker's own ethnographic study of the camp is titled *Lily Dale: The True Story of the Town That Talks to the Dead* (New York: HarperCollins, 2003).

4. Freud discussed the emotional valences and psychological significance of the uncanny in an etymological dissection of the German word *Das Unheimliche*, that which does not (*un-*) belong at home (*Heimliche*), in his 1919 essay "The Uncanny." Freud suggests that experiences of the uncanny ultimately point to repressed, which is to say, the familiar or "belonging-at-home," contents of the individual psyche.

5. The foundational study of Christian revivalism in nineteenth-century upstate New York is Whitney R. Cross's *The Burned-Over District: The Social and Intellectual History of Enthusiastic Religion in Western New York, 1800–1850* (Ithaca, NY: Cornell University Press, 1950).

6. Scholars of American religious history refer to this era as the Second Great Awakening. In and through thousands of Protestant revivals orchestrated throughout the first four decades of the nineteenth century, preachers reassured their flocks that Christ's sacrifice had atoned for the sins of all and taught them that their own acceptance or rejection of this divine gift constituted the pivotal moment in the drama of salvation. This teaching was a direct repudiation of Calvinist notions, inherited through the Puritans, of predestination. Intellectual leaders of the Second Great Awakening also prophesied a spiritual rebirth of the nation and the imminent Second Coming of Christ.

Several scholars have discussed how these newfound theological emphases reflected contemporaneous changes in the social and political landscape of an industrializing America. In *Revivals, Awakenings, and Reforms* (Chicago: University of Chicago Press, 1978), William G. McLoughlin builds on an anthropological model of "cultural revitalization" to interpret the Second Great Awakening as an adaptation to modernization. Similarly, in *The Democratization of American Christianity* (New Haven, CT: Yale University Press, 1991), Nathan O. Hatch reads evangelicalism as a Protestant response to the new political culture of the early American republic, particularly in its democratic exhortation to interpret Scripture in light of one's own personal experience.

The emergence of popular interest in mesmerism coincided with the Protestant revivals of the Second Great Awakening. Many Americans of this era looking for an Enlightenment-based rather than a Scripture-based rationale for religious belief embraced the uncanny displays of mesmerized subjects, including feats of clairvoyance and prognostication, as empirical demonstrations of the soul. For a further discussion of this topic, see chapter 2, "The Unconscious Discovered: The Mesmerists' Legacy," in Robert Fuller, *Americans and the Unconscious* (New York: Oxford University Press, 1986), 29–49.

Mesmerism was also perceived as a demonstration of the invisible chords of "sympathy" binding together the citizens of the United States during a period of rapid demographic change. See chapter 1, "Sleepwalking and Sympathy," in Robert S. Cox, *Body and Soul: A Sympathetic History of American Spiritualism* (Charlottesville: University of Virginia Press, 2003), 22–52.

7. Addressing the clairvoyant feats of mesmerized subjects, Cox observes, "In sympathetic terms clairvoyance offered more than just the expansion of the mental world; it offered the literal means of becoming a spectator of human relations" (*Body and Soul*, 41).

8. Joyce LaJudice and Paula M. Vogt, *Lily Dale Proud Beginnings: A Little Piece of History* (N.p.: n.p., 1984), 1–3.

9. The earliest national organization of Spiritualists in the United States was the National Convention of Spiritualists, which first convened in Chicago in 1864. This institution was dissolved, however, in 1873. The National Association of Spiritualists, predecessor to the National Spiritualist Association of Churches, was founded in 1893 in Chicago. See Marilyn Awtry, *History of National Spiritualist Association of Churches* (N.p.: National Spiritualist Association of Churches, 1983), 1.

10. Spear and his followers founded the utopian community of Harmonia, located just 25 miles south of Lily Dale, in 1850. In 1858, John and Carolyn Chase, both members of the settlement, received a message from the spirits of the place that 1,000 years previously, a civilization of web-footed Celtic Indians had lived on the banks of Kiantone Creek but had been swallowed up into the earth during a violent earthquake. On orders from these spirits, Spear and his followers went on to spend approximately $6,000 building a tunnel to unearth the remains of this civilization, which were never found. Harmonia was dissolved in 1863. When the Cassadaga Free Lake Association built its camp in 1879, many of Spear's former members who lived in the area became active members of the new Spiritualist community. For an extensive discussion of the life and thought of Universalist minister and Spiritualist leader John Murray Spear—including his utopian community in Kiantone, New York—see John Benedict Buescher, *The Remarkable Life of John Murray Spear: Agitator for the Spirit Land* (Notre Dame, IN: University of Notre Dame Press, 2006).

11. Awtry, *History of National Spiritualist Association of Churches*, 16–19.

12. George Lawton, "Spiritualism—A Contemporary American Religion," *Journal of Religion* 10 (January 1930): 37.

13. Michael P. Richard and Albert Adato, "The Medium and Her Message: A Study of Spiritualism at Lily Dale, New York," *Review of Religious Research* 22 (December 1980): 186–96.

14. Defining the "New Age" is no less complex an affair than pinpointing the meaning of Spiritualism, although for different reasons. The expression first surfaced in the mass media during the middle years of the 1980s, even though the social trend it was meant to describe had been brewing since the previous decade. From the start, "New Age" was an umbrella term. It referred to a burgeoning interest in a number of religious, psychological, and alternative healing teachings and practices that had previously been marginalized or simply ignored by modern institutions of power. Rather than compiling lists of *what* these subjects were, most scholars have found it more helpful to describe the New Age in terms of *who* its constituents were and *why* they sought out knowledge that had been stigmatized by their culture. In answer to the first, demographic question, New Agers were mostly white, college-educated members of the post–World War II babyboomer generation. At an earlier stage in their lives, they had been affected in some way by countercultural movements of the 1960s, particularly the antiwar, civil rights, and hippie movements. By the end of the decade, it was clear that these political and social experiments had failed to effect the sweeping revolution in American culture that they had envisioned. But by the end of the 1970s, an older if not more jaded generation had taken up a new strategy for change.

Many scholars have identified self-transformation as a defining ethos of the New Age. Boomers turned to a wide spectrum of teachings culled from non-Western cultures or subaltern traditions within the West to deepen self-awareness and heal the body and mind. While focused on the self, the New Age looked forward to broader changes in national and indeed planetary consciousness. But it resisted institutionalization. The movement took shape largely through the publication of books and through workshops and lectures organized by their authors. By the end of the 1970s, a small deluge of thematically similar works had appeared and with them a cast of highly sought-after authors/teachers. See James R. Lewis and Gordon Melton, eds., *Perspectives on the New Age* (Albany: State University of New York Press, 1992).

15. See Wade Clark Roof, *A Generation of Seekers: The Spiritual Journeys of the Baby Boom Generation* (San Francisco: Harper San Francisco, 1994).

16. See chapter 6, "Seekers," in Leigh Eric Schmidt, *Restless Souls: The Making of American Spirituality* (New York: HarperCollins, 2005), 227–68.

17. E. Lyell Earle, "Lily Dale, the Haunt of Spiritualists," *Catholic World* 68 (January 1899): 506–7.

18. Sir Arthur Conan Doyle was an enthusiastic supporter of Spiritualism from the turn of the twentieth century until his death in 1930, and his endorsement played a large role in Spiritualism's resurgence during the interwar years. His own two-volume *History of Spiritualism*, published in 1926, remains an authoritative account of the movement within NSAC circles. The main educational facility of the NSAC—the Morris Pratt Institute, based in Milwaukee,

Wisconsin—continues to include Doyle's *History* in its curriculum for the training of Spiritualist ministers.

19. For an account of how modern psychology grew out of and eventually distanced itself from early discourses about mesmerism, see Henri F. Ellenberger, *The Discovery of the Unconscious: The History and Evolution of Dynamic Psychiatry* (New York: Basic Books, 1970).

20. The history of modern parapsychology began in part as a scientific investigation of mediumship. The British Society of Psychical Research, founded in 1882, was the first organization of its kind to take up the empirical and rational study of six interrelated phenomena: mesmerism, thought transference, apparitions, haunted houses, mediumship, and a universal life energy proclaimed by German scientist Karl Ludwig von Reichenbach (the so-called Odic Force). Inspired by such efforts, a team of scientists formed the American Society of Psychical Research in 1885. In and through these developments, the various phenomena of mediumship were divorced from their original religious and cultural contexts, and parapsychology continues on as its own distinctive discourse. Since the formation of the American Society of Psychical Research, notable research projects on psychic phenomena have included J. B. Rhine's work on extrasensory perception at the Foundation for the Research on the Nature of Man at Duke University from 1924 to 1965; Montague Ullman's and Stanley Krippner's research at the Maimonides Medical Center in Brooklyn, New York, during the 1970s: and Charles Honorton's experiments at the Psychophysical Research Laboratories in New Jersey from 1979 to 1989.

For a historical discussion of the relationship between late nineteenth- and early twentieth-century Spiritualism and the beginnings of parapsychology, see R. Laurence Moore, *In Search of White Crows: Spiritualism, Parapsychology, and American Culture* (New York: Oxford University Press, 1977).

21. Ann Braude notes that "Spiritualism's conception of nature as permeated with divinity received earlier and more elegant expression within Unitarianism's more heterodox offshoot, Transcendentalism. Ralph Waldo Emerson's discovery in the 1830s that the divinity revealed in nature had no need of dogmas or rituals of an established church preceded the same discoveries by Spiritualists, and the hostility he encountered from his fellow Unitarian ministers when he questioned the divinity of Christ foretold the acrimony with which Spiritualism would be met even within the liberal denominations." Commenting on the Transcendentalists' disapproval of Spiritualism, Braude adds, "Yet, whatever disdain Emerson and Thoreau felt for Spiritualism, it spread some of their most cherished ideas far beyond the ranks of Transcendentalism" (*Radical Spirits*, 44–45).

22. A concise overview of the main developments within the field of parapsychology can be found in Robert M. Schoch and Logan Yonavjak, *The Parapsychology Revolution: A Concise Anthology of Paranormal and Psychical Research* (New York: Penguin Group, 2008).

23. Turner, a cultural anthropologist, coined the term "communitas" to describe a spontaneous experience among ritual initiates separated from the rest of society, suspended for a time in a liminal or antistructural state devoid of customary roles and obligations. See *The Ritual Process: Structure and Anti-Structure* (Chicago: Aldine, 1969).

24. "Ingenious Frauds at Lily Dale Séances: Psychical Research Society Investigates Reported Marvels at Famous Spiritist Stronghold and Exposes Fraudulent Methods of Mediums," *New York Times*, March 8, 1908.

CHAPTER 2

1. While some authors use the terms "mediumship" and "channeling" interchangeably, there is an important distinction in terms of the kinds of entities the medium or channeler claims to bring through. While mediums speak on behalf of deceased human beings, channelers deliver messages from other-than-human entities, usually of extraterrestrial origin. While such channelers proliferated in America after the first wave of UFO sightings in 1947, there were a handful of notable predecessors. Among these, one of the best known was the French psychic Helene Smith (née Catherine-Elise Muller), who claimed to have made telepathic contact with Martians. The content of Smith's messages—including samples of the Martian alphabet revealed through her sessions of automatic writing—appeared in the book *From India to the Planet Mars*, published in 1899 by psychologist Theodore Flournoy.

It was not until the early 1950s, however, that channeling arose as a perennial feature of American culture in and through the popular UFO craze. Modern-day channelers alleged that they had made contact with extraterrestrials through the same methods used earlier by Spiritualist mediums—relying on telepathy, automatic writing, visionary experiences, and dreams. Intended for humanity as a whole, their messages were almost always apocalyptic in content—either predicting the end of the human race or proposing ways to stave off such a calamity. Dorothy Martin, to cite but one famous example, wrote a letter in 1954 to a local Chicago newspaper claiming that she had been in telepathic contact with an extraterrestrial named Sananda. Martin, a Chicago housewife, wrote that Sananda had revealed to her that the end of the world was coming at the end of the year, on December 21, in the form of a great flood. She also promised that Sananda would rescue those who heeded her message and that a small group of about 15 to 20 followers were already making the necessary preparations for their departure from Earth. Martin eventually went on to found the Association of Sananda and Sanat Kumara. In 1965, she moved to Mount Shasta, California, and led a spiritual community there as "Sister Thedra." Until her death in 1988, she continued to bring through messages from Sananda and other extraterrestrials.

In ufological circles, channelers like Martin were lumped together with other individuals who claimed to have had physical as well as psychic contact with extraterrestrials. Collectively, these people were referred to as "contactees." One of the earliest Americans who claimed to have met an extraterrestrial in the flesh (and traveled aboard his UFO) was George Van Tassel. He narrated this experience in his 1952 book *I Rode a Flying Saucer* and organized one of the first UFO conventions—the Giant Rock Interplanetary Space Craft Convention—convened annually in the Mojave Desert until 1977. Another famous contactee was George Adamski, who claimed to have made physical contact with the "Space Brothers" and ridden with them on their ships. Like the channelers, Van Tassel, Adamski, and other contactees were obsessed with the apocalypse, particularly in the form of thermonuclear annihilation. Through them, extraterrestrials conveyed their distress over the direction humanity was taking and frequently assured humanity they were helping to avert the worst-case scenario. For an analysis of twentieth-century channeling, see Michael F. Brown, *The Channeling Zone: American Spirituality in an Anxious Age* (Cambridge, MA: Harvard University Press, 1999).

2. "When materialization replaced trance speaking as the most noteworthy public manifestation of Spiritualism, the meaning of mediumship changed. Like other forms of sensationalist mediumship, the new manifestations emphasized the medium's passivity in new and humiliating ways and downplayed her empowerment. . . . Mediums for materialization could not hope to inspire the same admiration that trance speakers elicited from their audiences. Letters of appreciation did not follow the appearance of a woman in a sack nailed to the floor." Ann Braude, *Radical Spirits: Spiritualism and Women's Rights in Nineteenth-Century America* (Boston: Beacon Press, 1989), 177.

3. All religions are implicitly social in nature, and yet many of the metaphysical movements that followed Spiritualism emphasized individual spiritual awakening as a necessary prelude to being of service to others. The Church of Christian Science and a number of different New Thought movements sought to heal the world one person at a time, deemphasizing the goals of broad social reform that had characterized antebellum Spiritualism. Theosophy, another offshoot of Spiritualism, went a step further in recognizing different levels of spiritual attainment from one individual to the next—even as it disseminated its teachings freely to the public and hoped for an eventual transformation in society. The Fourth Way, a metaphysical tradition imported from Europe into the United States after World War I, not only embraced a hierarchical notion of spiritual attainment but also kept its teachings guarded from noninitiates.

4. Not unlike the traditions of Christian Science and New Thought that came after it, Spiritualism has taken up its initial charge of social reform by emphasizing the transformation of individuals, one at a time. For a study of the unseen impact of metaphysical thought and practice in a host of modern professions, see Elizabeth Lloyd Mayer, *Extraordinary Knowing: Science, Skepticism, and the Inexplicable Powers of the Human Mind* (New York: Bantam, 2007). For a reflection on the tactics that members of mass society use to subvert the social order, see Michel de Certeau, *The Practice of Everyday Life*, trans. Steven Rendall (Berkeley: University of California Press, 2002).

5. "Pilgrimage may be thought of as extroverted mysticism, just as mysticism is introverted pilgrimage. The pilgrim physically traverses a mystical way; the mystic sets forth on an interior spiritual pilgrimage." Victor Turner and Edith Turner, *Image and Pilgrimage in Christian Culture* (New York: Columbia University Press, 1995), 33.

6. Henry David Thoreau, *Walden* (Boston: Beacon Press, 2004), 300.

7. Robert C. Fuller, *Americans and the Unconscious* (New York: Oxford University Press, 1986), 32–33.

8. "Passing from the *third* to the *fourth* state, a still greater and higher mental manifestation will be observed. . . . The mind becomes free from all inclinations which the body would subject it to, and only sustains a connexion by a very

minute and rare medium, the same that connects one thought with another. In this condition the patient progresses into the *fourth* state. Then the mind becomes free from the organization, except as connected by the medium before mentioned; and then it is capable of receiving impressions of foreign or proximate objects, according to the medium with which it particularly becomes associated." Andrew Jackson Davis, *The Principles of Nature, Her Divine Revelations, and a Voice to Mankind* (New York: S. S. Lyon and Wm. Fishbough, 1847), 36–37.

9. Ibid., 29.

10. In the opening of his essay "Circles," Emerson appropriates the circle from the writings of Augustine, who employs it as a metaphor for God, to use it as a symbol of (American) Nature: "The eye is the first circle; the horizon which it forms is the second; and throughout nature this primary picture is repeated without end. It is the highest emblem in the cipher of the world. St. Augustine described the nature of God as a circle whose centre was everywhere and its circumference nowhere." Ralph Waldo Emerson, *Essays* (New York: Harper & Row, 1951), 212.

11. Davis, *The Principles of Nature, Her Divine Revelations, and a Voice to Mankind*, 107.

12. Ibid., 675. Italics in original quote.

13. See Christopher Partridge, *UFO Religions* (New York: Routledge, 2003).

14. "But then what about the peddler's trunk, allegedly found at the same site and time as the bones? As a matter of fact, the trunk was never reported in any of the contemporary sources we uncovered. The earliest mention of it I have found is an account penned years later by one P.L.O.A. Keeler (1922), a Lily Dale medium who had a reputation for faking spirit writing and other phenomena.... I examined the trunk at the Lily Dale museum, whose curator Ron Nagy ... conceded there was no real provenance for it nor any proof of its discovery in 1904. And the trunk's condition appears far too good for its supposed half-century burial." Joe Nickell, "A Skeleton's Tale: The Origins of Modern Spiritualism," *Skeptical Inquirer* 32, no. 4 (July/August 2008), http://www.csicop.org.

15. Joe Nickell, "Riddle of the Crystal Skulls," *Skeptical Inquirer* 30, no. 4 (July/August 2006), http://www.csicop.org.

16. See Oliver Impey, *The Origins of Museums: The Cabinet of Curiosities in Sixteenth- and Seventeenth-Century Europe* (Oxford: Clarendon Press; New York: Oxford University Press, 1985).

17. See John Onians, "'I Wonder ...' A Short History of Amazement" in *Sight and Insight: Essays on Art and Culture in Honour of E. H. Gombrich at 85*, ed. John Onians (London: Phaidon Press, 1994), 11–32.

18. "Summing up the formal characteristics of play we might call it a free activity standing quite consciously outside 'ordinary' life as being 'not serious,' but at the same time absorbing the player intensely and utterly. It is an activity connected with no material interest, and no profit can be gained by it. It proceeds within its own proper boundaries of time and space according to fixed rules and in an ordinary manner. It promotes the formation of social groupings which tend to surround themselves with secrecy and to stress their difference from the common world by disguise or other means." Johan Huizinga, *Homo Ludens: A Study of the Play-Element in Culture* (Boston: Beacon Press, 1950), 13.

19. George P. Hansen, "CSICOPS and the Skeptics: An Overview," *Journal of the American Society of Psychical Research* 86, no. 1 (January 1992): 19–63.

20. Keel's work plays an important role in the history of ufology. Through the 1950s and 1960s, the dominant interpretation of UFOs assumed that they came from other solar systems within our galaxy. Keel's memoir supported the "ultra-terrestrial" hypothesis, returning ufology to its roots in the visionary realms of channeling. It also characterized the altered states of consciousness in a UFO experience as a "false illumination" induced by other-than-human entities bent on deceiving and confusing the human race. This interpretation of ufology has been taken up by self-identified Christian (conservative Protestant) ufologists in an elaborate theory of aliens as fallen angels. See chapter 12, "Games Non-People Play," in John Keel, *The Mothman Prophecies* (New York: Tom Doherty Associates, 1991), 151–71.

21. "The history of European relations with Native Americans is a history of murders, looted graves, illegal land transfers, and disruptions of sovereignty. Among these, land ownership may be the source of the nation's deepest guilt. Ownership itself—that is to say property—is a concept that haunts the American national mythos, repressed and erased in the Declaration of Independence in a manner that both denies and emphasizes its centrality to the republic. In the Declaration, Jefferson alluded to Locke, who had written of the fundamental rights of life, liberty, and property. But he changed the words to the more palatable formulation that we all know so well: life, liberty, and the pursuit of happiness. This erasure of the troublesome concept of property speaks volumes about the vexed relation that the United States has to its own territory. It also gestures toward one of the most basic reasons that American nationalism must be predicated on haunted grounds: the land is haunted because it is stolen." Renee L. Bergland, *The National Uncanny: Indian Ghosts and American Subjects* (Hanover, NH: University Press of New England, 2000), 8–9. Scholars have taken a similar analysis of the representation of African Americans in European American literature. See Toni Morrison, "Unspeakable Things Unspoken: The Afro-American Presence in American Literature," *Michigan Quarterly Review* 28 (Winter 1989): 1–34.

CHAPTER 3

1. See Rudolph Otto, *The Idea of the Holy: An Inquiry into the Non-Rational Factor in the Idea of the Divine and Its Relation to the Holy* (New York: Oxford University Press, 1923).

2. See Catherine L. Albanese, *Nature Religion in America: From the Algonkian Indians to the New Age* (Chicago: University of Chicago Press, 1991).

3. In Theosophical terminology, these eras or ages are referred to as "root races" and mark particular stages along humanity's continuous process of spiritual evolution. A root race simultaneously refers to a duration of time, a particular form of human life that existed during that era, and a geographical locale on the planet where human life was concentrated. As each root race comes to an end, a planetary cataclysm of some kind destroys the life forms of that era. See Helena P. Blavatsky, *The Secret Doctrine*, vol. 2, *Anthropogenesis* (Pasadena, CA: Theosophical University Press, 1977).

4. "The progenitors of Man, called in India 'Fathers,' Pitaras or Pitris, are the creators of our bodies and lower principles. . . . Primeval man would be 'the bone of their bone and the flesh of their flesh, if they had body and flesh.' As stated, they were '*lunar* Beings.'" Ibid., 88.

5. "The Sons of Wisdom, the Sons of Night . . . ready for re-birth, came down. They saw the (intellectually) vile forms of the first third (still senseless Race). 'We can choose,' said the Lords, 'we have wisdom.' Some entered the Chhayas. Some projected a spark. Some deferred till the Fourth (Race). From their own essence they filled (intensified) the Kama (the vehicle of desire). . . .' In these shall we dwell,' said the Lords of the Flame and of the Dark Wisdom." Ibid., 161.

6. Referring to Sanat Kumara, Leadbeater summarizes, "Our world is governed by a Spiritual King—one of the Lords of the Flame Who came long ago from Venus." Kumara presides over a certain initiation in which the Theosophical student is transfigured, as was Christ himself, into a divinized human being. "At this stage of the man's progress he has to be brought before the Spiritual King of the World, the mighty Head of the Occult Hierarchy, Who at this . . . step either confers the Initiation Himself, or deputes one of His pupils, the three Lords of the Flame Who came with Him from Venus to do so; and in the latter event the man is presented to the King soon after the Initiation has taken place. Thus the Christ is brought into the presence of His Father . . ." Charles Webster Leadbeater, *The Masters and the Path* (Whitefish, MT: Kessinger Publishing Rare Reprints) 321, 190.

7. Writing under his pen name, Godfré Ray King, Ballard elaborates that this antediluvian city was located on the banks of the Amazon River near the border between Brazil and Bolivia and ruled over by a descendent of the kings of Atlantis. See chapter 6, "Buried Cities of the Amazon" in Godfré Ray King, *Unveiled Mysteries* (Mansfield Centre, CT: Martino Publishing, 2011) 164-94. More than a decade earlier, Frederick S. Oliver, writing as "Phylos the Tibetan," wrote a similar narrative about a spiritually enlightened and technologically advanced antediluvian civilization. As it did in Ballard's visions, Mount Shasta figured prominently in Oliver's channeled narrative. See Frederick Spencer Oliver, *A Dweller on Two Planets; or, The Dividing of the Way, by Phylos the Tibetan* (Los Angeles: Poseid Publishing Company, 1920).

8. See Charles Berlitz and William L. Moore, *The Roswell Incident* (New York: G. P. Putnam's Sons, 1980).

9. James McAndrew, *The Roswell Report: Fact versus Fiction in the New Mexico Desert* (Washington, DC: Government Printing Office, 1995), http://www.airforcehistory.hq.af.mil/Publications/Annotations/roswellreport.htm.

10. James McAndrew, *The Roswell Report: Case Closed* (Ann Arbor: University of Michigan Library, 1997), http://contrails.iit.edu/history/roswell.

11. Stanton Friedman, "Scientist Challenges Air Force regarding UFOs," http://www.stantonfriedman.com/index.php?ptp=usaf_challenge (accessed November 4, 2010).

12. Jerome Clark, *The UFO Book: Encyclopedia of the Extraterrestrial* (Detroit: Visible Ink Press, 1998), s.v. "Chiles-Whitted Sighting."

13. Clark, *The UFO Book*, s.v. "Socorro."

14. Lynne D Kitei, *The Phoenix Lights: A Skeptics Discovery That We Are Not Alone* (Charlottesville, VA: Hampton Roads Publishing, 2004).

15. Edward Ruppelt, the air force officer who directed air force studies of UFOs from 1951 to 1953, wrote in 1955 that "of the several thousand UFO reports that the Air Force has received since 1947, some 15 to 20 percent fall into a category called unknown. This means that the observer was not affected by any determinable psychological quirks and that after exhaustive investigation the object that was reported could not be identified. To be classed as an unknown, a UFO report also had to be 'good,' meaning that it had to come from a competent observer and had to contain a reasonable amount of data." Edward Ruppelt, *The Report on Unidentified Flying Objects* (Charlestown, SC: Forgotten Books, 2008), 15. J. Allen Hynek, a professional astronomer and scientific consultant to the air force from 1948 to 1969, summarized in 1972 that "throughout the years, the percentage of Unidentifieds remained essentially the same" at 20 percent. J. Allen Hynek, *The UFO Experience: A Scientific Enquiry* (New York: Ballantine Books, 1972), 202.

16. John G. Fuller, *The Interrupted Journey* (New York: Berkley Publishing Corporation, 1966), 209.

17. Neil Barron, ed., *Anatomy of Wonder: A Critical Guide to Science Fiction*, 4th ed. (New York: Bowker, 1995).

18. *The X-Files* was the longest running science-fiction series in the history of American television, airing on Fox network from 1993 to 2002. Through its two main characters—FBI agents Fox Mulder (David Dechovny) and Dana Scully (Gillian Anderson)—the series popularized a wide range of ufological and paranormal themes, including the convoluted story line of the Roswell Incident itself. Dechovny played the "true believer" and Anderson the skeptic.

19. "UFO Bash No Letdown, Roswell Says," *Albuquerque Journal—Online Edition*, http://www.abqjournal.com (accessed November 4, 2010).

20. "The Whisperer of Darkness," in H. P. Lovecraft, *Tales* (London: Penguin Group, 2005), 433.

21. H. P. Lovecraft, *The Horror in the Museum and Other Revisions* (New York: Carroll & Graf Publishers, 2002), 134.

22. H. P. Lovecraft, *The Dream Quest of Unknown Kadath* (Las Vegas, NV: IAP, 2010), 4.

23. "The Call of Cthulhu," in Lovecraft, *Tales*, 167.

24. Ibid., 169.

25. Ibid., 167.

26. "When Reason and Science usurped God, Gothic [literature] rushed in to fill the resulting vacuum with the daemonic. The feeling most consistently evoked in Gothic tales is the terror of the life-threatening creature, wholly at the mercy of forces that are neither controllable nor understandable; a terror that at its most element level makes little distinction between 'natural' and 'supernatural' causes." Valdine Clemens, *The Return of the Repressed: Gothic Horror from the Castle of Otranto to* Alien (Albany: State University of New York Press, 1999), 2.

27. See chapter 2, "The Coming of the Saucers: Kenneth Arnold and the First Great Golden Age UFO Sighting," in Frank G. Wilkinson, *The Golden Age of Flying Saucers: Classic UFO Sightings, Saucer Crashes and Extraterrestrial Contact Encounters* (Raleigh, NC: Lulu.com, 2007), 13–16.

28. Richard Hall, "Signals, Noise, and UFO Waves," *The International UFO Reporter*, Winter 1999, http://www.cufos.org.

29. Donald Keyhoe, *The Flying Saucers Are Real* (N.p.: ReadaClassic.com, 2010), 23.

30. Ruppelt, *The Report on Unidentified Flying Objects*, 59.

31. The first mention of the "Estimate of the Situation" appears in Ruppelt's memoir, which was cleared by the air force for publication. "In intelligence, if you have something to say about some vital problem you write a report that is known as an 'Estimate of the Situation.' A few days after the DC-3 was buzzed [i.e., the Chiles-Whitted sighting], the people at ATIC [the Air Technical Intelligence Center] decided that the time had arrived to make an Estimate of the Situation. The situation was the UFO's; the estimate was that they were interplanetary!" Ruppelt, *The Report on Unidentified Flying Objects*, 52. No copy of this report, however, has ever been found.

32. "I wish to make only one assumption about all advanced technological civilizations: I believe they are all concerned about their own survival and security. Therefore, they must keep tabs on the primitives in the local neighborhood to assure they are not becoming a threat. . . . [B]y the end of World War II we had provided three signs that we would be a threat on the basis of our war-making tendencies. . . . The three signs of potential for interstellar travel in the very near future were:

1. The development and use of nuclear weapons. . . .
2. The development of even more powerful rockets as demonstrated by the many V-1 and V-2 rockets used by the Germans to attack England. . . .
3. Finally we have the amazing growth in the development of electronic systems. . . . I find it very interesting indeed that the only place on planet Earth where all three areas of new threatening technology could be checked out in July 1947 was southeastern New Mexico." Stanton T. Friedman, *Flying Saucers and Science: A Scientist Investigates the Mysteries of UFOs* (Franklin Lakes, NJ: Career Press, 2008), 164–66.

33. See Stanton T. Friedman, *Captured! The Betty and Barney Hill UFO Experience* (Franklin Lakes, NJ: Career Press, 2007). It was ufologist Marjorie Fish who first correlated Hill's star map with Zeta Reticuli, and Friedman builds on her work.

34. Friedman, *Flying Saucers and Science*, 167–68.

35. Humor, for Freud, is the result of the conscious mind giving expression to the socially forbidden and therefore repressed contents of the unconscious. See Sigmund Freud, *Jokes and Their Relation to the Unconscious* (New York: Norton, 1990).

36. Fort's four compendia, published during the interwar years, overlapped with the rise in popularity of pulp fiction. They include *The Book of the Damned* (1919), *New Lands* (1925), *Lo!* (1931), and *Wild Talents* (1932). Two years after Fort's death, the pulp magazine *Astounding Stories* published the entire text of *Lo!* in eight parts between April and November 1934. Aside from their entertainment value, Fort's books put forth a critique of science that anticipated Thomas Kuhn's argument in *The Structure of Scientific Revolutions* by many decades, namely, that science often excludes anomalies in defense of an extant paradigm

for reasons that are as much psychological, social, and political as they are rational. See Thomas Kuhn, *The Structure of Scientific Revolutions*, 3rd ed. (Chicago: University of Chicago Press, 1996).

CHAPTER 4

1. For a discussion of eighteenth- and nineteenth-century scientific expedition narratives and their relationship to romantic notions of Nature, see Richard Holmes, *The Age of Wonder: How the Romantic Generation Discovered the Beauty and Terror of Science* (New York: Pantheon Books, 2008).

2. See Marjorie Fish, "Journey into the Hill Star Map," MUFON UFO Symposium, 1974, http://www.nicap.org/hillmap.htm (accessed November 4, 2010).

3. Two books played an especially important role in popularizing the alternate-reality hypothesis: the first was Jacques Vallee's *Passport to Magonia*, published in 1969, and the second was John Keel's memoir *The Mothman Prophecies*, published in 1975. Vallee, an astronomer and computer scientist, became a ufologist in 1955 after sighting a UFO over his home in Pontoise, France. Vallee initially embraced the ETH but eventually came to reject it. The more he researched UFO encounters, the more he came across tales like Lonnie Zamora's encounter in Socorro, New Mexico, relating meetings with humanoid entities.

On the one hand, Vallee did not consider these experiences as completely hallucinatory or visionary because in many cases, like Zamora's, researchers found physical evidence corroborating the witnesses' reports. On the other hand, the sometimes whimsical, sometimes mischievous, and usually irrational behavior of the beings struck Vallee as having more in common with the tricksterish fairies and elves of Celtic folklore or the angels and demons of the Christian tradition than with the pulp-fiction–inspired renditions of aliens popularized by Donald Keyhoe and other ETH ufologists.

Passport to Magonia was an attempt to correlate close encounters of the third kind with these older folkloric tales. Vallee was *not* attempting to reduce ufology to a subspecies of legend, as some skeptics misread him. On the contrary, he was suggesting that both the various beings of folklore and the modern-day extraterrestrial were distinctive kinds of experiences/encounters that blur the normative boundaries in modern rational thought between subjective and objective "realities." In short, the extraterrestrials were *ultraterrestrials* that temporarily crossed over from a parallel or tangential universe into ours, kidnapped human victims, and returned back to their worlds with their captives. See Jacques Vallee, *Passport to Magonia: On UFOs, Folklore, and Parallel Worlds* (New York: McGraw-Hill/Contemporary, 1993).

John Keel's memoir of his experiences in Point Pleasant, West Virginia, popularized the ultraterrestrial hypothesis beyond what had by then become a ufological subculture. Keel was a journalist and ufologist who became interested in the strange experiences that residents in and around Point Pleasant were claiming to have during the years 1966 and 1967. These included sightings of UFOs, encounters with a freakish humanoid figure with red eyes and wings (later dubbed the "Mothman" after a character in the *Batman* comic book series), "men in black" (unidentified human beings, usually wearing ill-fitting clothes, reported to visit UFO witnesses after the event and to ask questions about their experiences), and parapsychological phenomena. Keel ended up living for several months in Point Pleasant. In coming to know some of the witnesses of these strange and terrifying events, he grew convinced that genuine occurrences of paranormal activity were happening. On December 15, 1967, the Silver Bridge—which spanned the Ohio River, connecting Point Pleasant to Gallipolis, Ohio—collapsed, killing 46 people. After the disaster, the paranormal activity in Point Pleasant ceased—a fact that led Keel to believe that the strange beings and ships had been a portent of impending calamity, one that the local residents had failed at the time to understand. See John Keel, *The Mothman Prophecies* (New York: Tor Books, 1991).

4. The ultraterrestrial hypothesis has also shaped both evangelical-fundamentalist Protestant and Catholic interpretations of UFOs. In the first case, a small but vocal number of conservative Protestant ufologists have come to identify the beings of ufology with the *nephilim*, or fallen angels, of Genesis 6 and the apocryphal Book of Enoch. They incorporate UFOs into a narrative of the Apocalypse: like the shape-shifting beings of Vallee's and Keel's accounts, the *nephilim* return in physical form to Earth in the Last Days as part of Satan's army, both tormenting human beings and luring them away from Christianity into metaphysical religions. The Roman Catholic interpretation of extraterrestrials has been decidedly more benign than the conservative Protestant one. Monsignor Corrado Balducci (1923–2008) was a theologian and exorcist who spoke openly about the reality of ultraterrestrials, primarily in interviews on Italian television and in Italian UFO journals. On several occasions, he suggested that aliens were angelic in nature. While Balducci's comments do not constitute an official— which is to say magisterial—pronouncement of the Church, it is noteworthy that his comments were never condemned. For an overview of conservative Protestant ufology from one of its more prominent spokespersons, see Zecharia Sitchin, *The End of Days: Armageddon and Prophecies of the Return* (New York: Harper, 2007).

5. Thomas E. Bullard, "UFO Abduction Reports: The Supernatural Kidnapping Narrative Returns in Technological Disguise," *Journal of American Folklore* 102 (1989): 147–70. In addition to discussing the basic narrative structure of abduction narratives, Bullard also drew one-to-one correlations between the eight stages of the visionary journey and those of otherworld journeys recounted throughout the world's religions—much like Vallee did in his seminal *Passport to Magonia*. See also Thomas E. Bullard, *The Myth and Mystery of UFOs* (Lawrence: University Press of Kansas, 2010), 138–39.

6. In abduction reports collected from the early 1980s on, the aliens' physical examination of their human captives takes on a highly sexualized dimension. They typically remove the clothes of their victims, whom they then place down on an operating table. After scrutinizing the surface of their captives' bodies, removing pieces of skin and/or hair, they proceed to conduct surgical procedures on their reproductive organs. For men, this may entail the collection of semen and, for women, the removal or fertilization of ova. Many abductees have recounted seeing alien-hybrid fetuses incubating in containers aboard the ships or meeting hybrid beings whom they recognize as their own offspring. Ufologist Budd Hopkins built on the examination narrative to popularize the idea of an alien-human hybridization

program as the raison d'être of abduction in his 1987 book *Intruders*. The thesis had been further developed in the works of ufologist David M. Jacobs, associate professor of history at Temple University. See Budd Hopkins, *Intruders* (New York: Ballantine, 1997), and David M. Jacobs, *Secret Life: Firsthand, Documented Accounts of UFO Abductions* (New York: Fireside, 1992).

7. Jonathan Z. Smith, "Close Encounters of Diverse Kinds," in *Religion and Cultural Studies*, ed. Susan L. Mizruchi (Princeton, NJ: Princeton University Press, 2001), 3–21.

8. Ibid., 7.

9. Tzvetan Todorov has analyzed the journals of Columbus as a simultaneous encounter and rejection of radical human difference. Obsessed with finding Paradise on Earth, Columbus passes over questions of the Indians' language, customs, and culture. The journals are replete with descriptions of *the landscape* that might confirm what he already believes to be true, that he has in fact wandered into Eden, but devoid of any attempt to explain who the *human others* are. In regard to Native American languages, for example, Todorov observes, "Columbus's failure to recognize the diversity of languages permits him, when he confronts a foreign tongue, only two possible, and complementary, forms of behavior: to acknowledge it as a language but to refuse to believe it is different; or to acknowledge its difference but to refuse to admit it is a language." Tzvetan Todorov, *The Conquest of America: The Question of the Other* (Norman: University of Oklahoma Press, 1999), 30.

10. Smith, "Close Encounters of Diverse Kinds," 15.

11. See Gary L. Ebersole, *Captured by Texts: Puritan to Postmodern Images of Indian Captivity* (Charlottesville: University of Virginia Press, 1995).

12. Mary Rowlandson, "True History of the Captivity and Restoration of Mary Rowlandson," in *Women's Captivity Narratives*, ed. Kathryn Zabelle Derounian-Stodola (New York: Penguin, 1998), 14.

13. John G. Fuller, *The Interrupted Journey* (New York: Berkley Publishing Corporation, 1966), 17.

14. Whitney Strieber, *Communion: A True Story* (New York: Avon Books, 1988), 9.

15. Richard Hofstadter, *The Paranoid Style in American Politics* (New York: Vintage, 2008).

16. John E. Mack, M.D., *Abduction: Human Encounters with Aliens* (New York: Macmillan, 1994).

17. While Mack remained noncommittal about the origins of abduction phenomena, he insisted that the abduction phenomenon can and should be studied as an aspect of the physical universe. He left unanswered whether the entities of his clients' encounters came from elsewhere from within our own universe or from realities tangential to ours.

18. "Nothing in my work on UFO abductions has surprised me as much as the discovery that what is happening to the earth has not gone unnoticed elsewhere in the universe. That the earth itself, and its potential destruction, could have an effect beyond itself or its own environment was altogether outside the worldview in which I was raised. But it would appear from the information that abductees receive that the earth has value or importance in a larger, interrelated cosmic system that mirrors the interconnectedness of life on earth. The alien abduction

phenomenon represents, then, some sort of corrective initiative." Mack, *Abduction*, 413.

19. Edward U. Condon, *Scientific Study of Unidentified Flying Objects* (New York: E. P. Dutton, 1969).

20. Of the 91 case studies reviewed in Condon's study, 30 remained unexplained. As ufologists ever since 1969 have never grown tired of pointing out, this is higher than the average percentage of unknowns reported by the air force throughout its UFO investigations during the mid-twentieth century. In the final analysis, the disagreements between skeptics and ufologists hinge on philosophical differences. British physicist and UFO skeptic Reginald Victor Jones explores this point in his essay "The Natural Philosophy of Flying Saucers," *Physics Bulletin* 19 (July 1968): 225–30, which was reprinted as an appendix to the Condon report. With refreshing honesty, Jones writes, "[UFO researchers] are left with assessing probabilities from what we know about the physical world, but we cannot reject the flying saucer hypothesis because it is unlikely. . . . I think this is where the natural philosopher must take his stand, for there is a well tried course in such a situation. This is to apply 'Occam's razor'—hypotheses are not to be multiplied without necessity. Of all the possible explanations for a set of observations, the one with the minimum of supposition should be accepted, until it is proved wrong. . . . *Of course, the difficulty in applying Occam's razor is in deciding which explanation of flying saucers involves the minimum hypothesis* [emphasis added]." Condon, *Scientific Study of Unidentified Flying Objects*, appendix 5, 930–31.

21. During the Apollo 14 mission in 1971, Edgar Mitchell experienced his own encounter with the *mysterium tremendum et fascinans* of Nature as an imminent manifestation of divinity. He subsequently helped to found the Institute of Noetic Sciences, a research institute for parapsychological investigation, located in Petaluma, California. In a July 28, 2008, interview with radio host Nick Margerrison of Britain's Kerrang! Radio, Mitchell publicly voiced his belief in a worldwide government cover-up of UFOs that began with the Roswell crash of July 1947. He claimed that he had been "briefed" by undisclosed authorities in "military circles and intelligence circles" that extraterrestrials have been regularly visiting the earth. This was also the content of his keynote address at the 2008 X Conference in April, held three months before the interview with Margerrison. Mitchell's interview on Kerrang! Radio can be heard online at http://www.youtube.com/watch?v=RhNdxdveK7c (accessed November 6, 2010).

Paul Hellyer gained overnight celebrity status within ufological circles when he testified to his belief in the Roswell Incident at the September 2005, Exopolitics Toronto symposium held in Canada. As Hellyer explained at the symposium, his curiosity about UFOs was piqued after watching the ABC television show "Peter Jennings Reporting: UFOs—Seeing Is Believing," aired earlier in the year. He began his own research on the topic and came across *The Day after Roswell*, in which author Colonel Philip Corso identified himself as a witness to the saucer and extraterrestrial bodies at the Roswell crash site. Corso further claimed that the Pentagon had subsequently reverse engineered weaponry from the metallic debris that military officials had sequestered in New Mexico. Hellyer contacted an unnamed, retired U.S. Air Force general to check up on Corso's claims and learned that the allegations of the book were true. Since 2005, Hellyer has spoken openly in a number of UFO venues about his belief in the Roswell Incident, a worldwide government cover-up of UFOs and extraterrestrial visitations, and classified plans within the U.S. government to defend the world militarily from alien visitations in the future. A portion of Hellyer's talk at the Exopolitics Toronto event can be viewed online at http://ufo-tv.com/exopolitics-toronto-paul-hellyer-speaks-of-ufo-disclosure-9252005-part-1 (accessed November 6, 2010).

CHAPTER 5

1. The exact type of tool does not affect the outcome, although forked sticks, metal rods, and pendulums are the most common implements used by American dowsers. The woodcut from the frontispiece of an eighteenth-century tract shows a dowser holding a tray of assorted tools—including scissors, a smoking pipe, and pincers. According to one history, German sausage has also been used. See William Barrett and Theodore Besterman, *The Divining Rod: An Experimental and Psychological Investigation* (London: Methuen, 1926), 2.

2. The logo appears on the very first issue of the ASD's *Activity Newsletter* 1, no. 2 (December 1, 1961): 1.

3. Paul Searls had discussed what he alternately calls the "imagined community of Vermont" in his cultural history of the state, *Two Vermonts*. The title refers to a division during the late nineteenth century between "uphill" and "downhill" cultures—or between agrarian and commercial societies, respectively. As a solution to the state's economic and demographic decline after the Civil War, professional downhillers seized on tourism, capitalizing on the state's rural stagnation to promote Vermont as a refuge from a rapidly modernizing world. This reinvention of the state began in the 1890s and continues to shape Vermont's twenty-first-century rural identity. As Searl summarizes, "Escalating urban misgivings about the consequences of modern 'progress' shaped the emergence of modern Vermont enormously. In the coming decades, Vermont remained marginal to the national economy. Its identity as the repository of ancient, simple republican values made Vermont central to the national psyche . . . Vermont became a focal point of the 'invention' of rural New England as an authentic representation of the lost agrarian republic. Downhill Vermonters had long prized their state as an agent of progress; outsiders, increasingly, prized it as uncontaminated by progress." What Searls refers to as the "lost agrarian republic" is the central trope of American pastoralism. Paul M. Searls, *Two Vermonts: Geography and Identity, 1865–1910* (Hanover, NH: University Press of New England, 2006), 99.

4. For an overview of American pastoralism in late eighteenth- and nineteenth-century literature and literary-inspired political thought, see Leo Marx, *The Machine in the Garden: Technology and the Pastoral Ideal in America* (New York: Oxford University Press, 1964), 6. Marx discusses the "yearning for a simpler, more harmonious style of life, an existence 'closer to nature' . . ." as particularly pronounced in America: "The soft veil of nostalgia that hangs over our urbanized landscape is largely a vestige of the once dominant image of an undefiled, green republic, a quiet land of forests, villages, and farms dedicated to the pursuit of

happiness." The image of America as an Edenic paradise dates back before the republic to the first accounts of the so-called New World by European voyagers.

5. "By 1785, when Jefferson issued *Notes on Virginia*, the pastoral ideal had been 'removed' from the literary mode to which it traditionally had belonged and applied to [social and political] reality." Marx, *The Machine in the Garden*, 73.

6. Old Home Week was inaugurated in 1901 when the state legislature passed a bill setting aside one week each August as the official time for the celebration. But efforts to steer the development of Vermont in the direction of its newfound image started a decade earlier. Railroad corporations were the first to embrace the idea that what was good for tourism was also good for mass transportation. In 1892, the Fish and Game Commission followed, acknowledging that it would need to manage the use and development of the state's natural resources to meet the expectations of tourists and began regulating accordingly. By the middle of the 1890s, the Vermont Board of Agriculture came to join the railroad companies in advertising the scenic beauty and wholesome values of its native state, and in 1895, *The Vermonter* magazine was founded to circulate the pastoral image even more extensively. In 1897, the Vermont Development Association was founded to coordinate further marketing efforts. Searls, *Two Vermonts*, 103–12.

7. Marsha Blackburn, "The View from Vermont Foliage: In the Northeast Kingdom, the Autumn Festival Is Not Simply about Leaves but about Taking the Beautiful Back Roads to a Simpler Time," *Baltimore Sun*, August 16, 1998, http://articles.baltimoresun.com/1998-08-16/features/1998228018_1_northeast -kingdom-rural-vermont-walden.

8. T. Edward Ross and Richard D. Wright, *The Divining Mind: A Guide to Dowsing and Self-Awareness* (Rochester, VT: Destiny Books, 1990), 66.

9. While there is no written record of the 1958 foliage festival, the first ASD bulletin mentions local dowsers using "whalebone stays, iron spikes, forked sticks, and bent wire" at the 1961 festival.

10. The early history of the ASD is recorded in its first bulletin—dated October 24, 1961—and its subsequent "activity newsletters." In 1964, the activity newsletters became quarterly digests, which have been published continuously since. The first bulletin lists the society's first 10 trustees, with five members from Vermont; one representative each from the states of Connecticut, Massachusetts, New York, and Virginia; and one member from New Jersey with a second home in Peacham, Vermont. The first activity newsletter, dated December 1, 1961, reported that membership in the society had grown to 1,000 members over the previous year.

11. "Dowser Convention," *Vermont Life*, Autumn 1961, 14–17.

12. ASD, *Activity Newsletter* 1, no. 2 (December 1, 1961): 1.

13. ASD, *Activity Newsletter* 2, no. 1 (May 1, 1962): 3.

14. Henry Gross of Biddeford, Maine, is the only speaker mentioned in the first, 1961 bulletin. In 1963, the ASD invited Dr. Joseph G. Pratt, assistant director of the Parapsychology Laboratory at Duke University, to join Biddeford, and from that point on the number of speakers has steadily grown. ASD, *Activity Newsletter* 3, no. 3 (August 15, 1963): 18.

15. Two questions have framed scientific research on dowsing. The first and more prosaic question involves the reasons for the movement of the rod. Most

researchers from the time of Agricola on have posited a somatic cause—rather than a property of the dowsing tools themselves. In more recent studies, the theory of unconscious muscular action prevails. The second and more central question concerns how or if the dowser obtains information about the target. Answers include the "normal inference" theory (i.e., dowsers are acute observers of their environment); physical causes, including sensitivity to electromagnetic fields; and parapsychological causes, particularly in the cases of off-site "informational dowsing" where a dowser locates water using only a map of the terrain. Distinct from these studies is a sociological theory that dowsing emerged and continues as a method of allaying anxiety in areas where water is scarce or where access to water is limited by economic restraints. Despite hundreds of studies on each one of these areas, the scientific literature on dowsing remains inconclusive. See George P. Hansen, "Dowsing: A Review of Experimental Research," *Journal of the Society for Psychical Research* 51, no. 792 (October 1982): 343–67.

16. The first sustained discussion of dowsing appears in Georgius Agricola's 1564 treatise *De Re Metallica* (On the Nature of Metals), a study of mining.

17. ASD, *Activity Newsletter* 1, no. 2 (December 1, 1961): 2.

18. The first reference to radiesthesia in ASD circles appears in the second newsletter in an advertisement for classes in "How to Develop Ability for Radiesthesic Perceptions" by a New York member. ASD, *Activity Newsletter* 2, no. 1 (May 1, 1962): 5.

19. Ibid., 1.

20. ASD, *Activity Newsletter* 3, no. 3 (August 15, 1963): 4.

21. ASD, *Activity Newsletter* 2, no. 1 (May 1, 1962): 3.

22. In 1986, the German Federal Ministry of Research and Technology (Bundesministerium für Forschung und Technologie [BMFT]) allotted roughly $165,000 (400,000 DM) to three Munich universities to research a long-standing belief among dowsers that converging streams of underground water radiate carcinogenic energy. As part of this study, two physicists and one biologist from three Munich universities oversaw experiments to ascertain the reliability of water dowsing in general. Between 1987 and 1988, they conducted around 10,000 preliminary tests on the abilities of approximately 500 self-identified dowsers, finally selecting 50 of the most promising candidates for the Scheunen ("barn") experiments. In these latter tests, scientists moved a pipe containing running water to random locations on the first story of a barn while dowsers on the second story attempted to locate the position of the water below them. The results, as summarized for the BMFT in a final 1990 report, suggested that "the success rate of average dowsers ... was ... in most cases indistinguishable (or nearly so) from chance"—but that a "few dowsers, in particular cases, showed an extraordinarily high rate of success, which can scarcely, if at all, be explained due to chance."

In light of the latter conclusion, the Scheunen experiments at first seemed to have proven the scientific validity of dowsing, at least among a small group of virtuosi. In a subsequent statistical analysis of the data, however, Jim T. Enright of the University of California at San Diego demonstrated that the German researchers had failed to report the *overall* success rate of the six dowsers they had singled out as extraordinary. While it is true that these dowsers had, *in particular cases*, obtained highly accurate readings, it is also true that in other cases they had performed poorly. Their success seemed to be "hit or miss"; in other words, it was both random and nonreproducible. Enright further pointed out that the researchers of the Scheunen experiments had never agreed to a method of statistical analysis *prior to* the tests. This omission allowed the authors of the BMFT report to use whatever model of assessing the data they could to emphasize certain test results over others. Enright argued that theirs was in fact a nonconventional method of statistical analysis, one that highlighted the best scores of the allegedly adept dowsers while keeping hidden their many failures. See J. T. Enright, "Water Dowsing: the *Scheunen* Experiments," *Naturwissenschaften* 82 (1995): 360–69.

23. Georgia Agricola, *De Re Metallica*, trans. Herbert Clark Hoover (Whitefish, MT: Kessinger Publishing, 2003), 38–41.

24. Christopher Bird, *The Divining Hand: The 500-Year-Old Mystery of Dowsing* (Atglen, PA: Whitford Press, 1993), 1.

25. Ibid., 2.

26. Ibid., 2–3.

27. Ross and Wright, *The Divining Mind*, 111.

28. "We now want to take one more step and consider an idea popularized by the late Itzhak Bentov, author of *Stalking the Wild Pendulum* (Rochester, VT: Destiny Books, 1987). He suggests that we think of this vast sea that lies behind our concept of the created universe not as a sea of energy but rather as a sea of consciousness—a sea of awareness, thought, or intention. In his view, it is this consciousness that, when put into a vibratory state, manifests as matter, from which the different forms we see around us are made. According to this approach, everything around you—your table or desk, your plants, even your own body—is made up of rapidly vibrating consciousness." Ibid., 58.

29. Ibid., 89.

30. Ibid.

31. S. W. Tromp, *Psychical Physics: A Scientific Analysis of Dowsing, Radiesthesia and Kindred Divining Phenomena* (New York: Elsevier Publishing Company, 1949), 441–503.

32. Chapter 7, "Physical or Sidereal: A Pendular Question," in Bird, *The Divining Hand*, 123–43.

33. Wade Clark Roof, *A Generation of Seekers: The Spiritual Journeys of the Baby Boom Generation* (New York: Harper San Francisco, 1994).

34. See Randall Sullivan, "American Stonehenge: Monumental Instructions for the Post-Apocalypse," *Wired Magazine*, April 20, 2009, http://www.wired .com/science/discoveries/magazine/17-05/ff_guidestones?currentPage=all (accessed November 6, 2010).

35. George P. Marsh, *Man and Nature or, Physical Geography as Modified by Human Action* (New York: Charles Scribner, 1864), 3.

CHAPTER 6

1. Dowsing is but one of the examples of magical thought and practice that Quinn includes in his history of Joseph Smith and the Book of Mormon, first published in 1987. Quinn's work has sustained heated criticism by many Mormon

historians since its initial publication but has been praised by other scholars, most of them non-Mormon, as a groundbreaking history. In 1993, Quinn, along with four other Mormon scholars, was excommunicated from the church for research that contradicted official church teachings. In Quinn's case, this research included but was limited to his work on Smith and magic. See D. Michael Quinn, *Early Mormonism and the Magic World View*, rev. ed. (Salt Lake City, UT: Signature Books, 1998).

2. Ibid., 35.

3. Ibid., 36.

4. See Giovanna Neudorfer, *Vermont's Stone Chambers: An Inquiry into Their Past* (Montpelier. VT: Vermont Historical Society, 1980).

5. William McNeil, *Visitors to Ancient America: The Evidence for European and Asian Presence in America Prior to Columbus* (New York: McFarland & Company, 2004), 165–69.

6. For a discussion of the archaeoastronomical features of the stonework of Calendar II and its environs, see James W. Mavor Jr. and Byron E. Dix, *Manitou: The Sacred Landscape of New England's Native Civilization* (Rochester, VT: Inner Traditions, 1989).

7. For a description of some of the more prominent lithic sites of New England, see Mary Gage and James Gage, *A Guide to New England Stone Structures: Stone Cairns, Stone Walls, Standing Stones, Chambers, Foundations, Wells, Culverts, Quarries and Other Structures* (Amesbury, MA: Powwow River Books, 2006). For a state-by-state listing of anomalous architecture sites (including but not confined to New England), see George M. Eberhart, *A Geo-Bibliography of Anomalies* (Westport, CT: Greenwood Press, 1980).

8. In 1969, James Whittall, an amateur archeologist, radiocarbon-dated the deepest of three separate soil deposits near the bottom of one of the North Salem structures. He also found a stone hammer and scraper—tools for working with stone—buried in the earth at this depth, suggesting that construction of the site had begun during the corresponding time. See James Whittall, "Megalithic Site—Mystery Hill North Salem, New Hampshire Radiocarbon Date Excavation October 1970." *NEARA Newsletter* 6, no. 1 (March, 1971): 19–20.

9. Barry Fell, *America B.C.: Ancient Settlers in the New World* (New York: Quadrangle/New York Times Book Company, 1977).

10. Madeleine L'Engle, *An Acceptable Time* (New York: Farrar, Straus and Giroux, 1989).

11. T. S. Eliot, "Little Gidding," in *Collected Poems, 1909–1962* (New York: Harcourt Brace Jovanovich, 1991), 208.

12. Stephen R. Riggs, ed., *Dakota-English Dictionary* (St. Paul: University of Minnesota Press, 1992), s.v. "ho."

13. Ibid., s.v. "aho."

14. The Earth Mysteries is an umbrella term covering a wide range of speculation on alleged, anomalous geophysical energies and their relationship with prehistoric architecture. In its present-day formulation, this discourse can be dated back to American and British metaphysical writings published in the mid-1960s. In Britain, a number of Earth Mysteries metaphysicists—including Paul Devereux, John Michell, Nigel Pennick, and Anthony Roberts—joined together to

found *The Ley Hunter* magazine in 1965. The journal became a forum for developing and popularizing the interrelated ideas of ley lines, geomancy, and Earth energies. Devereux served for a time as *The Ley Hunter*'s chief editor. See "Ley Lines, Earth Energies, and Other Mysteries," in Adrian J. Ivakhiv, *Claiming Sacred Ground: Pilgrims and Politics at Glastonbury and Sedona* (Bloomington: Indiana University Press, 2001), 22–43.

15. The Earth Mysteries appeared as the feature topic of the first ASD quarterly in 1980. Editor Tom Graves included the letter from Devereux to American dowser Sig Lonegren in its entirety. Devereux recollected his trip to Vermont the previous year: "I cannot let this opportunity pass without recording my delight at meeting you and your family, and the other marvelous members of the ASD and NEARA... I have a memory of New England that can be conjured up vividly by thoughts of brilliantly coloured foliage, wonderful, friendly, and hospitable people and mysterious, tree-shrouded stone artifacts." *American Dowser Quarterly Digest* 20, no. 1 (February, 1980): 22.

16. Peter Champoux, *Gaia Matrix: Arkhom and the Geometries of Destiny in the North American Landscape* (Washington, MA: Franklin Media, 1999).

17. Michell's chapter "Sacred Engineering" begins an overview of ancient scientists: "From what we have seen of the scientific methods practiced by the adepts of the ancient world it is possible to draw two conclusions. First, they recognized the existence of some force or current, of whose potential we are now ignorant, and discovered the form of natural science by which it could be manipulated. Secondly, they gained, apparently by means connected with their use of this current, certain direct insight into the fundamental questions of philosophy, the nature of God and the universe and the relationship between life and death." John Michell, *The View over Atlantis* (New York: Ballantine Books, 1969), 166.

18. Alfred Watkins, *The Old Straight Track: Its Mounds, Beacons, Moats, Sites and Mark Stones* (London: Abacus, 1974), xix.

19. The Nazis took up Watkins's theory of ley lines in a quest to map out the pre-Christian German landscape, eventually identifying a rock formation in Lower Saxony, where the leys allegedly converged, as the sacred hub of the Aryan homeland. See Ivakhiv, *Claiming Sacred Ground*, 23.

20. See Paul Devereux, *Shamanism and the Mystery Lines: Ley Lines, Spirit Paths, Shape-Shifting and Out-of-Body Travel* (Woodbury, MN: Llewellyn Publications, 1994).

21. Historian of religion Charles H. Long has written, "If Americans have exploited their world, it has been an exploitation of nature; if they have suffered, it has been through the forms of nature. It was precisely through theories of nature that the destruction of the Indian cultures took place, and a nation which at its inception proclaimed the equality of all human beings was able to continue the institution of slavery under the guise of nature.... It is from this concealment [of history] that the innocence and naiveté of the [mythical] American emerges. ... [T]his innocence ... is not a natural innocence, that innocence which is prior to experience; rather, this innocence is gained only through an intense suppression of the deeper and more subtle dimension of American *experience*." Charles H. Long, *Significations: Signs, Symbols, and Images in the Interpretation of Religion* (Philadelphia: Fortress Press, 1986), 143–44.

22. "[T]he theories of Darwin, which were then of topical interest, strongly attracted me, for they held out hopes of an extraordinary advance in our understanding of the world; and it was hearing Goethe's beautiful essay on Nature read aloud at a popular lecturer by Professor Carl Bruhl just before I left school that decided me to become a medical student." Sigmund Freud, *An Autobiographical Study*, trans. James Strachey (New York: Norton, 1989), 7.

EPILOGUE

1. William Carlos Williams, "The Red Wheelbarrow," Spring and All (Paris: Contact Publishing Company, 1923), reprinted in *The Collected Poems of William Carlos Williams*, vol. 1, *1909–1939*, ed. Christopher MacGowan and A. Walton Litz (New York: New Directions, 1991), 224.

Bibliography

Agricola, Georgia. *De Re Metallica*. Translated by Herbert Clark Hoover. White-fish, MT: Kessinger Publishing, 2003.

Albanese, Catherine L. *Nature Religion in America: From the Algonkian Indians to the New Age*. Chicago: University of Chicago Press, 1991.

Albanese, Catherine L. *A Republic of Mind and Spirit: A Cultural History of American Metaphysical Religion*. New Haven, CT: Yale University Press, 2008.

Awtry, Marilyn. *History of National Spiritualist Association of Churches*. N.p.: National Spiritualist Association of Churches, 1983.

Barkun, Michael. *A Culture of Conspiracy: Apocalyptic Visions in Contemporary America*. Berkeley: University of California Press, 2004.

Barrett, William, and Theodore Besterman. *The Divining Rod: An Experimental and Psychological Investigation*. London: Methuen, 1926.

Barron, Neil, ed. *Anatomy of Wonder: A Critical Guide to Science Fiction*. 4th ed. New York: Bowker, 1995.

Baudrillard, Jean. *America*. New York: Verso, 2010.

Bergland, Renee L. *The National Uncanny: Indian Ghosts and American Subjects*. Hanover, NH: University Press of New England, 2000.

Berlitz, Charles, and William L. Moore. *The Roswell Incident*. New York: G. P. Putnam's Sons, 1980.

Bird, Christopher. *The Divining Hand: The 500-Year-Old Mystery of Dowsing*. Atglen, PA: Whitford Press, 1993.

Blackburn, Marsha. "The View from Vermont Foliage: In the Northeast Kingdom, the Autumn Festival Is Not Simply about Leaves but about Taking the Beautiful Back Roads to a Simpler Time." *Baltimore Sun*, August 16, 1998, http://articles.baltimoresun.com/1998-08-16/features/1998228018_1_northeast-kingdom-rural-vermont-walden.

Blavatsky, Helena P. *The Secret Doctrine*. Vol. 2, *Anthropogenesis*. Pasadena, CA: Theosophical University Press, 1977.

Braude, Ann. *Radical Spirits: Spiritualism and Women's Rights in Nineteenth-Century America*. Boston: Beacon Press, 1989.

Brown, Michael F. *The Channeling Zone: American Spirituality in an Anxious Age.* Cambridge, MA: Harvard University Press, 1999.

Buescher, John Benedict. *The Remarkable Life of John Murray Spear: Agitator for the Spirit Land.* Notre Dame, IN: University of Notre Dame Press, 2006.

Bullard, Thomas E. "UFO Abduction Reports: The Supernatural Kidnapping Narrative Returns in Technological Disguise." *Journal of American Folklore* 102 (1989): 147–70.

Bullard, Thomas E. *The Myth and Mystery of UFOs.* Lawrence: University Press of Kansas, 2010.

Casey, Edward. *The Fate of Place: A Philosophical History.* Berkeley: University of California Press, 1998.

Certeau, Michel de. *The Practice of Everyday Life.* Translated by Steven Rendall. Berkeley: University of California Press, 2002.

Champoux, Peter. *Gaia Matrix: Arkhom and the Geometries of Destiny in the North American Landscape.* Washington, MA: Franklin Media, 1999.

Clark, Jerome. *The UFO Book: Encyclopedia of the Extraterrestrial.* Detroit: Visible Ink Press, 1998.

Clemens, Valdine. *The Return of the Repressed: Gothic Horror from the Castle of Otranto to* Alien. Albany: State University of New York Press, 1999.

Condon, Edward U. *Scientific Study of Unidentified Flying Objects.* New York: E. P. Dutton, 1969.

Cox, Robert C. *Body and Soul: A Sympathetic History of American Spiritualism.* Charlottesville: University of Virginia Press, 2003.

Cross, Whitney R. *The Burned-Over District: The Social and Intellectual History of Enthusiastic Religion in Western New York, 1800–1850.* Ithaca, NY: Cornell University Press, 1950.

Davis, Andrew Jackson. *The Principles of Nature, Her Divine Revelations, and a Voice to Mankind.* New York: S. S. Lyon and Wm. Fishbough, 1847.

Dean, Jodi. *Aliens in America: Conspiracy Cultures from Outerspace to Cyberspace.* Ithaca, NY: Cornell University Press, 1998.

Deloria, Philip J. *Playing Indian.* New Haven, CT: Yale University Press, 1999.

Devereux, Paul. *Mysterious Ancient America: An Investigation into the Enigmas of America's Pre-History.* London: Vega, 2002.

Devereux, Paul. *Shamanism and the Mystery Lines: Ley Lines, Spirit Paths, Shape-Shifting and Out-of-Body Travel.* Woodbury, MN: Llewellyn Publications, 1994.

"Dowser Convention." *Vermont Life.* Autumn 1961.

Earle, E. Lyell. "Lily Dale, the Haunt of Spiritualists." *Catholic World* 68 (January 1899): 506–7.

Eberhart, George M. *A Geo-Bibliography of Anomalies.* Westport, CT: Greenwood Press, 1980.

Ebersole, Gary L. *Captured by Texts: Puritan to Postmodern Images of Indian Captivity.* Charlottesville: University of Virginia Press, 1995.

Eco, Umberto. *Travels in Hyper Reality.* Translated by William Weaver. San Diego, CA: Harcourt Brace Jovanovich, 1986.

Eliade, Mircea. *The Myth of the Eternal Return, or, Cosmos and History.* Princeton, NJ: Princeton University Press, 1954.

Eliot, T. S. *Collected Poems, 1909–1962.* New York: Harcourt Brace Jovanovich, 1991.

Ellenberger, Henri F. *The Discovery of the Unconscious: The History and Evolution of Dynamic Psychiatry.* New York: Basic Books, 1970.

Emerson, Ralph Waldo. *Essays.* New York: Harper & Row, 1951.

Emmons, Charles. *At the Threshold: UFOs, Science and the New Age.* Columbus, NC: Granite Publishing, 1998.

Enright, J. T. "Water Dowsing: The *Scheunen* Experiments." *Naturwissenschaften* 82 (1995): 360–69.

Fell, Barry. *America Before Columbus: Ancient Settlers in the New World.* New York: Quadrangle/New York Times Book Company, 1977.

Fish, Marjorie. "Journey into the Hill Star Map." MUFON UFO Symposium, 1974, http://www.nicap.org/hillmap.htm.

Fort, Charles. *The Complete Books of Charles Fort: The Book of the Damned/Lo!/Wild Talents/New Lands.* New York: Dover Publications, 1974.

Friedman, Stanton T. *Captured! The Betty and Barney Hill UFO Experience.* Franklin Lakes, NJ: Career Press, 2007.

Friedman, Stanton T. *Flying Saucers and Science: A Scientist Investigates the Mysteries of UFOs.* Franklin Lakes, NJ: Career Press, 2008.

Friedman, Stanton T. "Scientist Challenges Air Force Regarding UFOs," http://www.stantonfriedman.com/index.php?ptp=usaf_challenge.

Freud, Sigmund. *An Autobiographical Study.* Translated by James Strachey. New York: Norton, 1989.

Freud, Sigmund. *Jokes and Their Relation to the Unconscious.* Translated by James Strachey. New York: Norton, 1990.

Freud, Sigmund. *The Uncanny.* Translated by David McLintock. New York: Penguin, 1993.

Fuller, John G. *The Interrupted Journey.* New York: Berkley Publishing Corporation, 1966.

Fuller, Robert C. *Americans and the Unconscious.* New York: Oxford University Press, 1986.

Gage, Mary, and James Gage. *A Guide to New England Stone Structures: Stone Cairns, Stone Walls, Standing Stones, Chambers, Foundations, Wells, Culverts, Quarries and Other Structures.* Amesbury, MA: Powwow River Books, 2006.

Grafton, Anthony. *New Worlds, Ancient Texts: The Power of Tradition and the Shock of Discovery.* Cambridge, MA: Belknap Press, 1995.

Greenblatt, Stephen. *Marvelous Possessions: The Wonder of the New World.* Chicago: University of Chicago Press, 1991.

Gunn, Giles. *New World Metaphysics: Readings on the Religious Meaning of the American Experience.* New York: Oxford University Press, 1981.

Hall, Richard. "Signals, Noise, and UFO Waves." *The International UFO Reporter,* Winter 1999, http://www.cufos.org.

Hansen, George P. "Dowsing: A Review of Experimental Research." *Journal of the Society for Psychical Research* 51, no. 792 (October 1982): 343–67.

Hansen, George P. "CSICOPS and the Skeptics: An Overview." *Journal of the American Society of Psychical Research* 86, no. 1 (January 1992): 19–63.

Hansen, George P. *The Trickster and the Paranormal.* Bloomington, IN: Xlibris, 2001.

Hatch, Nathan O. *The Democratization of American Christianity*. New Haven, CT: Yale University Press, 1991.

Hess, David J. *Science in the New Age: The Paranormal, Its Defenders and Debunkers*. Madison: University of Wisconsin Press, 1993.

Hofstadter, Richard. *The Paranoid Style in American Politics*. New York: Vintage, 2008.

Holmes, Richard. *The Age of Wonder: How the Romantic Generation Discovered the Beauty and Terror of Science*. New York: Pantheon Books, 2008.

Hopkins, Budd. *Intruders*. New York: Ballantine, 1997.

Hughes, Richard T. *Myths America Lives By*. Urbana: University of Illinois Press, 2004.

Huizinga, Johan. *Homo Ludens: A Study of the Play-Element in Culture*. Boston: Beacon Press, 1950.

Hynek, J. Allen. *The UFO Experience: A Scientific Enquiry*. New York: Ballantine Books, 1972.

Impey, Oliver. *The Origins of Museums: The Cabinet of Curiosities in Sixteenth- and Seventeenth-Century Europe*. Oxford: Clarendon Press; New York: Oxford University Press, 1985.

"Ingenious Frauds at Lily Dale Seances: Psychical Research Society Investigates Reported Marvels at Famous Spiritist Stronghold and Exposes Fraudulent Methods of Mediums." *New York Times*, March 8, 1908.

Ivakhiv, Adrian J. *Claiming Sacred Ground: Pilgrims and Politics at Glastonbury and Sedona*. Bloomington: Indiana University Press, 2001.

Jacobs, David M. *Secret Life: Firsthand, Documented Accounts of UFO Abductions*. New York: Fireside, 1992.

James, William. "Final Impressions of a Psychical Researcher." In *The Writings of William James*, edited by John J. McDermott, 787–99. Chicago: University of Chicago Press, 1977.

Jenkins, Philip. *Mystics and Messiahs: Cults and New Religions in American History*. New York: Oxford University Press, 2001.

Jones, Reginald Victor. "The Natural Philosophy of Flying Saucers." *Physics Bulletin* 19 (July 1968): 225–30.

Keel, John A. *The Mothman Prophecies*. New York: Tom Doherty Associates, 1991.

Keyhoe, Donald. *The Flying Saucers Are Real*. Las Vegas: IAP, 2009.

Kitei, Lynne D. *The Phoenix Lights: A Skeptic's Discovery That We Are Not Alone*. Charlottesville, VA: Hampton Roads Publishing, 2004.

Kristeva, Julia. *Powers of Horror: An Essay on Abjection*. Translated by Leon S. Roudiez. New York: Columbia University Press, 1982.

Kuhn, Thomas. *The Structure of Scientific Revolutions*. 3rd ed. Chicago: University of Chicago Press, 1996.

LaJudice, Joyce, and Paula M. Vogt. *Lily Dale Proud Beginnings: A Little Piece of History*. N.p.: n.p., 1984.

Lawton, George. "Spiritualism—A Contemporary American Religion." *Journal of Religion* 10 (January 1930): 37.

Leadbeater, Charles Webster. *The Masters and the Path*. Whitefish, MT: Kessinger Publishing Rare Reprints, n.d.

L'Engle, Madeleine. *An Acceptable Time*. New York: Farrar, Straus and Giroux, 1989.

Leonard, Todd Jay. *Talking to the Other Side: A History of Modern Spiritualism and Mediumship.* Lincoln, NE: iUniverse Inc., 2005.

Lewis, James R., and Gordon Melton. *Perspectives on the New Age.* Albany: State University of New York Press, 1992.

Long, Charles H. *Significations: Signs, Symbols, and Images in the Interpretation of Religion.* Philadelphia: Fortress Press, 1986.

Lovecraft, H. P. *The Horror in the Museum and Other Revisions.* New York: Carroll & Graf Publishers, 2002.

Lovecraft, H. P. *Tales.* London: Penguin Group, 2005.

Lovecraft, H. P. *The Dream Quest of Unknown Kadath.* Las Vegas, NV: IAP, 2010.

Mack, John E. *Abduction: Human Encounters with Aliens.* New York: Macmillan, 1994.

Marsh, George P. *Man and Nature or, Physical Geography as Modified by Human Action.* New York: Charles Scribner, 1864.

Marx, Leo. *The Machine in the Garden: Technology and the Pastoral Ideal in America.* New York: Oxford University Press, 1964.

Mavor, James W., Jr., and Byron E. Dix. *Manitou: The Sacred Landscape of New England's Native Civilization.* Rochester, VT: Inner Traditions, 1989.

Mayer, Elizabeth Lloyd. *Extraordinary Knowing: Science, Skepticism, and the Inexplicable Powers of the Human Mind.* New York: Bantam, 2007.

McAndrew, James. *The Roswell Report: Fact versus Fiction in the New Mexico Desert.* Washington, DC: Government Printing Office, 1995.

McAndrew, James. *The Roswell Report: Case Closed.* Ann Arbor: University of Michigan Library, 1997.

McClenon, James. *Wondrous Events: Foundations of Religious Beliefs.* Philadelphia: University of Pennsylvania Press, 1994.

McGrane, Bernard. *Beyond Anthropology.* New York: Columbia University Press, 1989.

McLoughlin, William G. *Revivals, Awakenings, and Reforms.* Chicago: University of Chicago Press, 1978.

McNeil, William. *Visitors to Ancient America: The Evidence for European and Asian Presence in America Prior to Columbus.* New York: McFarland & Company, 2004.

Michell, John. *The View over Atlantis.* New York: Ballantine Books, 1969.

Miller, Perry. *Nature's Nation.* Cambridge, MA: Harvard University Press, 1967.

Moore, R. Laurence. *In Search of White Crows: Spiritualism, Parapsychology, and American Culture.* New York: Oxford University Press, 1977.

Morrison, Toni. "Unspeakable Things Unspoken: The Afro-American Presence in American Literature." *Michigan Quarterly Review* 28 (Winter 1989): 1–34.

Nadis, Fred. *Wonder Shows: Performing Science, Magic, and Religion in America.* New Brunswick, NJ: Rutgers University Press, 2005.

Neudorfer, Giovanna. *Vermont's Stone Chambers: An Inquiry into Their Past.* Montpelier: Vermont Historical Society, 1980.

Nickell, Joe. "Riddle of the Crystal Skulls." *Skeptical Inquirer* 30, no. 4 (July/August 2006), http://www.csicop.org.

Nickell, Joe. "A Skeleton's Tale: The Origins of Modern Spiritualism." *Skeptical Inquirer* 32, no. 4 (July/August 2008), http://www.csicop.org.

O'Gorman, Edmundo. *The Invention of America: An Inquiry into the Historical Nature of the New World and the Meaning of Its History*. Bloomington: Indiana University Press, 1961.

Onians, John. "'I Wonder . . .' A Short History of Amazement." In *Sight and Insight: Essays on Art and Culture in Honour of E. H. Gombrich at 85*, edited by John Onians, 11–32. London: Phaidon Press, 1994.

Otto, Rudolph. *The Idea of the Holy; An Inquiry into the Non-Rational Factor in the Idea of the Divine and Its Relation to the Rational*. New York: Oxford University Press, 1923.

Paravisini-Gebert, Lizabeth, and Margarite Fernandez Olmos. *Creole Religions of the Caribbean: An Introduction from Vodou and Santeria to Obeah and Espiritismo*. New York: New York University Press, 2003.

Partridge, Christopher. *UFO Religions*. New York: Routledge, 2003.

Quinn, D. Michael. *Early Mormonism and the Magic World View*. Revised and expanded ed. Salt Lake City, UT: Signature Books, 1998.

Richard, Michael P., and Albert Adato. "The Medium and Her Message: A Study of Spiritualism at Lily Dale, New York," *Review of Religious Research* 22 (December 1980): 186–96.

Riggs, Stephen R. *Dakota-English Dictionary*. St. Paul: University of Minnesota Press, 1992.

Roof, Wade Clark. *A Generation of Seekers: The Spiritual Journeys of the Baby Boom Generation*. New York: Harper San Francisco, 1994.

Ross, T. Edward, and Richard D. Wright. *The Divining Mind: A Guide to Dowsing and Self-Awareness*. Rochester, VT: Destiny Books, 1990.

Rowlandson, Mary. "True History of the Captivity and Restoration of Mary Rowlandson." In *Women's Captivity Narratives*, edited by Kathryn Zabelle Derounian-Stodola, 1–52. New York: Penguin Classics, 1998.

Ruppelt, Edward. *The Report on Unidentified Flying Objects*. Charlestown, SC: Forgotten Books, 2008.

Schmidt, Leigh Eric. *Restless Souls: The Making of American Spirituality*. New York: HarperCollins, 2005.

Schoch, Robert M., and Logan Yonavjak. *The Parapsychology Revolution: A Concise Anthology of Paranormal and Psychical Research*. New York: Penguin Group, 2008.

Searls, Paul M. *Two Vermonts: Geography and Identity, 1865–1910*. Hanover, NH: University Press of New England, 2006.

Sitchin, Zecharia. *The End of Days: Armageddon and Prophecies of the Return*. New York: Harper, 2007.

Smith, Jonathan Z. "Close Encounters of Diverse Kinds." In *Religion and Cultural Studies*, edited by Susan L. Mizruchi, 3–21. Princeton, NJ: Princeton University Press, 2001.

Strieber, Whitney. *Communion: A True Story*. New York: Avon Books, 1988.

Sullivan, Randall. "American Stonehenge: Monumental Instructions for the Post Apocalypse." *Wired Magazine* 17, no. 5 (April 20, 2009), http://www.wired.com/science/discoveries/magazine/17-05/ff_guidestones?currentPage=all.

Thoreau, Henry David. *Walden*. Boston: Beacon Press, 2004.

Todorov, Tzvetan. *The Conquest of America: The Question of the Other*. Norman: University of Oklahoma Press, 1999.

Tromp, S. W. *Psychical Physics: A Scientific Analysis of Dowsing, Radiesthesia and Kindred Divining Phenomena*. New York: Elsevier Publishing Company, 1949.

Turner, Victor. *The Ritual Process: Structure and Anti-Structure*. Chicago: Aldine Publishing, 1969.

Turner, Victor, and Edith Turner. *Image and Pilgrimage in Christian Culture*. New York: Columbia University Press, 1995.

"UFO Bash No Letdown, Roswell Says." *Albuquerque Journal—Online Edition*, http://www.abqjournal.com.

Vallee, Jacques. *Passport to Magonia: On UFOs, Folklore, and Parallel Worlds*. New York: McGraw-Hill/Contemporary, 1993.

Vogt, Evon Z., and Ray Hyman. *Water Witching U.S.A.* Chicago: University of Chicago Press, 1959.

Watkins, Alfred. *The Old Straight Track: Its Mounds, Beacons, Moats, Sites and Mark Stones*. London: Abacus, 1974.

Weschler, Lawrence. *Mr. Wilson's Cabinet Of Wonder: Pronged Ants, Horned Humans, Mice on Toast, and Other Marvels of Jurassic Technology*. New York: Vintage, 1996.

Whitman, Walt. *Leaves of Grass: The First (1855) Edition*. New York: Classic Books, 2010.

Whittall, James. "Megalithic Site—Mystery Hill North Salem, New Hampshire Radiocarbon Date Excavation October 1970." *NEARA Newsletter* 6, no. 1 (March 1971): 19–20.

Wicker, Christine. *Lily Dale: The True Story of the Town That Talks to the Dead*. New York: HarperCollins, 2003.

Wilkinson, Frank G. *The Golden Age of Flying Saucers: Classic UFO Sightings, Saucer Crashes and Extraterrestrial Contact Encounters*. Raleigh, NC: Lulu.com, 2007.

Williams, Stephen. *Fantastic Archaeology: The Wild Side of North American Prehistory*. Philadelphia: University of Pennsylvania Press, 1991.

Williams, William Carlos. "The Red Wheelbarrow." *Spring and All* (Paris: Contact Publishing Company, 1923). Reprinted in *The Collected Poems of William Carlos Williams*. Vol. 1, *1909–1939*, edited by Christopher MacGowan and A. Walton Litz (New York: New Directions, 1991), 224.

Index

Page numbers in *italic type* indicate illustrations.

About the Author

DARRYL V. CATERINE, PhD, is an associate professor of religion in the Department of Religious Studies at Le Moyne College, having earned his degrees in religious studies from Harvard University and the University of California at Santa Barbara. Dr. Caterine's first book—*Conservative Catholicism and the Carmelites: Identity, Ethnicity, and Tradition in the Modern Church* (Indiana University Press, 2001)—was selected as a *Choice* Magazine Outstanding Academic Book of 2003.